LECTURES ON RELIGION AND THE FOUNDING OF THE AMERICAN REPUBLIC

Edited by John W. Welch with Stephen J. Fleming

Brigham Young University Press
Provo, Utah
– 2003 –

Brigham Young University, Provo, Utah 84602
© 2003 Brigham Young University Press.

Cover design: Kimberly Chen Pace
Cover painting: *The Tree of Life.* Hand-colored engraving, printed for John Hagerty, Baltimore, 1791, courtesy Maryland Historical Society, Baltimore, Maryland. John Hagerty (b. 1747) was a Methodist preacher and a printer-publisher in Baltimore in the 1790s, where he specialized in printing evangelical works, including a biography of John Wesley. In addition to *The Tree of Life,* Hagerty published the prints *The Tree of Virtues* and *The Tree of Vices,* motifs used in religious art for centuries. The Tree of Life, based on Revelation 22:2, brings forth twelve fruits of salvation. A large crowd is seen complacently strolling along the Broad Way to the Bottomless Pit, where the Devil and "Babylon Mother of Harlots" beckon. The sinners are labelled "pride," "chambering & wantonness," "quack," "usury," and "extortion." James H. Hutson, *Religion and the Founding of the American Republic* (Washington, D.C.: Library of Congress, 1998), iv; also available on-line at www.loc.gov/exhibits/religion/re107.html.

To contact the publisher, write to
403 CB, Brigham Young University, PO Box 24098, Provo, Utah 84602.

Library of Congress Cataloging-in-Publication Data

Lectures on religion and the founding of the American republic / edited
by John W. Welch with Stephen J. Fleming.
      p. cm.
Includes bibliographical references and index.
  ISBN 0-8425-2548-3 (alk. paper)
  1. United States—History—Revolution, 1775–1783—Religious aspects.
  2. United States—Church history—To 1775. 3. Statesmen—Religious
life—United States—History—18th century. 4. Church and state—United
States—History—18th century. 5. Freedom of religion—United
States—History—18th century. I. Welch, John W. (John Woodland) II.
Fleming, Stephen (Stephen J.)

E209.L43 2003
322'.1'097309033—dc21

2003011092

Printed in the United States of America
10 9 8 7 6 5 4 3 2 1

CONTENTS

ILLUSTRATIONS

INTRODUCTION

The lectures published in this volume were delivered at Brigham Young University from January to March 2002, when the Library of Congress exhibition entitled *Religion and the Founding of the American Republic* was on display at the university in Provo, Utah, during the same season in which the Winter Olympics were held in Salt Lake City. The exhibition in Provo was cosponsored by BYU Studies and the Harold B. Lee Library. It was a rare privilege for us to work with James Hutson, director of the exhibition and head of the Manuscripts Division of the Library of Congress.

The documents and artifacts in the exhibition show that America was settled by deeply religious men and women, who from 1620 to 1850 wrestled with the problem of how their personal religious convictions should manifest themselves in the social and political fabric of their new and dynamic nation. This exhibition, which can still be visited on line at loc.gov, vividly shows the religious dedication, the debates and choices, and the prayers and conflicts of many different peoples involved in the founding of the American republic.

Interestingly, the exhibition begins with documents concerning the persecution and execution of Jesuits in Europe and the flight of Puritans to America, and it ends with an account of the persecution and martyrdom of Joseph Smith and flight of the Latter-day Saints to the Rocky Mountains. But in the end, viewers are not simply back where they began. Between these bookends, this exhibition takes its guests on a fascinating journey of development and understanding. Religion played a much more significantly formative role in the history of the United States than is typically portrayed in the standard American history textbooks.

On Wednesday evenings during the ten weeks that the exhibition was open, the following lectures, organized by BYU Studies, were presented by scholars from various disciplines, including history, religion, law, political science, English, and other fields. They offer insights, enriching details, and clear explanations that not only augmented the enjoyment of the exhibition to visitors in 2002 but now allow all readers to approach the founding of America more perceptively.

The opening lecture was delivered by Chief Justice Richard C. Howe of the Utah Supreme Court, who gave a concise overview of the main themes presented in the exhibition. We express our deep gratitude not only to him and to the professors from Brigham Young University who participated in this lecture series, but we extend special thanks to James Hutson of the Library of Congress, Professor Laurie Maffly-Kipp from the University of North Carolina, Rabbi Fred Wenger from Salt Lake City, and the Most Reverend George Niederauer, Ph.D., Bishop of Salt Lake City, for their superb contributions.

We enthusiastically recommend that the present collection of lectures be read in conjunction with the richly illustrated exhibition catalogue, authored by James H. Hutson and still available from University Press of New England. Also valuable is another volume containing seven papers delivered at Library of Congress in connection with this exhibition and entitled *Religion and the New Republic: Faith in the Founding of America* (Lanham, Md.: Rowman and Littlefield, 2000). Edited by Hutson, that book examines mainly the history of separation of church and state. Its excellent articles discuss John Adams and the Massachusetts experiment, Thomas Jefferson and the wall of separation, the experiences of women and Evangelicals in the religious life of the early republic, and the religious character of the new American nation.

We are grateful to many people who made this exhibition and lecture series such a success, most notably Cali O'Connell of the Harold B. Lee Library staff and the generous donors who are friends of the library. We hope that the topics raised in the exhibition and explored in this volume will continue to stimulate reflection and strength for generations to come.

Randy J. Olsen
University Librarian

John W. Welch
Editor in chief of *BYU Studies*

Brigham Young University
Provo, Utah

RELIGION IN AMERICA
REMARKS AT THE OPENING OF THE EXHIBITION

Richard C. Howe
Chief Justice of the Utah Supreme Court

Early American history is replete with examples of people coming to this land for religious reasons. To be sure, it would not be accurate to assume that all the early settlers came for that reason. Many came for economic and other purposes, but a significant number sought refuge in a new land, away from oppression in Europe, to practice their religion in the way they deemed it should be practiced.

Perhaps the most widely known group to come to America for religious freedom was the Puritans. Every school boy and girl is familiar with the Puritans. The goal of the Puritans was to cleanse the Church of England of residues of Roman Catholicism, but there was no consensus among them how far reform should go. First, they left England and settled in Holland for a few years. From there, they sailed to Plymouth, Massachusetts, arriving in 1620. There, they quietly lived in a corner of Massachusetts in "sweet communion" with God.[1] It has been estimated that as many as 20,000 Puritans poured out of England by 1642, the majority congregating in New England and others spreading as far south as the West Indies.[2] The purpose of the Puritans was described by John Winthrop aboard a ship heading for Massachusetts in 1630 in the following words: "We shall be as a city upon a hill. We are commanded this day to love the Lord our God and to love one another to walk in His ways and to keep his Commandments and his Ordinance and his laws . . . that we may live and be multiplied, and that the Lord our God may bless us in the land whether we go to possess it."[3]

Once in control in New England, the Puritans relentlessly suppressed any dissent. It is ironic that once here the Puritans denied their neighbors the very religious freedom that brought them to the shores of North America. The most famous dissenter, Roger Williams, was driven out of Massachusetts when he would not retract controversial opinions that he held. Williams founded Rhode Island as a "shelter for persons distressed for conscience." The new colony protected even those whom Williams regarded as dangerously misguided, for nothing could change his view that "forced worship stinks in God's nostrils."

Not all who flocked to this new land were Christians. In 1658, Jews, who were objects of perennial persecution, came to Rhode Island to enjoy religious liberty. They were preceded four years earlier by a group of twenty-three brethren who landed in New Amsterdam fleeing persecution in Brazil. For some decades, Jews had flourished in Dutch-held areas of Brazil, but a Portugese conquest of the area in 1654 left them unwelcome in that country. A shipload of Jewish refugees from Dutch Brazil landed in New Amsterdam in the fall of 1654, and they threw themselves on the mercy of the community, which helped them survive the winter. Despite opposition from the Dutch governor, Peter Stuyvesent, they began to hold regular religious services the following year.[4]

Further down the Atlantic Coast, Pennsylvania was settled by Quakers, or the Religious Society of Friends as they prefer to be called. Under the leadership of William Penn, the charter of Penn's government gave religious freedom. He promoted a public relations campaign that flooded the European continent with books and pamphlets in Dutch, German, and French. His initial targets were sects sharing Quaker principles, who had long been persecuted in Europe. Penn assured this audience that Pennsylvania offered "liberty to all peoples to worship God according to their faith and persuasion." However, never one to underestimate the power of economic incentives, Penn also touted his colony as a place to make a good living. He was comfortable in mixing piety and the profit motive, believing that "while we sow spiritual seed, we shall reap carnal things in abundance."

Catholics flocked to the colony of Maryland. To a much lesser extent, religion played a part even in the establishment of the colony of Virginia. Virginia was settled for the most part, not by the religious visionaries who were in command in the northern colonies, but by businessmen operating through a joint stock company, the Virginia Company of London, who wanted to get rich. The colony looked very different from its American neighbors. Unlike New England and Pennsylvania, which were settled by families, Virginia was populated by single young men down on their luck. One Virginian, William Byrd II, writing about his countrymen early in the eighteenth century wrote, "Like true Englishmen they build a church that cost no more than 50 pounds and a tavern that cost 500." However, the businessmen of the Virginia Company kept their colony well supplied with ministers. One of these was Alexander Whitaker, who established a ministry to the Indians—fulfilling a goal written into the colony's first charter by James I. His most famous convert among the Indians was Pocahontas.[5]

Religion played a major role in the American Revolution by offering a moral sanction for opposition to the British—an assurance to the average American that opposition to the mother country was justified in the sight of God. Ministers of the gospel served the American cause in many capacities during the Revolutionary War: as military chaplains, as penmen for committees of correspondence, and as members of state legislatures, constitutional conventions, and the National Congress. Some even took up arms, leading continental troops in battle.

The Revolutionary War split some denominations, notably the Church of England, whose ministers were bound by oath to support the King, and the Quakers, who were traditionally pacifists. Prior to 1789, when the Constitution of the United States was adopted, America was governed by the Continental Congress, which operated under a charter called the Articles of Confederation. These articles did not officially authorize Congress to concern itself with religion, but there was no objection from the public about religious activities. It appears that both legislators and the public alike considered it appropriate for the national government to promote a kind of nondenominational Christianity. For example, Congress appointed chaplains for itself and the armed forces, sponsored the publication of a Bible, imposed Christian morality on the armed forces, and granted public lands to promote Christianity among the Indians. National days of thanksgiving or of "public humiliation, fasting and prayer" were proclaimed by Congress more than a dozen times during the Revolutionary War.[6]

The Continental Congress was guided by "covenant theology," a Reformation doctrine, especially dear to New England Puritans, which held that God bound Himself in an agreement with the nation and its people. This agreement stipulated that "a people should be prosperous or afflicted, according as their general Obedience or Disobedience thereto appears." Wars and revolutions were accordingly considered afflictions as divine punishments for sin from which a nation could rescue itself by repentance and reformation.

Many states joined with the Continental Congress in its Thanksgiving and Fast Day proclamations. The Massachusetts Constitution of 1780 declared that "the happiness of a people, and the good order and preservation of civil government, essentially depend on morality, religion, and piety." In Massachusetts, Connecticut, and New Hampshire, religious taxes were laid on all citizens, each of whom was given the option of designating his share to the church of his choice.[7]

When the Articles of Confederation proved to be inadequate, the Constitution of the United States was drafted and adopted in the summer of 1787. At the Constitutional Convention, the sessions were not opened or closed with prayer, apparently for the reason that the convention had no funds to engage the services of a chaplain. However, at one point in the convention, when the delegates seemed to be making little progress and were strongly divided over what this new government should look like, one of the delegates from Pennsylvania, Benjamin Franklin, made some remarks which have become perhaps the most famous made in that convention. After noting the deadlock and the searching for correct answers, Franklin said: "In this situation of this Assembly, groping as it were in the dark to find political truth, and scarce able to distinguish it when presented to us, how has it happened, Sir, that we have not hitherto once thought of humbly applying to the Father of Lights to illuminate our understandings?"[8] Franklin here reminded the convention how at the beginning of the Revolutionary War the Continental Congress had prayers for divine protection:

Our prayers, sir, were heard, and they were graciously answered. All of us who are engaged in the struggle must have observed the frequent instances of a Superintending providence in our favor. To that kind providence we owe this happy opportunity of consulting in peace on the means of establishing our future national felicity. And have we now forgotten that powerful friend or do we imagine that we no longer need his assistance? I have lived, Sir, a long time, and the longer I live, the more convincing proofs I see of this truth—*that God governs in the affairs of men.*[9]

Franklin continued:

If a sparrow cannot fall to the ground without his notice, is it probable that an empire could arise without his aid? We have been assured, Sir, in the sacred writings that "except the Lord build the House they labour in vain that build it." I firmly believe this; and I also believe that without his concurring aid we shall succeed in this political building no better than the Builders of Babel.[10]

No mention was made of religion in the original Constitution except in Article VI, which states that "no religious tests shall ever be required as a qualification" for federal office holders.[11] Because of the reluctance of some states, particularly Virginia, to adopt the Constitution without a bill of rights, the first ten amendments to the Constitution were promulgated by the first Congress meeting under the new constitution. In the very first amendment, two important guarantees of religion were provided. First, "Congress shall make no law respecting an establishment of religion" and, secondly, Congress shall not prohibit "the free exercise thereof."[12] With those constitutional guarantees, which we refer to generally as freedom of religion, the people of America have for the most part been a religious people and have been supportive of the church of their choice. Although many of the old established religions practiced in Europe were brought to America, new religions which are purely American sprang up here. Churches today are found in every city, town, and hamlet. Billions of dollars are voluntarily contributed annually for their building and maintenance.

Many of this nation's leaders after the colonial period have referred to the influence of religion in their lives and in their administration. Abraham

Lincoln, upon leaving his home in Springfield, Illinois, in February 1861 to travel to Washington to become the president, expressed his reliance upon God to guide him in his administration. South Carolina and other Southern states had seceded from the Union, and the nation was in crisis. Lincoln said, upon leaving Springfield:

> I now leave, not knowing when, or whether ever, I may return with a task before me greater than that which rested upon Washington. Without the assistance of that Divine Being who ever attended him, I cannot succeed. With that assistance, I cannot fail. Trusting in Him who can go with me and remain with you and be everywhere for good, let us confidently hope that all will yet be well. To His care commending you, as I hope in your prayers you will commend me, I bid you an affectionate farewell.[13]

There can be no doubt that religion has contributed significantly in the building of America and does so even today. I hope that these introductory comments will set the stage for many visitors, listeners, and future readers who find themselves drawn into this exhibition and lecture series on the role of religion in the founding of the American Republic.

These remarks were given on January 27, 2002, when Richard C. Howe was serving as Chief Justice of the Utah Supreme Court, at the formal opening of the Library of Congress exhibition entitled Religion and the Founding of the American Republic *at Brigham Young University. The author expresses appreciation to James H. Hutson for permission to draw generously from his exhibition catalogue,* Religion and the Founding of the American Republic.

Notes

1. James H. Hutson, *Religion and the Founding of the American Republic* (Washington, D.C.: Library of Congress, 1998), 4.

2. Hutson, *Religion and the Founding of the American Republic,* 6–7.

3. John Winthrop, *A Modell of Christian Charity,* quoted in Hutson, *Religion and the Founding of the American Republic,* 7, spelling modernized.

4. Material in preceding paragraphs is drawn, with permission, from Hutson, *Religion and the Founding of the American Republic,* 8.

5. Material in preceding paragraphs is used, with permission, from Hutson, *Religion and the Founding of the American Republic,* 8, 11–12, 15–17.

6. Hutson, *Religion and the Founding of the American Republic,* 46–47, 51, 117n3.

7. Hutson, *Religion and the Founding of the American Republic,* 53, 65–66.

8. Max Farrand, ed., *The Records of the Federal Convention,* 4 vols. (New Haven: Yale University Press, 1937), 1:451.

9. Farrand, *The Records of the Federal Convention,* 1:451, emphasis in original.

10. Farrand, *The Records of the Federal Convention,* 1:451.

11. United States Constitution, article 6.

12. United States Constitution, amendment 1.

13. Carl Sandburg, *Abraham Lincoln: The Prairie Years* in *Abraham Lincoln: The Prairie Years and the War Years,* 3 vols. (New York: Dell, 1954), 1:320.

"NURSING FATHERS"
THE MODEL FOR CHURCH-STATE RELATIONS IN AMERICA FROM JAMES I TO JEFFERSON

James H. Hutson

And kings shall be thy nursing fathers, and their queenes thy nursing mothers: they shall bow downe to thee with their face toward the earth, and licke up the dust of thy feete, and thou shalt know that I am the LORD; for they shall not be ashamed that waite for me.

Isaiah 49:23, King James Version (1611)

On April 15, 1775, four days before hostilities between British and American troops began at Lexington and Concord, the Massachusetts Provincial Congress proclaimed May 11 as a day of fasting and prayer throughout the colony. The fast day proclamation accused the British ministry of inciting the "Powers of Earth and Hell" to harass the Congregational Church in Massachusetts. Those, it asserted, "who should be Nursing Fathers become its Persecutors."[1] "Nursing Fathers"? Where did this peculiar phrase, more appropriate for an aberration in biology than statecraft, come from and what did it mean?

Those familiar with colonial Massachusetts would assume, correctly, that the phrase had theological roots. It comes from the prophet Isaiah and in 1775 had been in use for more

than two hundred years by British and American religious and political leaders (including two kings of England) to express their conviction that the government of any state must form a nurturing bond with religious institutions within its jurisdiction, that the civil authority must, in fact, become the "nursing father" of the church.

After the Declaration of Independence in 1776, substantial numbers of American citizens continued to use the nursing fathers metaphor to articulate their view about the proper relationship between government and religion, a view at polar opposites to Thomas Jefferson's assertion in 1802 that there should be a "wall of separation" between church and state.[2] Jefferson's phrase was an arresting one, but it languished, as a scholar has recently demonstrated, in relative obscurity until after World War II, when the Supreme Court embraced it in the *Everson* case (1947).[3] It is, therefore, no exaggeration to say that Jefferson's "wall" formulation has had a short and controversial run of only fifty years compared to the two hundred and fifty years in which the nursing fathers metaphor dominated the church-state dialogue in the Anglo-American world.

In *Provincial Congress*,

Concord, *April* 15, 1775.

WHEREAS it has pleased the righteous Sovereign of the Universe, in just Indignation against the Sins of a People long blessed with inestimable Privileges, civil and religious, to suffer the Plots of wicked Men on both Sides of the Atlantick, who for many Years have incessantly laboured to sap the Foundation of our public Liberties, so far to succeed; that we see the New-England Colonies reduced to the ungrateful Alternative of a tame Submission to a State of absolute Vassalage to the Will of a despotic Minister—or of preparing themselves speedily to defend, at the Hazard of Life, the unalienable Rights of themselves and Posterity, against the avowed Hostilities of their Parent State, who openly threatens to wrest them from their Hands by Fire and Sword.

In Circumstances dark as these, it becomes us, as Men and Christians, to reflect that, whilst every prudent Measure should be taken to ward off the impending Judgments, or prepare to act a proper Part under them when they come; at the same Time, all Confidence must be with-held from the Means we use; and reposed only on that GOD who rules in the Armies of Heaven, and without whose Blessing the best human Counsels are but Foolishness—and all created Power Vanity;

It is the Happiness of his Church that, when the Powers of Earth and Hell combine against it, and those who should be Nursing Fathers become its Persecutors—then the Throne of Grace is of the easiest Access—and its Appeal thither is graciously invited by the Father of Mercies, who has assured it, that when his Children ask Bread he will not give them a Stone:

THEREFORE, in Compliance with the laudable Practice of the People of GOD in all Ages, with humble Regard to the Steps of Divine Providence towards this oppressed threatened and endangered People, and especially in Obedience to the Command Heaven, that binds us *to call on him in the Day of Trouble,*——

RESOLVED, That it be, and hereby is recommended to the good People of this Colony, of all Denominations, That THURSDAY the Eleventh Day of *May* next be set apart as a Day of Public Humiliation, Fasting and Prayer; that a total Abstinence from servile Labor and Recreation be observed, and all their religious Assemblies solemnly convened, to humble themselves before GOD under the heavy Judgments felt and feared, to confess the Sins that have deserved them, to implore the Forgiveness of all our Transgressions, and a Spirit of Repentance and Reformation—and a Blessing on the Husbandry, Manufactures, and other lawful Employments of this People; and especially that the Union of the American Colonies in Defence of their Rights (for which hitherto we desire to thank Almighty GOD) may be preserved and confirmed.—that the Provincial and especially the Continental CONGRESSES, may be directed to such Measures at GOD will countenance.—That the People of *Great-Britain,* and their Rulers, may have their Eyes open'd to discern the Things that shall make for the Peace of the Nation and all its Connexions——And that AMERICA may soon behold a gracious Interposition of Heaven, for the Redress of her many Grievances, the Restoration of all her invaded Liberties, and their Security to the latest Generations.

By Order of the Provincial Congress,

JOHN HANCOCK, President.

In this fast-day proclamation, the Massachusetts Provincial Congress claimed that "those who should be Nursing Fathers [have] become its Persecutors," refering to perceived threats to the Congregational Churches by Britain. See the third paragraph.

PATRONS AND PROTECTORS FOR THE REFORMERS

Isaiah was a favorite book of the seminal thinkers of the Protestant Reformation of the sixteenth century, many of whom wrote commentaries on it: Zwingli (1529), Luther (1532), Munster (ca. 1540), Brenz (1550), Castiello (1551), Calvin (1551, 1552, 1559), Musculus (1557), and Bullinger (1567).[4] Most of these savants thought Isaiah 49:23 deserved only a few perfunctory remarks. For Luther

the verse meant little more than that "queens and wives of important men are to be converted to the Gospel."[5] John Calvin, however, was impressed by the possibility that the nursing father metaphor in verse 23 could promote the mission of the newly reformed churches. By giving the verse a militantly sectarian interpretation, he excited the imagination of English-speaking Reformers who, beginning in the 1560s, appropriated the metaphor and broadcast it across the British Isles.

Calvin's extensive comments on Isaiah 49:23, bristling with the belligerence of the early Reformers, locked in a lethal struggle with the Church of Rome. Princes who defended the true, reformed religion "obtained," Calvin declared, "this highest pinnacle of rank, which surpasses dominion and principality of every sort, to be 'nursing-fathers' and guardians of the Church." "The Papists," he continued, "have no other idea of kings being 'nursing fathers' of the Church than that they have left to their priests and monks very large revenues, rich possessions and prebends, on which they might fatten, like hogs in a sty." For the Protestant prince, "'nursing' aims at an object quite different from filling up those insatiable gulls"; rather it was "about removing superstitions and putting an end to all wicked idolatry, about advancing the kingdom of Christ and maintaining purity of doctrine, about purging scandals and cleansing from the filth that corrupts piety and impairs the lustre of Divine majesty." Of course, Protestant princes would "supply the pastors and ministers of the Word with all that is necessary for food and maintenance," but material support was incidental to a higher spiritual obligation. To "shew themselves to be 'nursing fathers,'" they must, above all, be "protectors of believers, and shall bravely defend the doctrine of the Word."[6]

It was Calvin's habit to work ideas from his numerous biblical commentaries, including his *Commentary on Isaiah,* into the multiplying and progressively expanding editions of his *Institutes of the Christian Religion.* In 1559 he introduced "nursing fathers" into book four of the *Institutes.* There

Calvin noted that "Isaiah, when he predicts that 'kings shall be nursing-fathers and queens nursing-mothers' to the Church, does not depose them from their thrones; but rather establishes them by an honourable title, as patrons and protectors of the pious worshipers of God."[7] This rather economical treatment of the passage would, no doubt, have encouraged contemporary readers to seek a fuller exposition of Calvin's views on Isaiah 49:23 by turning to his popular *Commentary.*

Confident, apparently, of obtaining an English audience, Calvin dedicated the first edition of his *Commentary* to the young Protestant king, Edward VI. Lamenting that the "Roman Antichrist, far and wide usurping and tyrannizing over the sanctuary of God, tears, crushes, and tramples under his feet all that belonged to God," Calvin urged Edward to devote himself to the promotion of "pure doctrine": "I expressly call upon, or rather, God himself addresses you by the mouth of his servant Isaiah, charging you to proceed, to the utmost of your ability and power, in carrying forward the restoration of the Church. . . . You daily read and hear that this duty is enjoined on you. . . . More especially Isaiah, as I have said, calls *Kings the nursing fathers of the Church,* (Is. xlix. 23) and does not permit them to withhold that assistance which her afflicted condition demands."[8]

When Queen Mary, a Catholic, ascended the English throne in 1553, she attempted to compel the country to return to Rome. According to Calvin, the "oppression of pure doctrine, which raged with prodigious violence for a short period" claimed as one of its victims his *Commentary,* which was "banished" from the realm.[9] Protestant fortunes revived in 1559, when Elizabeth became queen. Calvin dedicated his expanded 1559 edition of the *Commentary* to the new monarch, urging her to lay aside "all other kinds of business, a vast number of which, I have no doubt, will crowd upon you at the commencement of your reign" and concentrate with "invincible determination" on purifying the nation's religion. Entreated Calvin: "You ought to be stimulated, venerable Queen, by a sacred regard to Duty; for the Prophet Isaiah demands not only from *Kings* that they be *nursing fathers,* but also from *Queens* that they be *nursing mothers.* (Isa. xlix. 23.) This duty you ought to discharge . . . by removing the filth of Popery."[10]

Whether Elizabeth read Calvin's *Commentary* is unknown, but the Geneva Reformer's writings enjoyed a great vogue among her subjects. An English translation of his *Institutes of the Christian Religion* went through seven printings between 1561 and 1599. A translation of Calvin's sermons on Job was reprinted five times in ten years.[11] Both Elizabethan Puritan leaders and their opponents in the Anglican hierarchy appealed to Calvin's authority in theological disputes. The Puritan Thomas Cartwright, for example, arguing with the future Archbishop of Canterbury, John Whitgift, exclaimed that "we receive M. Calvin, and weigh of him, as of the notoblest [*sic*] instruments that the Lord hath stirred up for the purging of His Churches, and of the restoring of the plain and sincere interpretation of the Scriptures, which hath been since the Apostles' times."[12]

Calvin was personally acquainted with many of the Elizabethan Anglican leaders, who, during the Marian persecutions, fled to the European continent and found refuge in Switzerland and neighboring countries. These English exiles, it has been said, "came under the spell of Calvin's genius."[13] One of them, John Jewel, became Bishop of Salisbury upon Elizabeth's accession and began the administration of his diocese with "decided leanings to Calvinism." Jewel certainly knew Calvin's *Commentary on Isaiah,* for in 1562 he incorporated the nursing father metaphor into his *Apology for the Church of England,* a book that was "immediately adopted on all sides as the literary exposition of England's ecclesiastical position" and soon was considered so "authoritative" that it was chained to lecterns in churches throughout England.[14] By using the nursing father metaphor to describe the obligation of civil authorities to the church, Jewel embedded the concept in the consciousness of Anglicans, who habitually employed it during the following centuries; used by every priest from luminaries like Richard Hooker to the humblest parish curate, it became a mainstay of the church's vocabulary.[15]

A "Christian prince," Jewel declared,

> hath the charge of both tables committed to him by God, to the end he may understand that not temporal matters only but also religious and ecclesiastical causes pertain to his office; besides also that God by his prophets often and earnestly commandeth the king to cut down the groves, to break down the images and altars of idols, and to write out the book of the law for himself; and besides that the prophet Isaiah saith "A king ought to be a patron and nurse of the church" . . . we see by histories and by examples of the best times that good princes ever took the administration of ecclesiastical matters to pertain to their duty.[16]

The prophetic commission to the king as nursing father served, in Jewel's view, two purposes: it trumped the Church of Rome's pretensions, based on a theory of papal supremacy, to control English ecclesiastical affairs; and it authorized the English monarchy to impose its own brand of uniform religious truth throughout the realm. In response to attacks by Catholic theologians, Jewel issued a *Defense of the Apology* in 1567, which, like Calvin, he dedicated to Queen Elizabeth as the "nource" [nurse] of the church.[17]

However, neither Jewel's influence nor the term's appearance in the 1560 English Geneva Bible, which translated Isaiah 49:23 as "Kings shal be thy nourcing fathers," were sufficient to supersede a rival translation of the nursing father metaphor. Other authors, evidently uneasy about the propriety of a word picture of a suckling male, rendered it "foster fathers." The phrase Calvin used in the Latin versions of his *Commentary on Isaiah* and in his *Institutes* which Jewel[18] and the Geneva Bible translated as *nurse* and *nourcing fathers,* he (or his typesetters) spelled variously as *Ecclesiae nutritios, Ecclesiae nutricios, Ecclesiae nutricii,* and *nutritii tui.*[19] *Nutritios* and its variant spellings were derived from the Latin feminine noun *nutrix,* which a standard Latin-English dictionary translates as "a nurse, foster

mother."[20] Therefore, Thomas Norton, the translator of the frequently reprinted 1561 English edition of the *Institutes,* was on solid ground in rendering Calvin's "Ecclesiae nutritios" as "fosterfathers of the church."[21] William Allen in his *An Apologie . . . of Two English Colleges* (1581) employed the same locution. "Kings," wrote Allen, "are called by the Prophete [Isa: 49.23] her *foster fathers,* as Queenes be also named her *nources*: because it belongeth to the earthly power that God hath given them, to defend the lawes of the Church, to cause them to be executed, and to punish rebels and transgressors of the same."[22]

THE STUARTS AS ESTABLISHERS OF TRUE RELIGION

The royal prestige of James I secured the victory of the nursing fathers metaphor. In the course of his celebrated campaign to persuade the Dutch government to expel from its dominions the "wretch Heretique" Conrad Vorst, James issued his widely read *Declaration against Vorstius* (1610).[23] In this polemic, James declared "that it is one of the principal parts of that duetie which appertaines unto a Christian King, to protect the trew Church within his owne Dominions, and to extirpate heresies, is a maxime without all controversie." "Those honorouable Titles . . . Nutritius Ecclesiae, Nursing father of the Church," James asserted, "doe rightly belong unto every Emperour, King, and Christian Monarch."[24]

Charles I also called himself "an indulgent nursing father," giving the metaphor the cachet of a second royal patron.[25] The incessant use of the metaphor by the Anglican hierarchy to compliment the Stuart kings[26] and their successors—William III, for example, was extolled as "a Nursing Father to Zion the Church of God"[27]—put it in general circulation and secured it a place in the vocabulary of political controversy. The metaphor was used by two of the seventeenth century's most celebrated intellectual antagonists, political philosophers Robert Filmer and John Locke.[28] Through Locke's *Second Treatise of Government,* it came to the attention of a wide American audience. That it retained its vitality among eighteenth-century thinkers is attested by

Edmund Burke, who referred to the civil magistrate as a "Nurse and Increasor of Blessings."[29]

Puritan opponents of the Church of England under Elizabeth and the Stuarts differed among themselves on many issues, none more important than church government. Some Puritans favored a presbyterian form of church government, others a congregational one. Congregationalists were split between those who regarded themselves as a loyal opposition within the Church of England—the settlers of Massachusetts Bay belonged in this camp—and those "separatists" who utterly renounced the Church. Both wings of the Congregational movement subscribed to the Anglican interpretation of the ecclesiastical role of civil authority, as articulated by James I, that the ruler was obliged to establish true religion in his realm, and both appropriated the "nursing father" metaphor to convey this understanding.

The separatist position received its clearest formulation in the "Confession of 1596," a document issued in Amsterdam by men who had been driven out of England by political authorities who had executed their leaders and brutally persecuted their flocks. The authors of the "Confession," nevertheless, asserted that "it is the office and Duty of Princes and Magestrates . . . to suppress and root out by their authoritie all false ministries, voluntarie Relligions, and counterfeyt worship of God, to destroy the Idoll Temples, Images, Altares, Vestments, and all other monuments of Idolatrie and superstition" and to confiscate all church property of "anie false ministeries . . . And on the other hand to establish & mayntein by their lawes every part of Gods word his pure Relligion and true ministerie. . . . They accompt it a happie blessing of God who granteth such nourcing Fathers and nourcing Mothers to his Church."[30]

THE ENGLISH CIVIL WAR:
PROTECTORS OR ENFORCERS?

The religious dynamics of the English Civil War compelled the mainstream, nonseparating Congregationalists, now called Independents, to temper some of their earlier doctrinal zeal. On January 31, 1648, the day after the execution of Charles I, one of the most learned Independent ministers, Dr. John Owen, delivered a famous sermon in Parliament on the limits of religious toleration. According to Owen, scripture commanded "kings and judges to serve the Lord, in promoting the kingdom of the Lord Jesus Christ. And it is promised, Isa. xlix. 23, that 'they shall be nursing-fathers and nursing-mothers to the church' of Christ, even then when she shall 'suck the breasts of kings' (earthly things are the milk of kingly breasts)."[31]

Among the "earthly things" the nursing fathers were required to supply, Owen listed the following: the "providing or granting of places requisite for the performance of that worship which in the gospel is instituted"; "protection, as to peace and quietness in the use of the ordinances of the Lord Jesus Christ, from violent disturbers"; and "supportment and provision [for the gospel ministry] as to earthly things, where regularly failing."[32] Owen was as confident as the authors of the 1596 Confession that "it was the duty of the magistrate," as nursing father, "not to allow any public places for (in his judgment) false and abominable worship; as also, to demolish all outward appearances and demonstrations of such superstitious, idolatrous, and unacceptable service."[33] Those publicly and obstreperously propagating "uncouth" religious opinions were to be suppressed. But out of respect for the welter of Protestant religious opinions that had surfaced during the Civil War, Owen would permit the magistrate to allow the public airing of a variety of religious views (at least on matters indifferent) and would offer a wide latitude for the expression of religious opinions in private.

This was a position that many Presbyterians, especially those in Scotland, were not prepared to countenance. John Knox, the great pillar of Scottish Presbyterianism, was a disciple of Calvin who carried his preceptor's view on church-state relations directly from Geneva to the court of Queen Mary at Edinburgh. In an interview which the Reformer called "the first reasoning betwixt the queen and John Knox," September 4, 1561, Knox lectured the young monarch in the following manner: God "subjects people under princes, and causes obedience to be given unto them; yea, God craves of kings that they be as it were foster-fathers to his Church, and commands queens to be nurses to his people."[34] Knox's use of foster fathers gave the term as much prestige in Presbyterian circles as Jewel's simultaneous use of nursing fathers had done in the Anglican community. The metaphor eventually achieved a higher status among Presbyterians because it was incorporated by reference into the Westminster Confession of 1646,[35] for the past three centuries the basic creed of the denomination.

[80]

III. The Civill Magiſtrate may not aſſume to himſelf the Adminiſtration of the Word and Sacraments, or the power of the Keys of the Kingdom of Heaven e: yet he hath Authority, and it is his duty to take order, that Unity and Peace be preſerved in the Church, that the Truth of God be kept pure and intire, that all Blaſphemies and Hereſies be ſuppreſſed, all corruptions and abuſes in Worſhip and Diſcipline prevented or reformed: and all the Ordinances of God duly ſetled, adminiſtred and obſerved f. For the better effecting whereof he hath power to call Synods, to be preſent at them, and to provide that whatſoever is tranſacted in them be according to the mind of God g.

Courtesy Library of Congress

Humble Advice of the Assembly of Divines, Now by Authority of Parliament Sitting at Westminster (London, 1658). The position of the Westminster Confession on the role of the state in religious affiars.

The English Civil Wars did not make Presbyterians as malleable as the Independents, a point vividly illustrated by one of the classics in the literature of Presbyterian apologetics, Samuel Rutherford's *Lex, Rex*. Writing in 1644, Rutherford championed the nursing father metaphor (which in Scotland had by now supplanted Knox's foster fathers). He began his book with the strong, if conventional, assertion that "Kings and all Magistrates are Gods, and Gods deputies and lieutenants upon earth" as well as "nursing fathers of the Church." Later in his work Rutherford tackled the question of whether kings were fathers "univocally, or only

analogically." He concluded, "Though the Word warrant us to esteem King's fathers, Esa. 49. 23 . . . yet they are not essentially and formally fathers by generation . . . and yet are they but fathers metaphorically." Rutherford, in fact, preferred the term "Nurse-father" and applied it to kings, judges, and other civil officials. He took an uncompromising view of the role of the nurse-father, who was not only "appointed for Civill Policy, but for the maintenance of true religion, and for the suppression of idolatrie and superstition." "The King," Rutherford declared, "hath a chiefe hand in Church affaires, when he is a Nurse-Father, and beareth the Royall Sword to defend both the Tables of the Law." Rutherford made Henry VIII a posthumous "Nurse-father" because he had defended the faith "by his Sword."[36]

In 1652 a heated exchange occurred between an anonymous defender of the mainstream conception of the nursing father metaphor and Roger Williams, who was in England at the time defending Rhode Island's interests. A pamphlet, *The Examiner Examined,* contained a long subtitle asserting that the civil magistrate was obliged to "advance the true Religion." Quoting in justification the text from "Esay 49.22, 23," the anonymous advocate posed the following proposition: "Whether a Magistrate that knowes the Doctrine of Salvation by Christ Jesus, doe fulfill the Office of a Nursing Father, if he doe not cause this saving Food to be given to his Children; and Poyson, that is contrary Doctrine to be kept from them."[37] In an impassioned rejoinder, *The Examiner Defended,* Williams employed his distinctive, antitypological exegetical approach to argue that "this Prophesie of Kings and queens being nursing fathers and nursing mothers to the Saints" applied only to the Jews of the Old Testament. "Consequently," he asked

> Whether all those bloody persecutors (Papists and Protestants), who have used to drawn this shaft out of the Quiver of Scripture, whereby to pierce the tender heart of Jesus; yea and all that give a power to the Civil magistrate in Spirituals from this Scripture, Have not most ignorantly profaned the prophecy, and that to usurpation over the temple of God, the Consciences of Gods

own people; and to bloody violence against their Bodies, although under a cloak of providing wholesome food for their children and prohibiting poyson, etc.

After offering several more objections to the popular interpretation of Isaiah 49:23, Williams concluded by asking whether it

was not this very Doctrine that cost the late King Charles his Crown, and Life? Who being flattered and bewitched into this dream of a Nursing father, and a judge of wholesome food and poyson for his people; he forced poyson for food on the Scotch Nation . . . and prosecuting those fatal Wars, which (by a naked Hand from heaven) justly pluckt up root and branch, both Ceremonies, Bishops, and king together.[38]

A few years later an even more eminent advocate of liberty of conscience, John Milton, attacked the conventional understanding of Isaiah 49:23. Milton's eye was apparently caught by a passage in a precis of protestant theology, *Compendium Theologiae Christianae* (Basel, 1626) by the Swiss theologian Johannes Wolleb (Wollebius), which "caused a considerable sensation" in London in the 1650s, when it appeared in an English translation.[39] In his *Abridgement of Christian Divinitie*, as the translation was called, Wolleb asserted that "Magistrates are the Churches nursing-fathers, as they are keepers of the two Tables of the law, as they preserves Churches and Schools, and defend the Truth." In reply, Milton declared that "churches do not need the supervision of magistrates," or of kings, acting as "foster-fathers" (apparently, a deliberate substitution by Milton for what he considered the excessive Anglican, royalist usage of "nursing fathers"). "The magistrate should protect religion, not enforce it," because "Christ's kingdom is not of this world, it does not stand by force and constraint, the constituents of worldly authority. So the gospel should not be made a matter of compulsion, and faith, liberty and conscience cannot be."[40]

Americans in 1776 were unacquainted with—and could not have been influenced by—Williams's polemic against the nursing fathers; like his other theological writings it had long been forgotten, if, in fact, it had ever been known in the colonies. Nor is it likely that they would have been aware of Milton's strictures against the metaphor, since his essay attacking it was not published during his lifetime. But it is significant that men of the stature of Williams and Milton attempted to discredit the metaphor, for their efforts attest to its potency in seventeenth-century England.

The point in showing how firmly seventeenth-century Anglicans, Presbyterians, and Congregationalists-Independents were wedded to the nursing fathers metaphor is that they were the largest Protestant denominations in Great Britain and sent the largest number of settlers to North America.[41] By carrying the nursing fathers concept with them, members of these denominations established it as the model for church-state relations in most American colonies.

SUPPORTERS OF RELIGIOUS INSTITUTIONS IN EIGHTEENTH-CENTURY AMERICAN COLONIES

As the eighteenth century dawned in British North America, Anglicans routinely used the nursing father metaphor. Consider the controversy over the behavior of Francis Nicholson, appointed governor of Virginia in 1698. To his enemies among the Virginia planter elite, Nicholson was "a monstrous compound of . . . hypocrisy and profaneness."[42] Others, however, admired him for his financial generosity toward the Church of England and called him a "true son or rather Nursing Father of her in America."[43] At a meeting of Anglican clergymen in Philadelphia in 1704, Nicholson's conduct was strongly endorsed: "We cannot but with a Christian Indignation consider that so good a Nursing Father of our holy Mother, so unparalleled and munificent a promoter of it should be ungratefully traduced."[44] The next year, as controversial a figure as Nicholson, Lord Cornbury, Governor of New York, was commended for his financial generosity toward the church: "For his eminent care and protection of us; he is truly our Nursing Father."[45]

The most popular Anglican clergyman in eighteenth-century America, though an opponent of the church's hierarchy, was the famous evangelist George Whitefield, one of the principal promoters of the Great Awakening in the 1740s. Whitefield's partiality to the nursing fathers metaphor was exhibited in a sermon preached before a huge crowd in Philadelphia in 1746 in a recently erected revivalistic arena, the "New Building." George II, Whitefield declared, "deserved that great and glorious title which the Lord promises kings should sustain in the latter days, I mean *a nursing Father of the Church*."[46] Whitefield's sermon, immediately published, assured the metaphor the widest possible circulation in America.

Presbyterians did not begin emigrating to the American colonies until the second decade of the eighteenth century and did not become a critical mass in American public life until the 1760s. Their principal spokesman in the Revolutionary period was John Witherspoon, who arrived in the colonies from Scotland in 1768. Shortly thereafter, Witherspoon delivered the famous series of lectures to his students at Princeton which were frequently republished as *Lectures on Moral Philosophy*. In this work, Scottish Presbyterianism's traditional emphasis on nursing fathers and nursing mothers appeared in the following passage: "Many are of opinion, that besides all this, the magistrate ought to make public provision for the worship on God. . . . And indeed there seems to be a good deal of reason for it, that so instruction may be provided for the bulk of the common people. . . . The magistrates right in this case seems to be something like that of a parent."[47]

Nursing fathers was a central concept of New England Congregationalists. One of their early historians, Edward Johnson, composed an imaginary "proclamation for Volunties," which Christ himself was depicted as inspiring on the eve of emigration from England in 1628. The Saviour instructed the settlers that when "your feete are once safely set on the shores of America" they were to "provoke . . . all that are in authority to cast downe their Crownes at the Feet of Christ, and take them up againe at his command under his Standard as

nursing Fathers and nursing Mothers to the Churches."[48] Twenty years later, in 1648, New England church leaders adopted the Cambridge Platform, a creed as authoritative among the faithful as the Westminster Confession was among Presbyterians. The Platform asserted that the "Magistrates are nursing fathers & nursing mothers & stand charged with custody of both Tables."[49] Historians note that the patronage of Increase and Cotton Mather insured that notion of the nursing fathers continued to thrive in New England.[50]

Eighteenth century sermons teemed with the metaphor, as, for example, Elisha Williams's well-known *A Seasonable Plea for the Liberty of Conscience and the Right of Private Judgment* (1744), in which Williams, the rector of Yale College, 1726–1739, argued that "the civil authority of a state are obliged to take care for the support of religion, or in other words, of schools and the gospel ministry, in order to their approving themselves nursing fathers (as, I suppose, every body will own, and therefore I shall not spend any time in proving it)."[51] In the 1760s preachers of the Connecticut Election sermon featured the nursing fathers metaphor. In 1762, Joseph Bellamy, a stalwart in the "New Divinity" theological movement, described the ideal governor as exhibiting toward the citizens "all the good will and tenderness which are wont to reside in the heart of a nursing father or nursing mother toward an infant child."[52] Three years later, the election sermon was preached entirely from the text Isaiah 49:23. Calling his sermon *The Duty of Civil Rulers, to Be Nursing Fathers to the Church of Christ*, Edward Dorr listed a variety of ways in which the magistrates were to act as nursing fathers, the principal one being the paying of ministers' salaries from public revenues.[53] In 1771 a Congregational minister in Stonington, Connecticut, Joseph Fish, cited "Isa. 49.23 and kings shall be thy nursing fathers, and queens thy nursing mothers" as an example of God's "precious promise" to support the church. Fish gave the text what by that date had become a reactionary reading by suggesting that it would authorize political authorities to suppress the dissenting zealots who were plaguing his ministry. "As nurses or parents take care of their helpless children," Fish wrote, "carrying them in their arms, treating them with all tenderness and affection, and stretching out their hands for their protection and defence, so shall kings and queens treat the church of Christ."[54]

PAYMASTERS OF RELIGIOUS ESTABLISHMENT IN THE NEW REPUBLIC

After the Declaration of Independence, the calls for civil authorities to become nursing fathers of the church assumed a sense of anxious urgency in those states where the churches that had enjoyed exclusive state patronage during the colonial period were now under siege by reformers demanding their disestablishment. On September 13, 1783, an article appeared in the *Virginia Gazette, or, The American Advertiser* that contained, its author claimed, "the sentiments of the judicious Christians in this State." Religion was flagging, the "judicious Christians" declared, and "the friendly aid of the Legislature is wanting." Otherwise, God might inflict

> some severe stroke to rouse us to a sense of our duty and interest. Far be it from us to suppose that you [the legislators] conceive it beneath your dignity, to become nursing fathers of the church, and to promote true piety and devotion amongst us . . . and to raise up a numerous body of subjects, who will fear God and honor the Magistrates . . . and will become the best soldiers, the most industrious and wise citizens, that cannot fail to exalt these States to that degree of grandeur and happiness which will . . . raise the admiration of the whole earth.

In the same vein, the citizens of Amherst County adjured the General Assembly of Virginia on November 27, 1783, not to "think it beneath your Dignity to become Nursing Fathers of the Church" by funding religion in the state.[55]

In Revolutionary New England, the nursing fathers metaphor continued to be a coin of the realm. A member of the Massachusetts Constitutional Convention of 1780 asserted that on the convention floor one of the principal arguments

used for the continuation of public funding for the state's Congregational ministers was the reminder "that the prophet Isaiah, in speaking of gospel times, had declared, that kings should become nursing fathers and queens nursing mothers, to the church; which most certainly implied, that the civil authority would make suitable provision for the support and maintenance of public worship and teachers of religion."[56] Ezra Stiles, in his important 1783 sermon *The United States Elevated to Glory and Honor,* vented the post-independence anxiety of the Congregationalist establishment. Stiles worried that

> if even the Holy Redeemer himself and his apostles were to reappear among us, while unknown to be such, and importune the public government and magistracy of these states to become nursing fathers to the church, is it not to be feared that some of the states, through timidity and fearfulness of touching religion, would excuse themselves and dismiss these holy messengers.

"May we not humbly wish," Stiles asked his audience, the members of the Connecticut General Assembly, "that you would not repudiate the idea of being nursing fathers to our spiritual Israel, the church of God within this state? Give us, gentlemen," Stiles continued, "the decided assurance that you are friends of the churches, and that you are friends of the pastors."[57]

It is obvious from the evidence cited that by 1776, many Americans, especially those with pre-independence religious establishments, were preoccupied with what Calvin and his contemporaries regarded as a distinctly secondary duty of the civil authorities acting as nursing fathers: the use of public funds to provide financial support for the ministry. The reason for this change in focus is simple: the Toleration Act of 1689 and the subsequent commitment of many eighteenth-century lay and clerical leaders to freedom of conscience undercut the state's theoretical right to establish the true religion by eradicating the false. Under the new dispensation, what had previously been considered false was permitted to flourish, as the state stood impotently by. Calvin's, James I's, or Rutherford's concept of the nursing father, sword in hand, dispatching the heretics became instantly obsolete in 1689 and was succeeded in both England and America by the idea that the nursing father should become the preacher's paymaster.

The idea behind Calvin's concept of the nursing father was clear enough. By establishing the true religion, the civil authorities prepared the way for the eternal salvation of its citizens. By what rationale, however, did the state as nursing father confine itself solely to what John Owen called "supportment"? This question became especially pressing after 1776, when many of the new American state governments tried to pass general assessment acts, which laid religious taxes to pay a wide assortment of Protestant preachers. Since every denomination could not be the repository of the one true way to salvation, why should the nursing father pay any of them? The answer given by the intended ecclesiastical beneficiaries and their lay supporters was not, spiritually, a very edifying one: the state was urged to provide financial subventions to the churches as an act of self interest because the churches were uniquely qualified to help it achieve its secular objectives. This rationale turned on its head Calvin's case for the state as nursing father. To the great Reformer, the state, in its capacity as facilitator of salvation, acted as the agent of the church; after 1776, the church in many places came to be depicted as the agent of the state.

Most of the post-1776 arguments that stressed the civic contribution of the church were articulated by Dorr in his 1765 *Nursing Fathers* sermon. According to Dorr, "The civil interests of mankind, the safety of the state requires, that there be some religious establishments." He hammered away at this point: "The practice of religion and virtue, tends, above all other things, to promote those very ends, for which men entered into society"; "The public profession and practice of religion, was a benefit to the state, and absolutely necessary, to the safety and security of civil government"; religion was the "best security mankind can possibly have, of the quiet and peaceable enjoyment of their lives,

liberties and properties"; and it promotes "the public welfare and happiness of mankind."[58] Post-independence preachers did not improve much on Dorr. Religion was necessary, Phillips Payson declared in 1778, "to support and preserve order and government in the state;" it was the "great foundation of public prosperity and national happiness," John Witherspoon asserted in 1782; and it was "productive of really great and extensive public good," Bishop James Madison of Virginia claimed in 1799.[59] Statements such as these became hackneyed observations that tripped from the lips of every preacher and politician, including George Washington, in the Founding period.[60] The problem with the incessant argument for government support of religion on the grounds of its "public Utility" was that it reduced religion to the level of other activities that promoted the secular agenda of the state and resulted, finally, in speakers in the Massachusetts Constitutional Convention of 1820 equating religion with road building programs and the militia.[61] This degrading comparison, as a style of advocacy, became one of the many factors that produced the disenchantment that led to the disestablishment of religion in the commonwealth in 1833.

Since some of the talk after 1776 about the obligation of the state was obviously special pleading by Anglican and Congregational ministers, fearful that their publicly funded salaries would stop, it is a fair question to ask how broad, in fact, was the constituency for the nursing fathers metaphor? Elisha Williams claimed in 1744 that "ever body" agreed that civil magistrates should be nursing fathers of the church, but Williams meant "ever body" in New England, not throughout the colonies.[62] Isaac Backus, the New England Baptist leader, confirmed in 1768 that "many" of his fellow citizens, in justification of his area's entrenched system of religious taxation, "plead in this case that promise to the church, that *Kings shall be her nursing fathers and Queens her nursing mothers.*"[63] The metaphor continued to be on the tip of most New England tongues and was regularly encountered after 1776 in the region's political and theological controversies, as the following statement, made in 1785 by the future Chief Justice of Massachusetts Theophilus Parsons, demonstrates: "The Christian church was formed by Christ: she took her name from him, and was so far wedded to state policy as that he made 'kings and queens nursing fathers and mothers.'"[64] In fact, after 1776, to break the monotony of using the term nursing fathers, New Englanders began addressing their magistrates in print as "civil" and "political" fathers.[65] "The people call them fathers," said the preacher of the New Hampshire election sermon in 1791, "we are willing to be their political children, as long as they are good parents."[66] That all the New England states after 1776 laid some form of general religious tax indicates that the majority of legislators and their constituents must have believed that the state as nursing father was obliged to provide financial support to the church.[67]

THE "DEMOCRATIZATON" OF THE METAPHOR

What was the situation in the Episcopalian (formerly Anglican) colonies from Maryland southward? Here again we have the testimony of a leading Baptist, John Leland, about the power of the nursing fathers metaphor. Reflecting in 1791 on his recently concluded fourteen-year pastorate in Virginia, Leland observed that the "rulers" there, his friends Jefferson and Madison excepted, had been swayed by Episcopal ecclesiastical influence to try to promote the public financing of religion on the grounds that it would be "advantageous to the state" and that "this they often do the more readily when they are flattered by the clergy that if they thus defend the truth they will become nursing fathers to the church and merit something considerable for themselves."[68] That the Virginia and Maryland Assemblies were on the verge of passing a general religious tax in 1785, that the Georgia Assembly actually passed such a measure the same year, and that a similar measure failed by only a handful of votes in South Carolina a few years earlier demonstrate the existence in the South of a strong sentiment in favor of the state

assuming the role of the nursing father as paymaster of the church.[69]

General assessment taxes were defeated by the combined opposition of the Baptists and Presbyterians as well as that of civil libertarians like Jefferson. Baptists and Presbyterians considered general assessment taxes as a Trojan horse that would lead to the reestablishment of the Church of England in the full plenitude of its pre-1776 power, including the power to persecute "dissenters" which still occurred sporadically after independence. The Baptists and Presbyterians did not, however, repudiate the nursing fathers metaphor, for they valued the spirit of church-state relations that it signified. By redefining the metaphor, they tried to rescue it and make it relevant to the pluralistic religious environment that was emerging in the new American republic.

The Presbyterian act of redefinition was impressive because it involved an alteration in the denomination's creed, the Westminster Confession. In 1729, American Presbyterians adopted the text of the Confession as it had come from the pens of its authors in 1646. The General Assembly held in Philadelphia in 1788, called to align the church with the new American nation, put the spotlight on the nursing fathers metaphor by elevating it from a footnote reference to Isaiah 49:23 in the 1646 Confession to an exposition in the main body of the text in the section on the Civil Magistrate. According to the 1788 version of the Confession, "as nursing fathers, it is the duty of civil magistrates to, protect the Church of our common Lord, without giving the preference to any denomination of Christians above the rest . . . no law of any commonwealth should interfere with, let, or hinder, the due exercise [of religion] among the voluntary members of *any* denomination of Christians."[70] In other words, the state must be fair as well as solicitous, a position strongly supported by the Baptists, whose ministers, after 1776, imitated their Congregationalist counterparts by calling the civil authorities "political fathers."[71] "That promise that kings shall become nursing fathers and queens nursing mothers," Isaac Backus reminded his fellow

New Englanders, "carries in its very nature an *impartial care and tenderness for all their children*."[72] In a memorial to the Massachusetts Provincial Congress, December 2, 1774, the Baptists urged that "civil rulers ought undoubtedly to be nursing fathers to the church, by reproof, exhortation, and their own good and liberal example, as well as to protect and defend her against injustice and oppression."[73]

That there was, by 1788, substantial support for the Presbyterian-Baptist position among members of the old "established" denominations is demonstrated by the Massachusetts election sermon of 1788 in which the Congregationalist preacher David Parsons informed Governor John Hancock and the assembled civil and ecclesiastical dignitaries that rulers should "afford protection and encouragement" to all of the state's ministers:

> They should be patrons and nursing Fathers to the church of Christ; and use their utmost endeavors to advance his Kingdom. All the which they may do without binding the rights of conscience, or exerting their authority to impose articles of faith, or modes of worship; or enforcing these by penalties. Indeed such an exercise of power in a ruler would be to extend his commission beyond its limits, and to defeat its design, which was to protect and preserve the rights of conscience.[74]

Congregationalists in neighboring Connecticut endorsed this position. Possibly fearing that the United States might be infected by the antireligious violence of the French Revolution, the preacher of the 1795 election sermon, Andrew Lee, informed the dignitaries assembled at Hartford that their duty was to protect the state's churches, even as they guaranteed freedom of conscience to all. "It is," said Lee, "incumbent on those who are *set to rule for God* to be *nursing fathers* to the cause of God." "Let true religion only be defended from external violence," the preacher urged his audience.[75] In 1803 the preacher of the election sermon, Matthias Burnet, captured this shift in emphasis on the rulers' duty by saluting Connecticut's magistrates as the "venerable fathers of your country" who had "become nursing, protecting fathers to the church."[76]

What the Presbyterians and Baptists, with Congregationalist concurrence, were attempting to do was obvious: they wanted to democratize the nursing fathers by redefining their mission from the exertion of coercive authority on behalf of one church, to the exertion of the state's authority to guarantee to all communities of faith the equal protection of the law. According to the revised conception of the nursing fathers, the state ought to protect all churches within its jurisdiction from malefactors, bigots, and bullies. Furthermore, it ought to promote Christian worship in a variety of ways: by making public facilities—courthouses, post offices, federal office buildings—available on a nondiscriminatory basis for church services, by sponsoring the distribution of accurate editions of the Bible, by defending the sanctity of the Sabbath, and by providing religious instruction in the public schools.[77]

At the time, say, of Washington's first inauguration, Congregationalists, Episcopalians, Presbyterians, and Baptists composed the vast majority of the population of the United States. If the members of these denominations agreed with the positions of their leaders and spokesmen about relations between church and state—and there is no reason to suppose that they did not—a strong case can be made that in 1789 or at any time between 1776 and 1800 a substantial majority of the American people believed that relations between government and religion should be described by the nursing father metaphor. There was, to be sure, disagreement about how far the nursing father could employ coercive authority to support the church, but, at a minimum, all agreed that the state should have warm, paternal feelings for its religious institutions, and that civil authorities, in so far as the law allowed, should be friends, helpers, and protectors of the churches, should treat them as any good father would treat his children. Perhaps Isaac Backus expressed the prevailing sentiment best, when he asserted that a "sweet harmony" should exist between church and state.[78]

DIFFUSION AND DISAPPEARANCE OF THE PHRASE IN THE NINETEENTH AND TWENTIETH CENTURIES

America's attachment to the nursing father metaphor appeared to many to be threatened by the election of the alleged "atheist" Thomas Jefferson to the presidency in 1800. During the presidential campaign, John Mitchell Mason, a popular Presbyterian minister in New York City and a founder of Union Theological Seminary, admonished his fellow citizens that

> you are commanded *to pray for your rulers:* it is your custom to pray, that they may be men *fearing God and hating covetousness.* You entreat him to fulfill his promise, that kings shall be to his church *nursing-fathers, and queens her nursing-mothers.* With what conscience can you lift up your hands in such a supplication, when you are exerting yourselves to procure a president who does not fear God. . . . Do you think the church of Christ is to be nurtured by the dragon's milk of infidelity?[79]

Nevertheless, while it is certainly true that Jefferson did not, like James I, publicly exult in his role as a nursing father of the church, an argument can be made that, within the space imposed by his aversion to the use of state power to promote religion, he played the part. Jefferson, after all, attempted to give religion his symbolic support by conscientiously attending church services in the House of Representatives and, more to the point, he extended a helping hand to the infant churches in the raw, young city of Washington by permitting them to conduct services in government facilities, specifically, in the State Department and War Office buildings. In assisting these churches Jefferson was following the practice of public officials in his native Virginia, which was imitated throughout the South and West in the early years of the new republic. Having moved into a new capitol building in the underdeveloped city of Richmond on the heels of the passage of the Virginia Statute for Religious Freedom (1786), the state legislature threw open the capitol to religious groups of all complexions, including Catholics, who conducted in these official precincts everything from masses to vestry meetings.[80]

The nursing fathers metaphor continued to be used in the nineteenth century but its focus became diffuse. In 1826, for example, field representatives of the American Home Missionary Society asked the churches of New York state to redouble their efforts in the "new settlements" in the western United States. How much, they were reminded, "does Isaiah tell us of kings being nursing fathers, and queens nursing mothers, to the church, when he speaks of the wilderness and solitary place budding as the rose."[81] In 1833 the Reverend Jasper Adams, president of the College of Charleston, South Carolina, used the metaphor to explain why the Christian church was "taken under the protection" of the Roman Emperor Constantine in the fourth century A.D. "It was the prediction of ancient prophecy," wrote Adams, "that, in the last days, kings should become nursing fathers and queens nursing mothers to the Church;—and what was more natural than to understand this prophecy as meaning a strict and intimate union of the Church, with the civil government of the Empire."[82] A dispute among Virginia churches in 1844–45 about the wisdom of seeking a general incorporation act for the state's religious denominations revived the metaphor in its more familiar political setting. Opponents of the incorporation act, an innocuous measure similar to those in force throughout the United States, alleged that "a powerful State never grants privileges to the church without requiring, sooner or later, heavy payment. A State, nursing a church, has always been like a she-bear hugging a lamb."[83] The Baptist-Presbyterian attempt to democratize the nursing fathers metaphor had not, obviously, prevented demagogues from employing it to arouse atavistic anxieties about religious oppression.

By the 1850s, the metaphor was disappearing from public discourse. The practice which it represented continued, however, until well after the Civil War, most visibly in Congress, which did not lose its taste for helping local religious groups. In 1865, for example, Congregationalists in Washington, attempting to organize a church, approached the leadership of the House, which allowed the petitioners to use its chambers. The result was that by 1868, before the Congregationalists moved into their new church, "nearly 2000 assembled every Sabbath for the regular services in this large hall. . . . This audience was said to be the largest Protestant Sabbath audience then in the United States."[84]

By a curious coincidence, in the years immediately after World War II, the two principal models of church-state relations in American history crossed paths, heading in opposite directions. In a series of decisions beginning with *Everson v. Board of Education* in 1947, the Supreme Court announced its discovery that religion should be partitioned off from government by a "wall of separation," an enforced estrangement that most Americans in the Founding period would have found repugnant. At virtually the same time, in 1950 to be specific, the nursing fathers metaphor, having vanished from public discourse, disappeared from the printed page. In 1950 a new authorized Catholic English language translation of the Bible appeared, the New American Bible, followed two years later by a new authoritative Protestant English language translation, the Revised Standard Version. In both editions, nursing fathers in Isaiah 49:23 was replaced by its earlier competitor, foster fathers. (A new, authoritative Jewish translation of Old Testament dispensed with fathers altogether, rendering Isaiah 49:23 as "kings shall tend your children.")[85] In the numerous subsequent reprintings of both the Catholic and Protestant Bibles, foster fathers continued to hold its place. Postwar commentaries on Isaiah by distinguished biblical scholars followed the foster fathers trend, as did new scholarly translations of Calvin's *Institutes*.[86] The oblivion into which the nursing fathers metaphor fell is illustrated by a book, published in 1996, by a British scholar, *The Fifth Gospel: Isaiah in the History of Christianity,* in which the author surveyed the use of Isaiah by writers from the early Church fathers to modern feminism and found no references to Isaiah 49:23.[87] Another scholar has recently published a volume arguing that there was an "American revolution against patriarchal authority in the second half of the eighteenth century,"[88] unaware of the inconvenient (for his thesis) prominence of the nursing fathers metaphor during this precise period. Yet another illustration of modern amnesia is a volume published in 1984 by the political scientist Aaron Wildavsky, entitled *The Nursing Father: Moses as a Political Leader.* Wildavsky considered the title "nursing father" a compelling one, even for a modern audience—"what else," he remarked, "is a leader if not a 'nursing father'"—but he found the metaphor's scriptural locus, not in Isaiah, but in Numbers 11:12.[89]

Could the concept of the nursing fathers, as Professor Wildavsky hints, still be serviceable in modern America? This, of course, is a matter of speculation, but the question at least suggests that it may be premature to write an epitaph for the venerable metaphor. It was not vanquished by a competitor, the wall of separation, for it had receded from the national memory before *Everson* was decided. Nursing fathers, nevertheless, expressed the view of the Founders' generation toward the relations between government and religion far more accurately than Jefferson's catchy phrase in the Danbury Baptist letter. In other words, in the early years of the republic, Calvin, whom Jefferson hated with a passion that he reserved for few others, bested the master of Monticello.

Notes

1. Massachusetts Provincial Congress, Fast Day Proclamation, April 15, 1775, Broadside Collection, Rare Book and Special Collections Division, Library of Congress, Washington, D.C. Rare books that can be found in this collection will hereafter have the citation Rare Book and Special Collections, LOC.

2. The terms "church and state" and "government and religion" are used interchangeably in this paper. Professor Jon Butler, among others, insists there should be a distinction between the terms, especially in United States during the Founding period. In the context of the nursing fathers metaphor an argument could be made that church and state should be used until the passage of the Toleration Act of 1689 on the grounds that before that time the state, in the person of a king or republican civil magistrate, supported one church that was believed to embody the true faith. After 1689, and especially after 1776 in America, the state often undertook to support several (Protestant) denominations, an arrangement that might

justify speaking of the state and the *churches,* or, perhaps better, government and religion. Jon Butler, "Why Revolutionary America Wasn't a 'Christian Nation,'" in *Religion and the New Republic,* ed. James H. Hutson (Lanham, Md.: Rowan and Littlefield, 2000), 196.

3. Daniel L. Dreisbach, "Thomas Jefferson, a Mammoth Cheese, and the 'Wall of Separation between Church and State,'" in *Religion and the New Republic,* 89.

4. David C. Steinmetz, "John Calvin on Isaiah 6: A Problem in the History of Exegesis," in *Calvin and* Hermeneutics, ed. Richard C. Gamble (New York: Garland, 1992), 175.

5. Martin Luther, *Works,* ed. Hilton C. Oswald, 55 vols. (St. Louis: Concordia, 1955–86), 17:188.

6. John Calvin, *Commentary on the Book of the Prophet Isaiah,* trans. William Pringle, 4 vols. (Edinburgh: Calvin Translation Society, 1850), 4:39–40. Calvin published a Latin edition of his *Commentary on Isaiah* in 1551 and a French one the following year. In 1559 he brought out a new Latin edition, so extensively revised that he claimed it "ought justly to be reckoned a new work." Another Latin edition appeared in 1570, a French one in 1572, and other reprintings followed. Calvin, *Commentary on Isaiah,* 1:xvi.

7. John Calvin, *Institutes of the Christian Religion,* trans. John Allen, 6th American ed., 2 vols. (Philadelphia: Presbyterian Board of Christian Education, 1928), 2:637.

8. Calvin, *Commentary on Isaiah,* 1:xxii, xxiv, emphasis in original.

9. Calvin, *Commentary on Isaiah,* 1:xvi.

10. Calvin, *Commentary on Isaiah,* 1:xvii–xviii, emphasis in original.

11. Steinmetz, "John Calvin on Isaiah 6," 177.

12. John Whitgift, *The Works of John Whitgift,* ed. John Ayre, 3 vols. (Cambridge: Cambridge University Press, 1851–53), 1:243–47, quoted in Basil Hall, "Calvin against the Calvinists," in *John Calvin,* ed. G. E. Duffield (Grand Rapids, Mich.: Eerdmans, 1966), 35.

13. W. H. Fere, *The English Church in the Reigns of Elizabeth and James I* (London: Macmillan, 1924), 8, quoted in W. M. Southgate, "The Marian Exiles and the Influence of John Calvin," in *The Making of English History,* ed. Robert L. Schuyler and Herman Ausubel (New York: Dryden, 1952), 173. Southgate argued that scholars had exaggerated Calvin's influence on the Marian exiles, even though he admitted that "Calvin was probably the strongest single influence upon their thought." Southgate, "Marian Exiles," 173.

14. For more on Jewel, see Sidney Lee, ed., *Dictionary of National Biography,* 20 vols. (London: Oxford University Press, 1903–30), 10:815–19.

15. For Hooker's use of the metaphor, see Richard Hooker, *Of the Lawes of Ecclesiastical Polity,* in *The Folger Library Edition of the Works of Richard Hooker,* ed. W. Speed Hill, 7 vols. (Cambridge: Belnap Press of Harvard University Press, 1977–98), 3:233.

16. John Jewel, *An Apology of the Church of England,* ed. J. E. Booty (Ithaca, N.Y.: Cornell University Press, 1963), 115. Jewel wrote the *Apology* in Latin; Booty's text is the 1564 English translation by Lady Ann Bacon, considered the "official English version" of the book. Jewel, *Apology of the Church of England,* xlvi. For a copy of Jewel's tract, see the LOC on-line exhibition at loweb.loc.gov/exhibits/religion/re105.html.

17. John Jewel, *A Defense of the Apologie of the Churche of Englande* (London: Henry Wykes, 1570), preface (unnumbered), Rare Book and Special Collections, LOC.

18. Lady Ann Bacon translated Jewel's Latin into the English word *nurse.* Jewel, *Apology of the Church of England,* 115.

19. John Calvin, *Commentarii in Isaiam Prophetam* (Geneva: Apud Jo. Crispinum, 1551), 486, 495–96; John Calvin, *Commentarii in Isaiam Prophetam* (Geneva: Apud Jo. Crispinum, 1559), 426, 436–37; John Calvin, *Commentarii in Isaiam Prophetam* (Geneva: Apud Jo. Crispinum, 1570), 426, 436–37; John Calvin, *Institutio Christianae religionis* (Geneva: Olina Roberti Stephani, 1559), 551. These books can be found in the Folger Shakespeare Library, Washington, D.C.

20. D. P. Simpson, *Cassell's Latin Dictionary* (New York: Funk and Wagnalls, 1968), 400.

21. Norton's translation went though seven printings between 1561 and 1599. Cited here is the 1562 edition: John Calvin, *The Institution of the Christian Religion . . . Translated into Englishe . . . by T. N.* (London: Richarde Harrison, 1562), 551. This can be found in the Folger Shakespeare Library, Washington, D.C.

22. William Allen, *An Apologie and True Declaration of the Constitution of Two English Colleges* (Rheims: n.p., 1581), cited in Hooker, *Works of Richard Hooker,* 6:1029.

23. Conrad Vorst (Conradus Vorstius) was a reputed Socinian whom the Dutch government had appointed to succeed the famous Arminius on the theological faculty at the University of Leiden.

24. Bernhard Fabian, ed., *James I: The Workes* (Hildesheim: G. Olms, 1971), 349.

25. "Charles II," in *Encyclopedia Britannica,* 15th ed., 28 vols. (Chicago: Encyclopedia Britannica, 1979), 4:53. Charles's admirers believed "God had particularly made good his promise to our Part of his Church, that Kings should be its Nursing Fathers." Matthias Symson, *The Hanoverian Succession: One of the Blessings of the Restoration* (London: n.p., 1729), 8. This work can be found in the British Library.

26. For a reminder to Charles II that "to be a *Nursing Father of the Church* is one of the richest jewels in a Kings Crown," see Henry King, *A Sermon Preached at White-Hall on the 29th of May* (London: Henry Herringman, 1661), 16–17, Rare Book and Special Collections, LOC.

27. John James Caesar, *The Glorious Memory of a Faithful Prince* (London: J. H., 1702), 6. For Queen Mary as a "Nursing Mother of this Church of England," see Thomas Dawes, *A Sermon Preach'd at the Parish Church of St. Chad's in Shrewsbury, March 5. 1694/5 Being the Funeral Day of Our Most Gracious Sovereign Queen Mary* (London: F. C., 1695), 28–29. For Queen Anne "as a Nursing Mother to His Church and a Terrour to its Enemies," see Samuel Chandler, *England's Great Duty on the Death of their Josiah* (London: T. Parkhurst, 1702), 22. All these books can be found in the British Library.

28. For more on Filmer, see Robert Filmer, *Patriarcha and Other Writings,* ed. Johann P. Somerville (Cambridge: Cambridge University Press, 1991), 238. For Locke, see John Locke, *Two Treatises of Government,* ed. Peter Laslett, 2d ed. (Cambridge: Cambridge University Press, 1967), 360.

29. Edmund Burke, "Vindication of Natural Society," in *The Writings and Speeches of Edmund Burke,* ed. T. O. McLoughlin and James T. Boulton, 1 vol. to date (Oxford: Clarendon, 1997–), 1:140.

30. Williston Walker, ed., *The Creeds and Platforms of Congregationalism* (1893; reprint, New York: Pilgrim, 1991), 71–72.

31. John Owen, "Righteous Zeal Encouraged by Divine Protection; with a Discourse about Toleration," in *The Works of John Owen,* ed. William H. Goold, 16 vols. (1851; reprint, London: Banner of Truth Trust, 1967), 8:192.

32. Owen, "Righteous Zeal Encouraged," 8:192.

33. Owen, "Righteous Zeal Encouraged," 8:194.

34. William C. Dickinson, ed., *John Knox's History of the*

Reformation in Scotland, 2 vols. (London: Thomas Nelson and Sons, 1949), 2:17.

35. *The Confession of Faith* (1646; reprint, Edinburgh: Free Presbyterian Church of Scotland, 1967), 102.

36. Samuel Rutherford, *Lex, Rex: The Law and The Prince* (London: John Field, 1644), 6–7, 111, 141, 191, 430, 431, Rare Book and Special Collections, LOC.

37. Anonymous, *The Examiner Examined* (London: n.p., 1652), 3. This can be found in the Union Theological Seminary Library.

38. Roger Williams, *The Complete Writings of Roger Williams* (New York: Russell and Russell, 1963), 7:207–13.

39. For Wolleb, see J. J. Herzog and Phillip Schaff, eds., *The New Schaff-Herzog Encyclopedia of Religious Knowledge*, 13 vols. (New York: Funk and Wagnalls, 1908–14), 12:407.

40. John Milton, *Christian Doctrine*, in *Complete Prose Works of John Milton*, ed. Don M. Wolfe, 8 vols. (New Haven, Conn.: Yale University Press, 1953–83), 6:797, 799. For Wolleb, see Johannes Wollebius, *Abridgment of Christian Divinitie* (n.p., 1650), 1:26, quoted in Milton, *Christian Doctrine*, 797 n.

41. New England and the southern colonies were settled, respectively and almost exclusively, by Congregationalists and Anglicans. The overwhelming majority of inhabitants in each region retained its allegiance to its mother church until the eve of the American Revolution, although, beginning in the 1740s, Baptists began to make inroads in both sections. Presbyterians began immigrating to the middle colonies in substantial numbers early in the eighteenth century; by 1776 approximately 275,000 had arrived. James G. Leyburn, "Presbyterian Immigrants and the American Revolution," *Journal of Presbyterian History* 54 (spring 1976): 26. Figures on the exact number of members of religious denominations in colonial America are notoriously imprecise. The number of churches of each denomination correlates roughly with the proportion of members in society at large. In 1740, Congregationalist churches were the most numerous in the thirteen colonies, 423 in number, followed by 246 Anglican churches and 160 Presbyterian. In 1780, Congregationalists still led with 749 churches, followed by Presbyterians, 495; Baptists, 457; and Episcopalians (formerly Anglicans), 406. Edwin S. Gaustad, *Historical Atlas of Religion in America*, rev. ed. (New York: Harper and Row, 1976), 4–5.

42. Fouace (?) to the Bishop of London, September 28, 1702, Fulham Palace transcripts, Manuscript Division, Library of Congress.

43. John Talbot to SPG (Society for the Propagation of the Gospel), October 20, 1704, SPG transcripts, Manuscript Division, Library of Congress.

44. Pennsylvania Convention to the Bishop of London, August 31, 1704, in *Historical Collections Relating to the American Colonial Church*, ed. William Stevens Perry, 5 vols. (1870; reprint, New York: AMS, 1969), 2:506–7.

45. William Urquhart and John Thomas to SPG, November 14, 1705, SPG transcripts.

46. George Whitefield, *Britain's Mercies, and Britain's Duties*, 2d ed. (Boston: S. Kneeland and T. Green), reprinted in Ellis Sandoz, ed., *Political Sermons of the American Founding Era* (Indianapolis: Liberty, 1991), 125, emphasis in original.

47. Jack Scott, ed., *An Annotated Edition of Lectures on Moral Philosophy by John Witherspoon* (Newark: University of Delaware Press, 1982), 161.

48. J. Franklin Jameson, ed., *Johnson's Wonder-Working Providence, 1628–1651* (New York: Scribner's Sons, 1910), 24, 32.

49. See Walker, *Creeds and Platforms*, 221.

50. David D. Hall, *The Faithful Shepherd: A History of the New England Ministry in the Seventeenth Century* (Chapel Hill: University of North Carolina Press, 1972), 227, 240.

51. See Whitefield, *Britain's Mercies*, 109.

52. Joseph Bellamy, *The Works of Joseph Bellamy, D.D.*, 2 vols. (1853; reprint, New York: Garland, 1987), 1:584.

53. Edward Dorr, *The Duty of Civil Rulers, to Be Nursing Fathers to the Church of Christ* (Hartford: Thomas Green, 1765), Rare Book and Special Collections, LOC. For a copy of Dorr's tract, see James H. Hutson, *Religion and the Founding of the American Republic* (Washington, D.C.: Library of Congress, 1998), 60.

54. Joseph Fish, *The Examiner Examined* (New London: Timothy Green, 1771), 57–58, Rare Book and Special Collections, LOC.

55. Revolutionary Religious Petitions, Library of Virginia, Richmond, Virginia.

56. A Member of the Convention, *Boston Independent Chronicle*, February 10, 1780.

57. Ezra Stiles, *The United States Elevated to Glory and Honor* (New Haven, Conn.: Thomas and Samuel Green, 1783), reprinted in John W. Thornton, ed., *The Pulpit of the American Revolution* (1860; reprint, New York: Da Capo, 1970), 490, 512.

58. Dorr, *Duty of Civil Rulers*, 10, 11, 17, 24.

59. Phillips Payson, *A Sermon Preached before the Honorable Council* (Boston: John Gill, 1778), reprinted in Thornton, *Pulpit of the American Revolution*, 340. John Witherspoon, Thanksgiving Proclamation, October 11, 1782, in *Journals of the Continental Congress, 1774–1789*, ed. Galliard Hunt, 34 vols. (Washington, D.C.: United States Government Printing Office, 1904–37), 23:647. Bishop James Madison, *An Address to the Members of the Protestant Episcopal Church, in Virginia* (Richmond: T. Nicolson, 1799), 23.

60. Washington asserted that religion and morality were the "great pillars" of human happiness and public prosperity. Farewell Address, 1796, broadside, Rare Book and Special Collections, LOC.

61. The idea of the "public Utility" of religion was everywhere during the Revolutionary period. See James H. Hutson, *Religion and the Founding of the American Republic* (Washington, D.C.: Library of Congress, 1998), 61–65. Heman Lincoln, speech, December 26, 1820, in *Journal of Debates and Proceedings in the Massachusetts Constitutional Convention, 1820–1821* (1853; reprint, New York: Da Capo, 1970), 423. For the equation of religion and the militia, see "Defence of the Third Article," in *The Christian Examiner and General Review* 13 (January 1833): 353.

62. See Whitefield, *Britain's Mercies*, 109.

63. Isaac Backus, *A Fish Caught in His Own Net* (Boston: Edes and Gill, 1768), reprinted in William G. McLaughlin, ed., *Isaac Backus on Church, State, and Calvinism: Pamphlets 1754–1789* (Cambridge: Harvard University Press, 1968), 238, emphasis in original.

64. [Theophilus Parsons], *An Answer to a Piece, Entitled, "An Appeal to the Impartial Public"* (Salem: S. Hall, 1785), 19, Rare Book and Special Collections, LOC.

65. See, for example, Payson, *Sermon Preached before the Honorable Council*, 340; Samuel Cooke, *A Sermon Preached at Cambridge* (Boston: Edes and Gill, 1770), reprinted in Thornton, *Pulpit of the American Revolution*, 179, 181; Simeon Howard, *A Sermon Preached before the Honorable Council* (Boston: John Gill, 1780), 393, reprinted in Thornton, *Pulpit of the American Revolution*, 393; David Tappan, *A Sermon Preached before His Excellency John Hancock* (Boston: Thomas Adams, 1792), reprinted in Sandoz, *Political Sermons*, 1118, 1121; Stephen Peabody, *Sermon before the General Court of New*

Hampshire (Concord N.H.: George Hough, 1797), reprinted in Sandoz, *Political Sermons*, 1336. Thomas Stone, *A Sermon Preached before His Excellency Samuel Huntington* (1792; reprint, New York: Readex Microprint, 1985), 29, microfiche.

66. Israel Evans, *A Sermon, Delivered at Concord* (Concord, N.H.: George Hough, 1791), reprinted in Sandoz, *Political Sermons*, 1070.

67. Thomas Curry, *The First Freedoms: Church and State in America to the Passage of the First Amendment* (New York: Oxford University Press, 1986), 163–92.

68. John Leland, *The Rights of Conscience Inalienable* (New London: T. Green and Son, [1791]), in Sandoz, *Political Sermons*, 1091.

69. Curry, *First Freedoms*, 134–58.

70. Presbyterian Church in the U.S.A., *The Constitution of the Presbyterian Church of the United States of America* (Philadelphia: Board of Christian Education of the Presbyterian Church in the U.S.A., 1955), 67.

71. Caleb Blood, *A Sermon* (Rutland, Vt.: Anthony Haswell, 1792), 34, quoted in Curry, *First Freedoms*, 190.

72. Isaac Backus, *An Appeal to the Public for Religious Liberty* (Boston: John Boyle, 1773), reprinted in McLaughlin, *Isaac Backus on Church, State*, 323, emphasis in original.

73. Memorial to the Massachusetts Provincial Congress, December 2, 1774, in Alvin Hovey, *A Memoir of the Life and Times of the Rev. Isaac Backus* (1858; reprint, New York: Da Capo, 1972), 217.

74. David Parsons, *A Sermon Preached before His Excellency John Hancock* (Boston: Adams and Nourse, 1788), 12–13, Rare Book and Special Collections, LOC.

75. Andrew Lee, *A Sermon, Preached before His Excellency Samuel Huntington* (1795; reprint, New York: Readex Microprint, 1985) 16–17, microfiche.

76. Matthias Burnet, *An Election Sermon, Preached at Hartford* (1803; reprint, Worcester, Mass.: American Antiquitarian Society, 1965), 22, microfiche.

77. For the Baptists' support of these positions, see Lucy Warfield Wilkinson, "Early Baptists in Washington, D.C.," in *Records of the Columbia Historical Society* 29–30 (1928), 215–16; William G. McLoughlin, *Isaac Backus and the American Pietist Tradition* (Boston: Little, Brown, 1967), 149–50; and Curry, *First Freedoms*, 190.

78. Backus, *A Fish Caught in Its Own Net*, 191.

79. John Mitchell Mason, *The Voice of Warning, to Christians, on the Ensuing Election of a President of the United States* (New York: G. F. Hopkins, 1800) reprinted in Sandoz, *Political Sermons*, 1471, emphasis in original.

80. See James H. Hutson, "Thomas Jefferson's Letter to the Danbury Baptists: A Controversy Rejoined," *William and Mary Quarterly*, 3d series, 56 (October 1999): 787.

81. *Constitution of the American Home Missionary Society* (New York: D. Fanshaw, 1826), 73.

82. Jasper Adams, *The Relation of Christianity to Civil Government in the United States* (Charleston, S.C.: A. E. Miller), reprinted in Daniel Dreisbach, ed., *Religion and Politics in the Early Republic: Jasper Adams and the Church-State Debate* (Lexington: University Press of Kentucky, 1996), 40.

83. Thomas Buckley, "After Disestablishment: Thomas Jefferson's Wall of Separation in Antebellum Virginia," *Journal of Southern History* 61 (August 1995): 462.

84. Everett O. Alldredge, *Centennial History of the First Congregational United Church of Christ, Washington, D.C., 1865–1965* (Baltimore: Port City, 1965), 10.

85. *Tanakh: A New Translation of the Holy Scriptures According to the Traditional Hebrew Text* (Philadelphia: Jewish Publication Society, 1985), 725. Compare to the 1941 Jewish Publication Society edition: "And kings shall be thy foster-fathers, And their queens thy nursing mothers," 539.

86. Walter Brueggemann, *Isaiah*, 2 vols. (Louisville: Westminster, 1998), 2:117–19. John Calvin, *Institutes of the Christian Religion*, ed. John T. McNeill, trans. Ford Lewis Battle (Philadelphia: Westminster, 1960), 2, 490.

87. John F. A. Sawyer, *The Fifth Gospel: Isaiah in the History of Christianity* (Cambridge: Cambridge University Press, 1996).

88. Jay Fliegelman, *Prodigals and Pilgrims: The American Revolution against Patriarchal Authority, 1750–1800* (Cambridge: Cambridge University Press, 1982), 267.

89. Aaron Wildavsky, *The Nursing Father: Moses as a Political Leader* (University: University of Alabama Press, 1984), 57–58.

THE ENGLISH REVOLUTION, MILTON, AND THE ROOTS OF RELIGIOUS LIBERTY IN AMERICA

John S. Tanner

In the spring of 1786, Thomas Jefferson, then serving as ambassador to France, traveled to London to visit John Adams, then serving as minister to the Court of St. James's. On April 4, during a delay in trade and treaty negotiations, the two patriots set off for a coach tour of the English countryside. Among other places of interest they visited were Edgehill and Worcester, sites of the first and last battles of the English Revolution in the mid seventeenth century. From his diary it is clear that Adams was deeply moved to walk "the Scænes where Freemen had fought for their Rights." "This was history he knew in detail," observes Adams's recent biographer David McCollough. It was a history well known to Jefferson as well. Both men recognized that the seeds of political and religious liberty in America had been sown more than a century before on English soil. Hence Adams was dismayed to discover the locals at Worcester were "so ignorant and careless" regarding the sites where seventeenth-century Englishmen had, like eighteenth-century Americans, thrown off the yoke of monarchy. "I was provoked," Adams records, "and asked, 'And do Englishmen so soon forget the Ground where Liberty was fought for?

Tell your Neighbours and your Children that this is holy Ground. . . . All England should come in Pilgrimage to this Hill, once a Year."[1]

Modern Americans may well feel equally rebuked under Adams's censure. For we, too, remain largely oblivious of the struggles where "Liberty was fought for" in mid-seventeenth-century England. This anecdote reminds us that the English Revolution served as a prelude to the American Revolution and that this connection was well known by the Founders, not to mention by their foes.[2] Examples abound of the ongoing influence of the English Revolution on Adams, Jefferson, and their compatriots. Adams credited James Harrington, Algernon Sidney, Marchamont Needham, John Milton, and other English Commonwealthmen with having convinced him "that there is no good government but what is Republican."[3] Likewise, Thomas Jefferson drew heavily from Milton's anti-prelatical tracts when drafting legislation on religious freedom for Virginia.[4] Similarly, Jefferson specifically summoned up the rhetoric of the English Revolution when, just two weeks before his death, he celebrated the jubilee of the Declaration of Independence by declaring "the palpable truth, that the mass of mankind has not been born with saddles on their backs"—an image which was derived from a speech that one of Oliver Cromwell's soldiers, Richard Rumbold, delivered from the scaffold just before his execution.[5] These examples illustrate the way that the rhetoric, principles, people, places, and historical events of the so-called "Good Old Cause" resonated across the years and over the sea to American shores. My purpose is to trace how Milton and, more broadly, the English Revolution served as conduits conveying principles of civil and religious liberty to the early American republic.

Since the time of English historian Thomas Babington Macaulay it has become commonplace to think of the abortive English Revolution as completed in the Glorious Revolution of 1688. However, it might be more accurate to say, as does historian Lydia Dittler Schulman, "The real victory of the English Commonwealth was the American Revolution." The influences of the English Revolution on the American Revolution included "natural and inalienable rights, the contractual nature of government, the subjection of magistrates to law, the legitimacy of revolution when rulers cease to govern for the good of the people, the superiority of mixed and balanced government, and the importance of education." Schulman concludes, "The body of political thought generated by the Great Rebellion and the Glorious Revolution is now generally recognized as a major ideological influence on the American Revolution."[6]

Milton and the English Revolution played a significant role in the story of religion and the founding of the American republic, though this chapter is often overlooked in accounts of its founding. Too often, the intellectual origin of the American Revolution has been understood narrowly in terms of the triumph of Enlightenment values. In Enlightenment meta-narratives, religion typically figures as a villain that visited vicious sectarian violence on Europe during the sixteenth and seventeenth centuries until it was restrained by secular values of tolerance, separation, disestablishment, and freedom of inquiry during the eighteenth century. Such explanations, however, oversimplify and distort the intellectual genealogy of religious toleration. As the theme of the Library of Congress exhibition implied, and as is abundantly evident when one considers the influence of a figure like Milton upon the Founding, religion was not simply the source of intolerance. It also played a positive role in the rise of tolerant democratic republics such as ours. In Milton we see how apparently secular Enlightenment principles were powerfully and proleptically articulated within an older religious discourse of Christian liberty.[7]

Commitment to such shared civic virtues fostered a special sense of kinship in the Founders toward their seventeenth-century English forebears, particularly Milton. In Milton, Americans could discern civic virtues framed in what became a distinctively American idiom, which Nathan Hatch calls "civil millennialism" or "Christian republicanism," by which Hatch means the "convergence of millennial and republican thought."[8] Early Americans heard this convergence in Milton's prose. A good example can be found in Milton's tract for press liberty, *Areopagitica*, which situates a proto-Jeffersonian call for freedom of speech—"Give me the liberty to know, to utter, and to argue freely according to conscience, above all liberties"—within a rhetoric of Protestant millennialism that could have come straight out of Puritan New England.[9] Similarly, early American readers heard the strains of Christian republicanism sounding in Milton's poetry, particularly *Paradise Lost*. Milton's epic is said to have "supplied some of the core mythology of . . . the revolutionary enterprise" in early America;[10] and similarly, to have served as "a natural literary handbook of revolutionary polemicists."[11]

My argument is that the English Revolution served as a well-known prelude to the American Revolution in early America, playing an important role in the origin of our conception of civic and religious liberty; and that Milton served as the "leading authority on republican ideas" in early America. This is not because he was "the most original or systematic of the Commonwealthmen," but because he, more than any other, championed liberty in soaring prose and sublime poetry calculated to survive the failure of his cause and to speak to early Americans with a familiar voice.[12] Milton made seventeenth-century revolutionary thought available to subsequent generations on both sides of the Atlantic. As Scott Simkins argues,

> Milton's poetry and prose . . . ran through colonial consciousness like a vein of gold through a mine. Rather than looking at the colonists' political inheritance as a layer cake, with Rousseau stacked on Montesquieu stacked on Locke, consider it like a marble cake, with swirls of related ideas from Magna Carta to *Areopagitica* to *L'Esprit des Lois.*

Thus, according to Simkins, a "link existed between Puritan and American revolutions due largely to Milton."[13]

MILTON AND THE DEFENSE OF AMERICAN LIBERTY

To discern the Miltonic marbling that runs through the American republic's concept of religious liberty, one needs to "ring the bell backward," in T. S. Eliot's phrase, conjuring the life and times of "one who died blind and quiet."[14] Milton felt that he lost his eyesight in the defense of liberty. But for the leniency of Charles II and the intervention of friends, he could well have lost his life in the cause as well. Although his life and works are more complex and dynamic than can be fully accounted for under any single idea, Christian liberty surely lays claim to be a lodestar guiding his career. Milton took considerable pride in his role as heroic defender of liberty. For example, in an autobiographical account of his prose writing, he characterized his rather disparate prose pamphlets as a deliberate, coherent, and systematic effort to "advance the cause of true and substantial liberty . . . which is best achieved, not by the sword, but by a life rightly undertaken and rightly conducted."[15] Likewise, in his poetry he frequently presents himself as a defender of true Christian liberty. To cite but one example, consider Sonnet 12, "I did but prompt the age to quit their cloggs," in which he presents himself to his nation

as a spokesmen for the "rules of antient libertie." True liberty must be distinguished from license: "For who loves that [liberty], must first be wise and good."[16] A brief rehearsal of Milton's biography reveals why Americans looked to Milton as a natural ally in their own struggle for liberty and the great exponent of the English Revolution.

Born in 1608, Milton's life-experiences and thought "arise from the same set of cultural circumstances" that led Puritan separatists to migrate to Plymouth Plantation and other colonists subsequently to break away to found Rhode Island.[17] While Milton did not emigrate, religiously his life traces an arc of separation from established religion. With the advantage of hindsight, it is of course possible to exaggerate the young Milton's Puritan sympathies. Even so, one can scarcely fail to notice indications in his early life of the Puritan trajectory Milton would follow.

Milton likely inherited his feelings for religious liberty from his father. John Milton Sr. was something of a martyr for the cause of religious freedom, having been disinherited when he embraced Protestantism. His famous son would likewise prove himself willing to suffer for truth's sake and would celebrate this particular kind of courage as a high heroic virtue.[18] The young Milton may have also imbibed a love for religious liberty from his local minister and tutor. He was raised in a left-leaning Church of England parish, which chose its own minister, Richard Stock, a man of Puritan sympathies. Of perhaps even greater influence on young Milton was his tutor, Thomas Young. A Scottish Presbyterian, Young manifested some of "the same disaffection" that led John Winthrop to leave England. Young left England for Germany in 1620, the same year the pilgrims set sail in the *Mayflower.* In Elegy 4 (1627), Milton depicts Young sympathetically as a religious exile. And much later, in an anti-prelatical tract, Milton defended his old tutor's attack on church hierarchy. The fires of religious liberty thus seem to have been lit in Milton even as a boy.

And they grew brighter in college. Cambridge was at the epicenter of Puritan discontent. In 1629, when Milton received his B.A. from Cambridge, the Reverend John White urged the graduates to consider migrating to Massachusetts Bay. Milton, of course, chose to stay in England—but ultimately not in the Church of England. Soon after Milton received his M.A. and should have been ordained, William Laud became archbishop. Laudian reforms, which imposed High Church ceremonialism on the Church of England, "plunged many a Puritan into a crisis of conscience, John Milton among them." Milton's growing recognition that he could not enter the ministry as both he and his parents had intended from childhood is evident in his university poem "Lycidas" (1637), which attacks the corrupt clergy in the Laudian church. The forces that drove some across the sea to New England led Milton to feel "church-outed." This discontentment with the state church was a critical factor in his decision to embrace a literary vocation as a poet.[19]

Milton did not, however, immediately pursue a poetic vocation. Rather, he chose to put his poetic career on hold during his middle years specifically to defend the cause of liberty, even though this meant temporarily restricting himself to the "left hand" of prose. Milton spent the 1640s and 1650s writing pamphlets in the defense of liberty, first as a private citizen and subsequently as a minister in Cromwell's Council of State. In his early anti-prelatical tracts, like *Of Reformation* and *The Reason of Church-Government*, Milton opposed the lordly power of bishops. Subsequently, verifying James I's fear that "no bishop" would mean "no king," Milton opposed political tyranny in such tracts as *Eikonoklastes* and *The Tenure of Kings and Magistrates*. Milton's unwavering opposition to tyranny moved him ever leftward, politically and religiously—from nominal Anglican, to Presbyterian, to Independent, to church of one.

The Tenure proved especially attractive to early American patriots. In it, well before Locke, Milton advanced a contract-theory of government upon which he argued for the right of a people to depose tyrants. A phrase from *The Tenure* may have influenced Jefferson's famous opening lines of the Declaration of Independence, the first draft of which reads: "We hold these truths to be sacred and undeniable; that all men are created equal and independent, that from that equal creation they derive rights inherent and inalienable." Similarly, Milton bluntly asserted: "No man who knows ought, can be so stupid to deny that all men naturally were borne free, being the image and resemblance of God himself."[20] Notably, both Milton and Jefferson grounded the natural right to personal liberty in a religious understanding of Creation and human nature, though the religious basis for natural rights was more muted by Jefferson. Supplying a Miltonic context for the Declaration foregrounds the religious origin of what became a secular Enlightenment idea—namely, the inalienable right to liberty.

Another important liberty tract for Americans from Milton's middle years is *Areopagitica*, a ringing defense of toleration. Tradition has it that Roger Williams personally brought a copy of *Areopagitica* to Rhode Island. A century later, *Areopagitica* was the first of Milton's works to be printed in America—published, not coincidentally, on the eve of the Revolution (1774).[21] *Areopagitica*, which contains Milton's loftiest prose on liberty, appealed to revolutionaries across the Channel as well as across the Atlantic. It was rendered into French by Honoré Mirabeau, in a translation which, in deference to French Enlightenment tastes, suppressed the profoundly religious basis of its argument. Mirabeau's translation of *Areopagitica* was read at the opening of the "States General" in 1788.[22] Thus Milton's defense of religious toleration was sounded at the beginning of both the American and French Revolutions.

The greatest labor of Milton's middle years was his *Defensio pro populo Anglicano* (*Defense of the English People*). This treatise defended, before an international tribunal and against attack by the learned Continental scholar Salmasius, the English people's right to overthrow a monarchy and to establish a commonwealth. Writing *Defensio* took a toll on Milton, whose eyesight by then was rapidly failing. He believed that preparing this long erudite defense of liberty cost him his sight. Nevertheless, he expressed his willingness to lay this terrible offering on the altar of freedom, comparing his choice to that of Achilles, who preferred glory and early death over ignominy and long life.[23] *Defensio* established Milton's international reputation as Europe's most learned champion of republican principles.

Milton continued to espouse "that which is call'd not amiss *the good Old Cause*" to the end of his days, however unpopular the cause ultimately became.[24] In February 1659, he published another discourse on religious toleration, *A Treatise on Civil Power*. And soon thereafter, he published and republished a desperate appeal to the English people not to abandon the republic for monarchy. The most courageous and at the same time foolhardy act of Milton's life was publishing *The Readie and Easie Way to Establish a Free Commonwealth* in March 1659, and then again in May, only weeks before Charles II was to be restored to the throne. During these perilous times, when other regicides were scrambling for cover, Milton bravely called attention to himself as an unrepentant Commonwealthman. Faced with what he regarded as the enormous calamity of his countrymen, who had been Providentially led out of bondage, now "chusing them . . . a captain back for *Egypt*," Milton felt compelled to utter what he feared may be the last words of "reviving liberty" to his backsliding English nation. And this he did in a politically naive, pragmatically futile, but grandly prophetic gesture: "Thus much I should perhaps have said though I were sure I should have spoken only to trees and stones; and had none to cry to, but with the Prophet, *O earth, earth, earth!* to tell the very soil it self, what her perverse inhabitants are deaf to."[25]

These should have been the last lines Milton ever published, but against all odds, he survived the restoration of Charles II. From the Restoration to end of his life, Milton remained an unreformed

republican and advocate of religious toleration. Not only did he publish a prose tract entitled *Of True Religion,* which forcefully reprised his earlier defenses of religious toleration and disestablishment, but he championed Christian liberty obliquely in his great last poems: *Paradise Lost, Paradise Regain'd,* and *Samson Agonistes.* Issued under the state censor's watchful eye, these poems are necessarily circumspect about the poet's republican sympathies. Nevertheless, their author's libertarian principles are clear enough to have made the poems suspect to Tories, like Samuel Johnson and T. S. Eliot, as well as dear to Whigs like John Toland and patriots like Thomas Jefferson. Though masked, the "Good Old Cause" continues to animate Milton's great last poems. The poems are not merely timeless monuments, but speak to the particular conditions of religious dissent during the Restoration. One measure of this is evinced by the chapter subtitles of a recent book about the literature of Non-Conformity, each of which is drawn from *Paradise Lost.*[26] Similarly, literary critics over the last three decades have been busily recovering the radical and, more recently, republican subtexts of Milton's great final poems.[27] There is now abundant evidence that Milton's poetry and prose served as conduits of Commonwealth ideas to subsequent generations of readers.

MILTON'S INFLUENCE ON THE FOUNDING

Nowhere was Milton's influence more apparent than in early America. Milton was not only the most important spokesperson of the English Commonwealth period, but he was possibly the most influential of any literary figure. Several important book-length studies have demonstrated Milton's importance in early America. George Sensabaugh's pioneering book *Milton in Early America* thoroughly documents Americans' extensive knowledge and use of Milton during the colonial and early republican periods. Sensabaugh concludes that, after Isaac Watts, Milton was the most quoted modern poet in colonial America and that no other author, ancient or modern, "impressed on Americans distinct modes of feeling and speaking; none etched on their minds visions of a transcendent world" more than Milton, whose reputation eclipsed even that of Homer and Vergil.[28]

Nancy Armstrong and Leonard Tennenhouse corroborate Sensabaugh's assertions in *The Imaginary Puritan*. They claim that Milton was "the most widely read author in eighteenth-century America. . . . If a home in the American colonies possessed any books besides the Bible, they were likely to be *The Pilgrim's Progress* and *Paradise Lost*."[29] Moreover, Milton's significance cannot adequately be measured merely by cataloguing how frequently his works were cited, sold, or found in personal libraries. Milton's influence in early America was as profound as it was pervasive, impressing itself deeply on the American character. The power of his impact is partly a function of timing, for Milton's shaping influence was greatest precisely as America was fashioning its national identity. It is also partly a function of the mythic appeal of his works and life. Armstrong and Tennenhouse argue for the presence of something they call the "mind of Milton" in our national life, functioning as an ongoing vehicle for transmitting the impact of the English Revolution on American culture.[30]

Similarly, Keith W. F. Stavely argues, in a book entitled *Puritan Legacies:* Paradise Lost *and the New England Tradition, 1630–1890,* that Milton imparted a "structure of feeling" with respect to such revolutionary principles as antinomianism and Arminianism—principles that lasted for hundreds of years in America.[31] Stavely ingeniously illustrates the continuing impact of Milton in his final chapter, which undertakes an ethnographic study of Charles F. Morse, a "secularized Puritan as country editor" in late nineteenth-century Marlborough, Massachusetts. In the quotidian experience of Morse's life and New England town, Stavely delineates the continuing presence of a Miltonic "structure of feeling."[32]

If Milton's influence was evident, even in attenuated forms, at the end of the nineteenth century, it was even more pronounced during the Revolutionary era.[33] The ideological influence of *Paradise Lost* on those who first fashioned this country has been most ably set forth in Lydia Dittler Schulman's book entitled *Paradise Lost and the Rise of the American Republic.* Schulman traces the profound and enduring impact of Milton's distinctive formulation of republican principles on the Founders. She is especially attentive to the appeal implicit in Milton's idea of Christian liberty, which conjoins notions of freedom with self-discipline. As Shulman notes, Milton's appeal to American patriots such as John Adams lies precisely in the fact that Milton, like Adams, saw humans as at once rational, free, empowered with self-transcendence, and hence capable of self-government; and at the same time as fallible, corruptible, subject to temptations, and hence in need of personal and political checks and restraints. Put another way, Milton's special appeal derives from the fact that he emphasizes both human *ameliorability,* the fulfillment of which requires political and religious freedom, and human *fallibility,* the presence of which necessitates the need for self-discipline, political restraints, and virtuous leadership.[34] By espousing republican values in terms of this complex ideal of Christian liberty, Milton spoke to both ends of the political spectrum occupied by the early patriots. For Jefferson and his intellectual heirs, Milton became a champion of religious freedom and opponent of political oppression. For Adams and those of his disposition, Milton embodied the idea of liberty based in reason and self-discipline and thus was adduced as an opponent of demagoguery and other forms of "individualism gone awry."[35] This distinction is developed below in my discussion of Adams and Jefferson.

It should be clear from this brief survey of the scholarship on Milton in America that no single paper can hope to provide anything like a full account of Milton's influence on the Founding, much less of the broader impact of the English Revolution for which he was a spokesperson. I must therefore skip over such fascinating historical details as the fact that Benjamin Franklin adapted Milton's hymn to creation from Book 5 of *Paradise Lost* for his own private liturgy[36] and devote the balance of the paper to Milton's influence on four figures featured in the Library of Congress exhibition: two from the colonial period, Roger Williams and Jonathan Mayhew; and two whose impact was greatest during the Revolution and early republic, John Adams and Thomas Jefferson.

Roger Williams and Jonathan Mayhew

Unlike Mayhew, Adams, and Jefferson, Roger Williams was Milton's contemporary. Moreover, Williams and Milton knew each other personally: they read each other's works, shared each other's political and religious sympathies, and studied languages together on Williams's trips back to old England. And they made common cause in the defense of religious freedom, an alliance illustrating the origins of our religious liberty in the English Revolution. In 1644, both Williams and Milton published similar defenses of religious toleration. In February and July, Williams published *Queries of Highest Consideration* and his famous *The Bloudy Tenent, of Persecution, for Cause of Conscience Discussed,* an eloquent early appeal for untrammeled religious toleration. In November of the same year, Milton published his equally famous attack on censorship, *Areopagitica,* which argued as well for freedom of conscience and religious toleration. It was likely at this time and through this circumstance that Milton and Williams first became personally acquainted.[37]

Though ideological allies, Milton and Williams did not espouse identical positions on religious toleration in *Areopagitica* and *The Bloody Tenent.* Milton's focus is on press freedom, and specifically on the opprobrious practice of prior restraint. He proposed broad but limited freedom for Protestants to publish their beliefs. However, he excepted "Popery" and books "absolutely either against faith or manners."[38] By contrast, Williams advocated complete toleration; he included Catholic, Jew, Muslim, and pagan. Nevertheless, both Williams and Milton were clearly allied in the cause of toleration and separation. Both men roused the same enemies

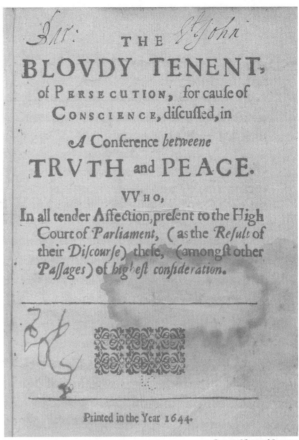

Roger Williams's *The Bloudy Tenent [Bloody Tenet]* was one of the earliest pleas for religious liberty in the colonies.

and raised the same concerns from the establishment; both were regarded as radical and dangerous by Parliament and singled out for censure and suppression.[39] Written within months of each other, *The Bloody Tenent* and *Areopagitica* constitute the most important calls for religious freedom in Early Modern English. Each helped shape the concept of religious tolerance for the early American republic. It is no coincidence that both these seminal texts emerged during the tumultuous 1640s from controversies engendered by the English civil wars, which served as a seedbed for religious liberty in America.

During the Commonwealth period in the early 1650s, Roger Williams was again in England and was again linked with Milton in the defense of religious toleration, along with Henry Vane the Younger, Milton's friend and ally in the English Revolution and erstwhile governor of Massachusetts. All three opposed efforts by Cromwell's regime, in response to the proliferation of radical sects, to limit religious toleration and reestablish a state church.[40] Although it is possible to romantically exaggerate the degree of friendship between Milton and Williams, there is no doubt that the two were on amicable terms. In 1652, Williams taught Milton Dutch while Milton, in exchange, helped him with "many more languages."[41] At this time they may have also discussed Williams's antinomianism. Like Williams, Milton would subsequently endorse a "qualified antinomianism . . . as a concomitant of Christian liberty."[42]

Milton also had a major influence on Jonathan Mayhew (1720–89), a Congregationalist minister in Boston, whose sermons during the decades prior to 1776 played a key role in preparing the country for revolution. As the Library of Congress exhibition notes, Mayhew's *Discourse concerning Unlimited Submission and Resistance to Higher Powers* (1750) was considered by John Adams to be the first shot of the American Revolution. If so, it is a salvo that explicitly continued the battles waged during the English Revolution between Royalist and Roundhead. The sermon was given in connection with the centennial of the execution of Charles I, in response to Tory eulogies of Charles I that condemned seventeenth-century regicides such as Milton and that argued for unlimited submission to monarchs.[43] Furthermore, there is a significant and demonstrable connection between Mayhew and Milton. The story of how this came about constitutes a fascinating chapter in the annals of the Founding's intellectual history.

After Milton's death, his legacy was continued primarily by the Whigs.[44] Some Whig admirers, like Addison, downplayed Milton's radical politics, on the whole ignoring his prose and regicide past while celebrating his poetry as sublime, timeless, and apolitical. However, Milton's radicalism was not entirely suppressed. It was admired by a faction called the Real Whigs, which deliberately set about to preserve and transmit Commonwealth ideals into the eighteenth century.[45] Key figures in this effort were the deist John Toland, who published a collection of Milton's prose in 1697, and the Nonconformist Thomas Hollis, who disseminated Commonwealth literature broadly, on both sides of the Atlantic—including Toland's edition of Milton's prose. Eventually, Hollis became a correspondent with Jonathan Mayhew in Boston, sending him so-called "liberty books" from the English Revolution, including generous selections of Milton's defenses of "civil, religious, and domestic liberty." So effective was Hollis in fomenting revolutionary sentiment in the colonies that the great Tory critic Samuel Johnson blamed the American Revolution upon the mischief created by Hollis, "because he had rescued so many tracts of the Interregnum and presented these 'liberty books' to impressionable Americans."[46] In Johnson's eyes, the American rebellion was the baleful progeny of men such as Milton. American patriots were in effect English Commonwealthmen *redivivus*.

There's reason to believe that Johnson got the etiology of the American Revolution right, at least with respect to Mayhew's *Discourse concerning Unlimited Submission*. This "first shot" of the Revolution confirms Johnson's suspicion that the rebellion in America constituted a revival of the convulsive political turmoil of the English Revolution. After all, the sermon was preached in connection with the centennial of Charles I's execution, specifically in an effort to counter Tory readings of this watershed event. And it borrowed heavily from the arguments of a notorious regicide, John Milton. George Sensabaugh provides several pages of side-by-side analysis demonstrating Milton's specific influence on this and other revolutionary sermons by Mayhew.[47] Thus it is fair to see Mayhew's *Discourse* as recontesting the great unresolved religious and political questions of mid-seventeenth-century England: Do subjects have an obligation to obey a monarch, however corrupt? Are Christians ever justified in throwing off a tyrant? Are there any legitimate religious grounds for rebellion? American Tories, like their seventeenth-century cousins the English Royalists, responded to these questions by urging quietism, consistent with the teachings by

St. Paul that servants should obey masters. Mayhew, like Milton and his fellow republicans, argued that it was not only lawful for Christians to resist tyrants, but their duty. Properly considered, tyrants are not to be counted among the legitimate powers Christians are duty-bound to obey. Rather, oppressors are to be numbered among the powers in high places against whom Christians are to wrestle, according to Paul (Eph. 6:12).

The connection between Milton and Mayhew's *Discourse* then is clear. Moreover, the evidence for the nexus is not only referential but explicit. Hollis wrote to Mayhew that "it is to Milton, the divine Milton, and such as him, in the struggles of the civil wars and the Revolution, that we are beholden" for our liberty.[48] Further, Mayhew distributed Milton's prose and other "liberty tracts" around the colonies with the specific intent of fostering republicanism. Included among the recipients of Milton's republican prose were the president of Harvard and the provincial lieutenant governor of Massachusetts.[49] Thus, if Mayhew's *Discourse* may be described as the first shot of the American Revolution, then Milton may be said to have provided the ammunition.

From his Boston pulpit, Mayhew kept firing rounds fashioned out of the same material. A decade after the *Discourse,* Mayhew took up arms against the so-called "Bishops Plot."[50] He opposed the Church of England's attempt to establish an American episcopate by sneaking Anglican bishops onto America's shores. It was impossible for Mayhew and others steeped in the liberty books not to see the Bishops Plot in terms of the Stuarts' efforts to impose prelatical control over religious worship in seventeenth-century England. That is, Mayhew saw the plot very much in the context of Milton's anti-prelatical tracts. Similarly, Mayhew interpreted forced taxes imposed by the Sugar Act (1764) and Stamp Act (1765) in terms of forced tithes, against which Milton also inveighed more than a century before. As Schulman puts it, "In the minds of Mayhew and other Nonconforming colonists, as for the seventeenth-century Commonwealthmen,

the issues of ecclesiastical and civil oppression, tithes and unlawful taxes, became inextricably entwined."[51] Mayhew thus vividly exemplifies the ongoing presence of Milton and the English Revolution in Colonial America. Mayhew prepared Americans to see their cause against the Crown as an extension of the Good Old Cause, their revolution as a reenactment of the English Revolution, and themselves as new Commonwealthmen bearing the banner of liberty once borne by John Milton.

John Adams and Thomas Jefferson

As young men, both Adams and Jefferson read and responded enthusiastically to Milton but in distinctly different ways. Their contrasting youthful responses to *Paradise Lost* prefigure political differences which would come to divide these men who defined the "North and South Poles of the American Revolution."[52] Their responses also describe, with virtually paradigmatic precision, two sides of an enduring literary crux in Milton studies regarding the nature of Milton's Satan: Is he a legitimate hero, the Romantic champion of liberty against the tyranny of an unjust Heavenly Monarch, as Jefferson saw him? Or is he a villainous demagogue, the proponent of not liberty but its counterfeit, license, as Adams thought? These contrasting readings of *Paradise Lost,* as is so often the case, reveal as much about the reader's politics as Milton's.

Adams first read *Paradise Lost* as a young man of twenty-one. His journal entry for April 30, 1756, rhapsodizes that Milton's "Powr over the human mind was absolute and unlimited" and that "His Genius was great beyond Conception, and his Learning without Bounds."[53] Although he would subsequently find Milton wanting as a practical political theorist, Adams said that his early reading of Milton's political tracts helped convince him "that there is no good government but what is Republican."[54] Likewise, Thomas Jefferson was deeply impressed with Milton's *Paradise Lost* when he first read it as a young man. He filled his commonplace book with some forty-seven quotations

Twenty times, in the course of my late reading, have I been up on the point of breaking out, "This would be the best of all possible Worlds, if there were no Religion in it"!!! But in this exclamati I should have been as fanatical as Bryant or Cleverly. Without Religion this World would be Something not fit to be mentioned in Polite Company, I mean Hell. So far from believing in the total and universal depravity of human Nature; I believe there is no Individual totally depraved. The most abandoned Scoundrel that ever existed never yet Wholly extinguished his Conscience, and while Conscience remains there is Some Religion. Popes, Jesuits and Sorbonists and Inqui sitors have Some Conscience and Some Religion.

In this letter to Thomas Jefferson, April 19, 1817, John Adams expresses his views on religion and human nature.

from Milton's epic—many taken from Satan's speeches. Subsequently, Jefferson also read and responded positively to Milton's republican prose. As we have seen, Jefferson may have borrowed from Milton's *Tenure of Kings and Magistrates* for the Declaration of Independence, and he explicitly drew from Milton's tracts for his arguments in behalf of religious toleration and separation of church and state.

It is telling that what most impressed young Adams was Milton's sublimity, grandeur, and learning; Adams was struck by the scope of *Paradise Lost*'s grand design. Adams was also impressed by Milton's insistence that true liberty is inseparable from virtue. Jefferson, by contrast, fills his commonplace book with admiring citations of the grandly defiant speeches by Milton's Satan, such as:

> What though the field be lost?
> All is not lost; the unconquerable Will,
> And study of revenge, immortal hate,
> And courage never to submit or yield.[55]

Unlike Adams, what Jefferson most admired in Milton's prose was not his erudition, not his rational republicanism, nor the grounding of liberty in virtue, but Milton's passionate support of rebellion, religious toleration, and intellectual freedom.[56]

With respect to the relative power of the president versus the Congress, Adams once wrote to Jefferson, "You are afraid of the one, I, the few. . . . You are apprehensive of monarchy; I, of aristocracy."[57] This remark forecast the political differences that would ultimately divide Federalist from Republican. It is also consistent with the way each man read *Paradise Lost*. Adams and Americans of his persuasion found in Milton's Satan not a hero, but an example of the dangers of demagoguery. For Federalists like Adams, the poem's Council in Hell became a "central warning symbol" against the tyranny of those who would invoke language of revolution against tyranny in order to justify their own passion for social distinction and tyranny.[58] Likewise, the Puritan Adams responded warmly to Milton's assertion that only good people could be truly free and hence fit to entrust with political power.[59]

By contrast, Jefferson celebrates *Paradise Lost*'s rhetoric in behalf of the untrammeled freedom of the mind, even when the arguments are advanced by Satan. Jefferson's admiration for Milton's Satan anticipates the Romantic reaction. Jefferson would likely have agreed with Blake, who argued that Milton was "of the Devil's party without knowing it," and that he "wrote in fetters when he wrote of angels and God," while he spoke from his own political experience and with true poetic inspiration when he described Hell's revolt against the supposed tyranny of Heaven.[60] Jefferson was profoundly impressed with Satan as defiant spokesperson of Romantic individualism, while Adams was most impressed with "Milton himself"—his commitment to liberty restrained by reason and virtue, his godlike ability to comprehend a "Stupendous Plan" of "him who rules the universe."[61] In their early contrasting responses to Milton, we discern the contours of the American parties that each patriot would eventually lead. In Adams's early response to Milton, we see a nascent American Federalist, while in Jefferson's early response, we see a proto-Republican—a darling of Jacobins and subsequent Romantic revolutionaries.

Milton continued to figure in the mature work of both Adams and Jefferson through the Revolution, the Constitutional Convention, and into the nineteenth century. As Adams studied republican models of government, he understandably expressed disappointment with Milton. For Milton was no political theorist, nor a good source for practical advice about how to build political institutions—perhaps because he believed that personal virtue was ultimately more important to good government than political structure. Adams justly faults Milton for his slapdash proposal for a perpetual council in *Readie and Easie Way*. He thinks that Milton ought to have followed the lead of Commonwealthman James Harrington in advocating bicameralism. Yet despite his disaffection with Milton as a practical political thinker, Adams still turned to Milton the moralist and martyr when he, like Milton, faced political attack in his later years. Adams approvingly quoted Milton's sonnet "I did but prompt the age" when he defended himself against the vicious partisan attacks attending the rise of parties in the early republic.[62]

Jefferson also combed Milton's prose for political ideas during the Revolutionary and Republican eras. Jefferson drew most heavily from Milton in the debates over disestablishment in the State of

Virginia. Milton, who fought mandatory tithes, would have been pleased that his work helped Jefferson win approval for "An Act for Exempting Dissenters from Contributing to the Anglican Church" (1776). Similarly, Jefferson again drew from Milton's prose to construct arguments for "A Bill for Religious Freedom" (1786)—an accomplishment Jefferson regarded as so important that he stipulated it be inscribed on his tomb. Jefferson borrowed extensively from Milton in the notes about religious toleration he made, entitled "Outline of Argument."[63] Jefferson was particularly attracted to the anti-clericalism expressed by Milton in *Of Reformation* and *Reason of Church Government*. He admired Milton's insistence that laymen were capable of expounding scripture and offering religious opinions, noting Milton's scholarly opinion that, in the primitive church, bishops were elected by believers rather than appointed by popes. And he concurred with Milton's view that Christianity fell into apostasy both when and *because* it became officially established under Constantine.[64] Both men concluded from this fact about primitive Christianity that true religion not only did not need state support but may actually be harmed by establishment. As Milton avers at the end of *Paradise Lost*, to enforce faith by "secular power" leads to the decline of true faith.[65] In light of Milton's manifest contributions to Jefferson's views regarding religious liberty, George Sensabaugh concludes: "It is therefore safe to say that Milton, through Jefferson, contributed tangibly to the settlement of religious freedom in Virginia; and this contribution, in turn, established a clear path between the Puritan to the American Revolution."[66]

CONCLUSION

This remark about Jefferson and Milton may well serve to summarize the general lines of my argument. Having established that Milton and the English Revolution contributed to religious freedom in America, let me offer a concluding caution. One ought not to exaggerate the influence of either Milton or the English Revolution on the Founding. The Founders did not slavishly follow any one figure—whether Milton or Montesquieu. Nor did they seek republican principles only in English Commonwealth of the previous century. They also looked nearer at hand to Enlightenment political theory, and farther afield to classical republicanism as well as to the Florentine and Dutch republics. This said, the English Revolution as a whole, and Milton's poetry and prose in particular, clearly did play a significant role in the history of religious freedom and the founding of the American republic.

Moreover, Milton's influence persisted beyond the Founding well into the nineteenth century. In conclusion, let me cite but two brief examples. First, consider a comment by Margaret Fuller. After quoting with approval R. W. Griswold's opinion that, paradoxically, Milton is our most American writer, Fuller adds her own explanation and encomium:

> Mr. Griswold justly and wisely observes: "Milton is more emphatically *American* than any author who lived in the United States." He is so because in him is expressed so much of the primitive vitality of that thought from which America is born, though at present disposed to forswear her lineage in so many ways. He is the purity of Puritanism. . . . He is one of the Fathers of this Age, of that new Idea which agitates the sleep of Europe, and of which America, if awake to the design of Heaven and her own duty, would become the principal exponent. But the Father is still far beyond the understanding of his children."[67]

Second, consider Ralph Waldo Emerson's view of Milton as an "apostle of freedom." Emerson calls Milton "the sublimest bard of all," adding that "no man can be named whose mind still acts on the cultivated intellect of England and America with an energy comparable to that of Milton."[68]

Truly Milton and the English Revolution were formative influences that shaped the founding of the American Republic. Their influence stretched from seventeenth-century English battlefields like Worcester, on whose hill "liberty was fought for," over the ocean and across the years to Bunker Hill. The Founding was wrought under the aegis of Milton and his Revolution. To some degree, we live under that banner still. We can discern traces of its influence in our national character to the extent that America still fuses today, as it did in De Toqueville's time, the "spirit of religion" with the "spirit of liberty." This is the spirit of the English Commonwealth. It is the spirit of Milton.

Notes

1. John Adams, *Diary and Autobiography of John Adams*, ed. L. H. Butterfield, 4 vols. (Cambridge: Belknap Press of Harvard University Press, 1961), 3:185; David McCullough, *John Adams* (New York: Simon and Schuster, 2001), 359.

2. For a political cartoon linking the American Revolution and the English Revolution, see *The Yankee Doodles Intrenchments* [sic] *Near Boston 1776*, in James H. Hutson, *Religion and the Founding of the American Republic* (Washington D.C.: Library of Congress, 1998), 42.

3. John Adams, *The Papers of John Adams*, ed. Robert J. Taylor, 10 vols. to date (Cambridge: Belnap Press of Harvard University Press, 1977–), 4:87.

4. George F. Sensabaugh, *Milton in Early America* (1964; reprint, New York: Grodian, 1979), 137–45.

5. McCollough, *John Adams*, 645.

6. Lydia Dittler Schulman, Paradise Lost *and the Rise of the American Republic* (Boston: Northeastern University Press, 1992), 15, 97.

7. That the Founding had religious origins is, of course, not an entirely novel claim. A number of political and literary historians have called attention to the pre-Enlightenment roots of American Revolution, particularly the English Revolution. I have in mind the work of political historians like Nathan O. Hatch, *The Sacred Cause of Liberty: Republican Thought and the Millennium in Revolutionary New England* (New Haven: Yale University Press, 1977), and Caroline Robbins, *The Eighteenth-Century Commonwealthman* (Cambridge: Harvard University Press, 1959), as well as of literary historians such as Schulman, Paradise Lost *and the Rise of the American Republic* and Keith W. F. Stavely, *Puritan Legacies:* Paradise Lost *and the New England Tradition, 1630–1890* (Ithaca, N.Y.: Cornell University Press, 1987).

8. Hatch, *Sacred Cause of Liberty*, 3.

9. John Milton, *Areopagitica*, in *The Riverside Milton*, ed. Roy Flanagan (Boston: Houghton Mifflin, 1998), 1018–19. All subsequent references to Milton are to *The Riverside Milton*.

10. Tony Davies, "Borrowed Language: Milton, Jefferson, Mirabeau," in *Milton and Republicanism*, ed. David Armitage and others (Cambridge: Cambridge University Press, 1995), 260.

11. Schulman, Paradise Lost *and the Rise of the American Republic*, 100.

12. Schulman, Paradise Lost *and the Rise of the American Republic*, 99.

13. Scott Simkins, "Puritan, Poety, and Political Radical," *Colonial Williamsburg Interpreter* (May 1993), ocean.st.usm.edu/~wsimkins/milton.html.

14. T. S. Eliot, "Little Gidding," *Four Quartets:* ll. 182, 179.

15. John Milton, *Second Defense of the English People*, in *Riverside Milton*, 1117.

16. John Milton, Sonnet 12, in *Riverside Milton*, 251–52.

See also John Milton, *The Tenure of Kings and Magistrates,* "For indeed none can love freedom heartilie, but good men; the rest love not freedom, but license," in *Riverside Milton,* 1057.

17. My summary of the Puritan influences on young Milton borrows from Stavely, *Puritan Legacies,* 3–5. Otherwise, my chief source on Milton's life is Barbara Lewalski, *The Life of John Milton: A Critical Biography* (Oxford: Blackwell, 2000).

18. See John Milton, *Paradise Lost,* 12:569–70.

19. Stavely, *Puritan Legacies,* 3–5.

20. Milton, *Tenure of Kings and Magistrates,* 1060. See Davies, "Borrowed Language," 261; and Walter Isaacson, *Benjamin Franklin: An American Life* (New York: Simon and Schuster, 2003), 312. Isaacson explains that it was Franklin who struck out "sacred and undeniable" and inserted instead "self-evident." This was a deliberate attempt to relocate the ground of human liberty from religion to rationality. In a single stroke, Franklin reoriented America's charter of freedom so its largest claims sound not scriptural but scientific, not Miltonic but Cartesian.

21. Lewalski, *Life of John Milton,* 541; Sensabaugh, *Milton in Early America,* 37.

22. Davies, "Borrowed Language," 266, 269. Mirabeau's translation went through three editions in four years. In addition, *Areopagitica* was evidently also published in 1831 in Greek, in connection with the creation of a free Greek republic. Davies, "Borrowed Language," 270.

23. Milton, *Second Defense,* 1107–9.

24. John Milton, *The Readie and Easie Way to Establish a Free Commonwealth,* in *Riverside Milton,* 1148, emphasis in original.

25. Milton, *Readie and Easie Way,* 1148.

26. N. H. Keeble, *The Literary Culture of Non-Conformity in Later Seventeenth-Century England* (Leicester, Eng.: Leicester University Press, 1987).

27. See, for example, Christopher Hill, *Milton and the English Revolution* (New York: Viking, 1977) and David Norbrook, *Writing the English Republic, 1627–1660* (Cambridge: Cambridge University Press, 2000).

28. Sensabaugh, *Milton in Early America,* viii, 4.

29. Nancy Armstrong and Leonard Tennenhouse, *The Imaginary Puritan: Literature, Intellectual Labor, and the Origins of Personal Life* (Berkeley: University of California Press, 1992), 11.

30. Armstrong and Tennenhouse, *Imaginary Puritan,* 27–46.

31. Stavely, *Puritan Legacies,* 9–10, 19–33.

32. Stavely, *Puritan Legacies,* 220–70.

33. On Milton's "Diminishing Stature" after the period of the early republic, see Sensabaugh, *Milton in Early America,* 282–306.

34. Schulman, Paradise Lost *and the Rise of the American Republic,* 3–17, 127–31.

35. Schulman, Paradise Lost *and the Rise of the American Republic,* 19.

36. Davies, "Borrowed Language," 263.

37. Lewalski, *Life of John Milton,* 180.

38. Milton, *Areopagitica,* 1022.

39. Lewalski, *Life of John Milton,* 178–79, 182.

40. Lewalski, *Life of John Milton,* 285–86.

41. Quoted in Lewalski, *Life of John Milton,* 285.

42. Lewalski, *Life of John Milton,* 430.

43. Sensabaugh, *Milton in Early America,* 59–61. For a copy of Mayhew's tract, see Library of Congress's on-line exhibition at lcweb.loc.gov/exhibits/religion/rel03.html.

44. Schulman, Paradise Lost *and the Rise of the American Republic,* 113–16. See also Patricia Bonomi, *Under the Cope of Heaven* (New York: Oxford University Press, 1986), 189–90, and Nicholas von Matlzahn, "The Whig Milton: 1667–1700," in *Milton and Republicanism,* 229–53.

45. This history is told most fully in Caroline Robbins's *The Eighteenth-Century Commonwealthman* (Cambridge: Harvard University Press, 1959). It is also summarized in Schulman, Paradise Lost *and the Rise of the American Republic,* 114–16. Complete religious freedom was one of the planks of the Real Whigs.

46. Schulman, Paradise Lost *and the Rise of the American Republic,* 118.

47. Sensabaugh, *Milton in Early America,* 52–66.

48. Schulman, Paradise Lost *and the Rise of the American Republic,* 122. Near the end of his life, Mayhew specifically acknowledged that he had been taught "the doctrine of Civil liberty" in his youth by Milton. Sensabaugh, *Milton in Early America,* 54.

49. Schulman, Paradise Lost *and the Rise of the American Republic,* 121–23.

50. For a political cartoon depicting the "Bishop's Plot," see *An Attempt to Land a Bishop in America* in Hutson, *Religion and the Founding,* 41.

51. Schulman, Paradise Lost *and the Rise of the American Republic,* 125.

52. Quoted in McCollough, *John Adams,* 604.

53. Adams, *Diary and Autobiography,* 1:23.

54. Adams, *Papers,* 4:87.

55. Milton, *Paradise Lost,* 1:105–8.

56. Schulman, Paradise Lost *and the Rise of the American Republic,* 127–31; Sensabaugh, *Milton in Early America,* 136–37; Davies, "Borrowed Language," 258–60.

57. McCullough, *John Adams,* 380.

58. Schulman, Paradise Lost *and the Rise of the American Republic,* 186.

59. Schulman, Paradise Lost *and the Rise of the American Republic,* 102–3.

60. William Blake, *The Marriage of Heaven and Hell,* in *Selected Writings of William Blake,* ed. Robert F. Gleckner (New York: Meredith, 1967), 73.

61. Adams, *Diary and Autobiography,* 23–24.

62. Schulman, Paradise Lost *and the Rise of the American Republic,* 176.

63. Sensabaugh, *Milton in Early America,* 139–45.

64. Sensabaugh, *Milton in Early America,* 143.

65. See Milton, *Paradise Lost,* 508–40.

66. Sensabaugh, *Milton in Early America,* 145.

67. Margaret Fuller, *Papers on Literature and Art* (1846), quoted in Stavely, *Puritan Legacies,* vi.

68. Quoted in Lewalski, *Life of John Milton,* 545.

69. "This civilization is the result . . . of two quite distinct ingredients which anywhere else have often ended in war but which Americans have succeeded somehow to meld together in wondrous harmony; namely, *the spirit of religion* with *the spirit of liberty.*" Alexis de Tocqueville, *Democracy in America,* trans. Gerald E. Bevan (London and New York: Penguin Books, 2003), 55.

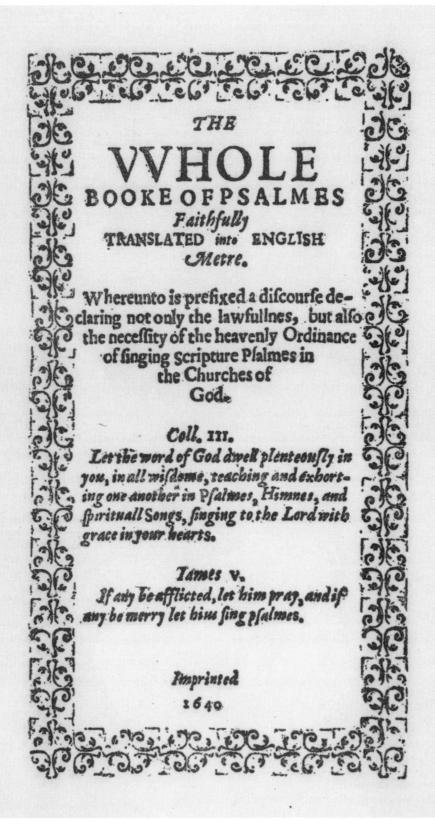

The Bay Psalm Book, translated from Hebrew into English, was the first book printed in the colonies.

The Influence of the Hebrew Scriptures on the Founders and the Founding of the American Republic

Andrew C. Skinner

From the earliest periods of the republic's history to the present day, both the Hebrew scriptures (also known as the Old Testament) and the Christian New Testament have exerted tremendous influence on American life. However, the evidence indicates that American political life and culture were, from their earliest beginnings, grounded as much, or more, in the Hebrew scriptures than in the New Testament. Of course, Christians have generally used the Old Testament, but the particular focus on the Hebrew scriptures by both the Puritans and the Founding Fathers is remarkable. In fact, the further back one goes in American history, the more saturated with Hebraic references and allusions one finds American culture to be. Indeed, it is this Hebraic milieu, rather than one grounded in the Christian New Testament, which most fueled the fires of imagination and motivation among early American Christian colonists and Founders of the Republic. As Cecil Roth put it, "Deprive modern Europe and America of [their] Hebraic heritage and the result would be barely recognizable."[1] This paper, therefore, emphasizes the importance of the Hebrew

scriptures in early American life, from the early Puritans to the Founding Fathers.

THE PURITANS AND THE EARLY COLONISTS

Many of the early American settlers were good Hebraists and were deeply rooted in the *original* biblical literature. This is true for churchmen, laymen, and political leaders alike.[2] Hebrew was far from being an alien tongue on American Christian soil. Among political figures, William Bradford (1590–1657), one of the original *Mayflower* pilgrims and second governor of the Plymouth Colony, is said to have studied Hebrew *most* of all other languages because it allowed him to "see with his own eyes the ancient Oracles of God in their native beauty."[3] Bradford regarded Hebrew as "that most ancient language, and holy tongue, in which the Law and Oracles of God were writ; and in which God, and angels, spake to the holy patriarchs, of old time." The study of Hebrew consoled the governor in his old age.[4] Looking back to the landing at Plymouth in the harsh December of 1620 and reviewing the desperate predicament of the colonists, Bradford attributed their sustenance and ultimate success to the spirit and grace of God. He then emphasized his point by citing biblical quotations—taken not from Jesus or some other passages from the New Testament, but, rather, from the Old Testament, specifically the book of Deuteronomy and the Psalms.[5]

In 1648, Thomas Shepard made a similar argument when defending the Bay Colony against charges of cowardice leveled by the Puritans in England who were fighting the Cavaliers. Shepard appealed to the Old Testament: "What shall we say of the singular providence of God bringing so many shiploads of His people, through so many dangers, as upon eagles' wings, with so much safety from year to year?" He then supported his thesis with citations from Exodus and Micah.[6]

An English interpretation of the Psalms' poetic structure, the Bay Psalm Book, was printed in 1640, making it the first book printed in the colonies.[7] The first Hebrew grammar printed in America was published in 1735 by Judah Monis, a Jewish convert to Christianity and the first full-time instructor of Hebrew at Harvard University.[8] Colonial America's first colleges attached particular importance to Hebrew scholarship. At Harvard University, the nation's oldest institution of higher learning (founded in 1636), great value was placed on the study of Hebrew as part of the curriculum, and an oration in Hebrew was delivered every year at the annual commencement ceremonies until 1817.[9] Samuel Johnson, the first president of what was to become Columbia University, said in 1759 that the study of Hebrew was a "gentlemen's accomplishment" because Hebrew was "the mother of all languages."[10] Such a declaration was a far cry from the medieval Christian belief that Hebrew was the language of the diabolical, since the Jews themselves were the children of the devil.[11]

The effects of this Hebrew linguistic and literary dispersion on colonial culture were tremendous. Professor Randall Stewart's assertion, which has become almost axiomatic, is instructive: "The Bible has been the greatest single influence on our [American] literature."[12] But more to the point, it was not the Christian Bible (which emphasizes the New Testament) that formed the foundation of this influence educationally, but the Hebrew scriptures. Carlos Baker, in a brilliant essay entitled "The Place of the Bible in American Fiction," confirms our observation:

> Well into the early national period, when our prose fiction began, the New England mind was saturated with the Old Testament rather than the New. All children were raised on the Bible from the cradle, and writers could assume, as we can no longer do, that the stories of Moses in the bulrushes, or Lot's wife, or Ruth amid the alien corn, or Abraham's sacrifice, were known to them as our children know the complex lore of missiles and moon-conquest. Professor [Perry] Miller has observed, "There are hundreds of Edens, Josephs, Elijahs for every rare crucifixion or still more rare recreation of the Manger, while Madonnas, are, of course, non-existent."[13]

The Hebraic mood created and promoted by colonial leaders became so well entrenched in American life that one twentieth-century American author would declare that New England itself was also a "holy land."[14] The break with England in 1776 apparently even prompted some revolutionaries to suggest that Hebrew be adopted as the official language of the newborn country.[15]

Hebraic influence on colonial education, both formal and informal, was tremendous. George Washington, for example, received tutoring that contained liberal doses of Old Testament literature and lore. His half brother, Lawrence, discussed with young George "the hero-prophets" of the Hebrew scriptures. And it is most significant to note that the young future president was taught to look for answers in the Old Testament. On one of the pages of Washington's schoolboy notebooks, penned in his own distinctive handwriting, is the instruction, "If you can't find it in the Book of Ezekiel, look in Israel."[16] "Israel" was the group name generally applied in the eighteenth century to the first five books of the Old Testament. One biographer has written that this is proof indeed that young Washington was thinking in biblical terms in those early days.[17] I would note additionally that it was the Hebrew testament in which Washington was immersed.

In 1781, while the Revolution was in progress, Ezra Stiles, president of Yale University, delivered his public commencement address in Hebrew. He took for a text Ezra 7:10: "For Ezra had set his heart to seek the law of the Lord, and to do it, and to teach it." According to Charles Seymour, himself a former president of Yale, Stiles was fluent in Hebrew, which he spoke with a "grace unusual even for those days."[18] When he became president of the university in 1777, Stiles assigned Hebrew study to a prominent place in the college curriculum. Naturally, the best collection of readings for the language class was to be found in the Hebrew Bible. Little wonder, then, that the official seal of Yale University is engraved with the words *urim ve-tumim* ("light and perfection").

WHY THE INTEREST?

Early on, the Puritans thought of themselves as the children of Israel. The Hebrew scriptures were not so important to the colonists because they liked the Jews, but, rather, because several of the colonial founders believed they were a continuation of Israel, that they were Israel restored. Along with seeing themselves as the children of Israel, the Puritans adopted an Exodus motif with regards to themselves. As Perry Miller explained, "They identified themselves and their destiny within the focus of biblical history: King James I was their Pharaoh, America was Canaan, and the Atlantic Ocean was the Red Sea."[19] This motif not only resonated with the early Puritans but would become a central idiom during the Revolutionary era. Thus, many of the colonists and founding leaders of this land centered their lives around this defining episode they called *their* Exodus and deliverance.

Not only did the colonial founders call America the new Promised Land, but, according to Perry Miller, "They grew to regard themselves as so like the Jews that every anecdote of tribal history seemed like a part of their own recollection."[20] From Benjamin Franklin's grandfather, Peter Folger

of Rhode Island, came a little ditty coined in 1676: "New England they are like the Jews, as like as like can be."[21] Therefore, it was only natural that colonial settlers would regard the Old Testament as a rule of life and the source of instruction in difficult political times. The Hebrew scriptures constituted for them an important guide in most aspects of life—faith as well as political practice. The cornerstone of the "New Jerusalem" which the Puritans yearned to establish in the wilderness of America was the Hebrew Bible.[22] These colonists really applied the names they found in the Hebrew scriptures to their own life circumstances. They named their communities after towns mentioned in Hebrew scripture, and they chose Old Testament names for their children. An examination of place names in modern America reveals that half the states contain a Bethel, around twenty states have a Goshen or a Hebron, and there are at present about thirty Jerusalems or its derivative, Salem.[23] Other common biblical place names include Sharon, Damascus, Moriah, Jordan, Canaan, Lebanon, and Carmel. On the other hand, the name Nazareth, which seems specifically Christian since it does not appear anywhere in the Old Testament, is not so common in America.[24]

Thus, the identification with the children of Israel was the fundamental motive behind the particular importance the Puritans placed on the Hebrew scriptures. This sense of chosenness has resonated throughout American history, and the Exodus motif was to become a major motif throughout the American Revolution.

COLONIAL POLITICS

The Exodus motif continued its influence on various aspects of American politics. It is nowhere better demonstrated than in Revolutionary-period political commentary. Political satire in the form of biblical parodies became especially popular in New England during the pre-Revolutionary years owing to increasing American dislike of British governmental interference. Bernard Bailyn tells us that no fear, no accusation, no warning was more common among the voices of opposition than those which spoke of tyranny and attempted enslavement on the part of the British government. British actions were viewed as "the attempts of a wicked administration to enslave America."[25] With slavery present throughout the colonies, American reacted strongly to such images. The First Continental Congress, in a letter to the British people, expounded on "the ministerial plan for enslaving us," and the Second Continental Congress justified its actions by references to "the rapid progress of a tyrannical ministry."[26]

Such denouncements had a special resonance in the colonies where people generally were acquainted with the biblical book of Esther. Here they possessed a ready-made model for a wicked, tyrannical, and ministerial conspiracy, attempting to usurp sacred rights and enslave an entire people, namely, the bloodthirsty Haman at the court of Ahasuerus. In 1775, a Newbury, Massachusetts, minister, Oliver Nobel, wrote:

> Haman the Premier, and his junto of court favorites, flatterers, and dependents in the royal city, together with governors of provinces, councilors, boards of trade, commissioners and their creatures, officers and collectors of REVENUE, solicitors, assistants, searchers, and inspectors, down to tide-waiters and their scribes, and the good Lord knows whom and how many of them, together with the coachman and servants of the whole . . . Not that I am certain the Persian state had all these officers . . . or that the underofficers of state rode in coaches or chariots . . . But as the Persian monarchy was despotic . . . it is highly probable [they did] . . . Now behold the DECREE obtained! The bloody PLAN ripened! [The] cruel perpetrators of the horrid PLOT and a banditti of ministerial tools through the provinces [had everything in readiness.] But behold! . . . A merciful GOD heard the cries of this oppressed people.[27]

This was not the first time a British leader had been associated with the Esther story. As early as 1747 Cadwallader Colden, acting governor of New York, had been described as New York's Haman by an angry patriot, Philip Livingston.[28]

Colonial propaganda often took the form of biblical imitation to review and criticize specific enactments of the British government. In what has been described as "the most ambitious and nearly successful of half a dozen Biblical imitations which appeared in the Revolutionary period," The First Book of the American Chronicles of the Times reviewed the six months following the passage of the Port Bill. The American Chronicles was published serially in Philadelphia during the winter of 1774–1775 and according to Bruce Granger "catches the accent of the Old Testament chronicles books, though sometimes the diction has a synthetic ring."[29] However, the American Chronicles is so clever and complete in its characterization that identification of the intended protagonists becomes an engaging exercise.

Bruce Granger summarizes the American Chronicles as follows:

> When the men of Boston learned that the great Sanhedrim [British government] had passed "a decree that their harbours be blocked up" and that Rehoboam the king [King George III of England] had sent Thomas the Gageite to enforce it, they "entered into a solemn league and covenant, that they would obey the book of the law, and none other."

The parody continues as the Israelite tribes (that is, the colonies) "take pity on the Bostonites":

> And they got ready their camels and their asses, their mules and their oxen, and laded them with their meat, their fine wheaten flour, their rice, their corn, their beeves and their sheep, and their figs and their tobacco abundantly, and six thousand shekels of silver, and threescore talents of gold, and sent them, by the hands of the Levites, to their brethren, and there was joy in the land.

Continuing his description of Chronicles, Granger explains,

> In letters to Rehoboam, Thomas complains that the Americanites are "giants, men of great stature, and we seemed but as caterpillars in their sight." Rehoboam [King George III of England] replies, "My Grandfather corrected them with rods, but I will chastise them with scourges." When Thomas lays siege to Boston, a man of the town declares that they do not mean to sell their birthright 'for a dish of TEA.'

The *American Chronicles* ends with Mordecai (Benjamin Franklin) lamenting, "Wo unto the land whose king is a child, whose counsellors are madmen, and whose nobles are tyrants, that devise wicked counsel, for they shall be broken like potters clay."[30] It was reported by the *North Carolina Gazette* that *The First Book of the American Chronicles of the Times* sold upwards of three thousand copies in just a few days.[31]

The New Republic

Cecil Roth has pointed out that the Hebraic conception of the tripartite agreement between God, his people, and their earthly ruler formed the basis of support for constitutional government in England. This was taken over by colonial leaders, and, in turn, "by the fathers of the American Revolution, who were inspired at every turn by the ideas of the Bible." Professor Roth continues,

> The "Pilgrim Code" of Plymouth Colony (1636) and the "Body of Liberties" of Massachusetts (1647) were confessedly based on the Hebrew scriptures, and the leaders of the American Revolution, from Benjamin Franklin downwards, were imbued with Hebrew conceptions.
>
> It was Hebraic mortar . . . that cemented the foundations of the republic.[32]

Without question, the Exodus motif remained an effective metaphor during the Revolution and was prominent in the minds of its leaders as well as common supporters of the Revolution. On July 5, 1776, the Liberty Bell was rung to signal the Continental Congress's adoption of the Declaration of Independence. Commissioned in 1751 by the Pennsylvania Provincial Assembly to hang in the new State House (renamed Independence Hall) in Philadelphia, the Liberty Bell was inscribed with the words of Leviticus 25:10: "And proclaim liberty throughout all the land unto all the inhabitants thereof." It is significant that this potent symbol of the nation's freedom bore a verse from the Hebrew scriptures and not something from one of the sayings of Jesus or Paul on freedom and liberty. During the Revolution, references to ancient Israel as a symbol of the American colonies were constant, especially in

New England. The Boston *Gazette*, for example, ran a communication in 1782 which began, "My dear countrymen, my sincere wish and prayer to God is, that our Israel may be saved from the rapacious jaws of a tyrant."[33]

On the same day that the Declaration of Independence was adopted, Thomas Jefferson, John Adams, and Benjamin Franklin were assigned the task of formulating an official seal for the new nation.[34] They and other national founders, including the Reverend Thomas Hooker (who wrote the constitution for Connecticut), believed that a presentation of the Exodus motif would be the most substantive and appropriate image to display on the Great Seal of the new republic, because it symbolized the ideals of the new nation.[35] Similar is Franklin's description of the way he thought it should be portrayed:

> Moses standing on the Shore, and extending his Hand over the Sea, thereby causing the same to overwhelm Pharoah who is sitting in an open Chariot, a Crown on his Head and a Sword in his Hand. Rays from a Pillar of Fire in the Clouds, reaching to Moses, to express that he acts by Command of the Deity.
>
> Motto, *Rebellion to Tyrants is Obedience to God.*[36]

Jefferson's proposal was very similar.

> Pharoah sitting in an open chariot, a crown on his head and a sword in his hand passing thro' the divided waters of the Red sea in pursuit of the Israelites: rays from a pillar of fire in the cloud, expressive of the divine presence and command, reaching to Moses who stands on the shore and, extending his hand over the sea, causes it to overwhelm Pharoah. Motto. Rebellion to Tyrants is Obedience to god.[37]

Jefferson's scheme seems to have derived from Franklin's, but this was not his only proposal, at least not according to John Adams, who presents us with added insight. In writing to Mrs. Adams on August 14, 1776, Adams reported that for the image of the Great Seal, "Mr. Jefferson proposed the children of Israel in the wilderness, led by a cloud by day and a pillar of fire by night; and on the other side, Hengist and Horsa, the Saxon chiefs from whom we claim the honor of being descended, and whose political principles and form of government we have assumed."[38] According to one writer, Jefferson, who had studied the institutes of Anglo-Saxon government, believed that they were very close to, and an extension of, those principles of representative government practiced by ancient Israel under the leadership of Moses.[39]

THE OLD TESTAMENT AND THE FOUNDING FATHERS

Benjamin Franklin

Not only does Benjamin Franklin's proposal for the Great Seal of the United States reflect a significant understanding and application of the Exodus motif as found in the Hebrew scriptures, but several of his other papers and letters also convey a sense of Franklin's thorough knowledge of the Old Testament and its influence upon him as well as his contemporaries.

One of the more interesting examples is a letter to Samuel Cooper, dated May 15, 1781, wherein Franklin extolled the virtues of a sermon that Cooper had preached to celebrate the inauguration of the new government. Franklin noted:

> Nothing could be happier than your Choice of a Text, and your Application of it. It was not necessary in New England, where everybody reads the Bible, and is acquainted with Scripture Phrases, that you should note the Texts from which you took them; but I have observed in England, as well as in France, that Verses and Expressions taken from the sacred Writings, and not known to be such, appear very strange and awkward to some Readers.[40]

Since the text of Samuel Cooper's sermon was taken from Jeremiah 30:20–21, "Their Congregation shall be established before me: and their Nobles shall be of themselves, and their Governor shall proceed from the midst of them," one wonders how accurate Franklin's comment "everybody . . . is acquainted with Scripture Phrases" would be in our day. However, one also wonders if Franklin was not really telling us that in his day New Englanders knew the biblical references to every passage of scripture that applied to their situation as a new nation in the context of the Exodus motif.

The Exodus motif remained a powerful metaphor for Franklin throughout his life. In a letter to the editor of the *Federal Gazette*, dated 1788, Franklin unequivocally applied the circumstances of ancient Israel to those of the American colonists. Franklin drew heavily on the Exodus motif for what turns out to be a comparison of the ancient Israelites and the anti-federalists in America.

> One would have thought that this Appointment of Men, who had distinguish'd themselves in procuring the Liberty of their Nation, and hazarded their Lives in openly opposing the Will of a powerful Monarch, who would have retain'd that Nation in Slavery, might have been an Appointment acceptable to a grateful People; and that a Constitution framed for them by the Deity himself might, on that Account, have been secure of a universal welcome Reception. Yet there were in every one of the *thirteen Tribes* some discontented, restless Spirits, who were continually exciting them to reject the propos'd new government, and this from various Motives.

> Many still retain'd an Affection for Egypt, the Land of their Nativity; and these, whenever they felt any Inconvenience or Hardship, tho' the natural and unavoidable Effect of their Change of Situation, exclaim'd against their Leaders as the Authors of their Trouble; and were not only for returning into Egypt, but for stoning their deliverers.[41]

The parallels between the ancient Israelites and the American colonists are unmistakable: a new nation seeking to secure liberty from a powerful monarch, a new constitution framed with God's help, and the disaffected of the new nation seeking to return to the land of their nativity and captivity. Franklin concluded his letter by affirming his belief in the divinely inspired nature of the federal Constitution and the influence of Providence upon the General Convention. He could hardly conceive of such a momentous transaction as was undertaken by the Constitutional Convention being left to chance.[42]

Thomas Jefferson

Jefferson, like John Adams, did not possess a very high regard for sole reliance on the biblical text. As historian Edwin Gaustad explains, if God had spoken literally to humankind at one time, "the vagaries of centuries of translation and transmission had left the contemporary reader of the Bible with imperfect texts, meaningless phrases, corrupted manuscripts."[43] Jefferson's counsel was to read the Bible as one would read Livy or Tacitus. Those ideas "which contradicted the laws of nature, must be examined with more care, and under a variety of faces." Jefferson cited the story of Joshua commanding the sun to stand still, as a case in point. As anyone could plainly discern, such an event would be contrary to natural law. Examine all the circumstances, Jefferson advised, and then ask which is more probable: an error in reporting or a violation of nature's law?[44] The surest course was trust in reason, which, in the words of Adams, was "a revelation from its Maker which can never be disputed or doubted."[45] Yet, Jefferson definitely was *not* an atheist as some have charged—nor was he an agnostic.

For all of Jefferson's cautions, he was still greatly influenced by the Bible, as his proposal for the Great Seal of the new nation testifies. And with regard to the ideological foundations of the new nation, we find him making more direct references to the Hebrew scriptures than to the New Testament. For him the opening phrases of the Declaration of Independence were neither idle or rhetorical: under "the Laws of Nature and of Nature's God . . . all men are created equal, . . . they are endowed by their creator with certain unalienable rights." Thus, Jefferson exulted in the words of Psalm 148—recommending them to John Adams "as an excellent portrayal of Nature's God"[46] (recapitulating the famous phrase he used in the Declaration of Independence):

> Praise the Lord!
> Praise the Lord from the heavens, praise him in
>   the heights!
> Praise him all his angels, praise him, all his host!
> Praise him, sun and moon, praise him, all you
>   shining stars!
> Praise him, you highest heavens, and you waters
>   above the heavens!
> Let them praise the name of the Lord!
> For he commanded and they were created.
> And he established them for ever and ever;
> He set a law which cannot pass away.

Jefferson was also fond of Psalm 18:9–10 because the words of that passage spoke of Nature, which itself spoke the language of God.

Scholars have devoted considerable time trying to understand where Jefferson got the phrase "pursuit of happiness" that is included in the Declaration (that is, "all men are . . . endowed by their creator with certain unalienable rights . . . Life, Liberty, and the pursuit of Happiness"). Likewise, commensurate effort has been expended in determining what he meant. As Pauline Maier explains, the Hebrew scriptures tremendously influenced colonial thinking on this point: "For Jefferson and his contemporaries, happiness no doubt demanded safety or security, which would have been in keeping with the biblical phrase one colonist after another used to describe the good life—to be at peace under their vine and fig tree with none to make them afraid (Micah 4:4)."[47]

So even though Jefferson may not have been a biblical literalist, nor did he accept every verse as inspired, he was, without question, deeply influenced by the texts of the Hebrew scriptures. They were, so to speak, "in the air" he breathed. In his second inaugural address, he called for "the favor of that Being in whose hands we are, who led our fathers, as Israel of old, from their native land, and planted them in a country flowing with all the necessaries and comforts of life."[48] In the words of one of Jefferson's biographers, "Jefferson not only knew his Bible, he also knew when it seemed most appropriate to evoke its imagery."[49] That imagery most relevant to America's circumstances came in healthy measure from the Hebrew scriptures. In fact, in at least one of his writings, Jefferson seems to distinguish the Old Testament from the New Testament by referring to the first as *the* Bible, while the New Testament was simply the "Testament." Both, he said, are part of the common law.[50]

Other Founders

Others who shared the views of Jefferson and Adams regarding the excellence of reason over revelation also demonstrated their familiarity with the

Hebrew scriptures. Ethan Allen of Vermont, who published *Reason the Only Oracle of Man* in 1784, quoted Job 11:17 when he acknowledged that scripture implied that "none by searching can find out God," and inferred that even reason could not resolve *every* issue.[51]

From among the updated papers of Alexander Hamilton we read his following incomplete comment about the Jewish people:

> [The] *progress of the Jews* . . . from their earliest history to the present time has been & is, intirely [*sic*] out of the *ordinary course* of human affairs. Is it not then a fair conclusion that the *cause* also is an *extraordinary one*—in other words that it is the effect of some great providential plan? The man who will draw this Conclusion will look for the solution in the Bible. He who will not draw it ought to give us another fair solution.[52]

Such a reference can only be to the Hebrew scriptures, which presents the destiny of Israel, specifically the Jews, as following a divinely appointed or providential plan. The New Testament, on the other hand, sometimes portrays the Jews in a very unfavorable light—some would even say in diabolical terms (compare John 8:44 where the Jews are called the children of the devil by Jesus).

AFTER THE WAR

After the war was over, the stories and themes of the Hebrew scriptures continued to be used by many as vehicles to inform and teach the public about historical events and political issues. Thomas Jefferson, who made explicit reference to certain passages in the Old Testament, was himself referred to symbolically in the context of those scriptures by others. Medford, Massachusetts, pastor David Osgood employed bitter invective against Jefferson as president. If George Washington was the nation's King David, said Osgood, Jefferson was the rebellious son Absalom. In 1801 the Reverend Nathanael Emmons preached a fast-day sermon on the radical and regrettable change of leadership in *Israel,* but of course everyone understood that he meant the United States.[53]

Timothy Dwight

Perhaps the most impressive presentation of national history cast in the guise of Hebrew narrative events was published in 1785 by Timothy Dwight. Entitled *The Conquest of Canaan,* this American epic poem, written in eleven books in rhymed pentameters, retells the story of Joshua's leadership of Israel during their conquest of the promised land. But, in fact, it is a colossal and symbolic account of Washington's conquest of the British and the establishment of America. Dwight wanted to give the New World an epic poem of their own such as the *Iliad* was to Greece or the *Aeneid* to Rome. And though he was a rigid Calvinist, and "a Yankee Christian gentleman," he chose an episode from the Hebrew scripture as the pattern for his work.[54]

As the poem opens, the reader understands that Joshua is the hero, "Chief," and "Leader" of the action, divinely appointed.

> THE Chief, whose arm to Israel's chosen band
> Gave the fair empire of the promis'd land,
> Ordain'd by Heaven to hold the sacred sway,
> Demands my voice and animates the lay.[55]

The Israelites, in accord with sacred history as outlined in the Book of Joshua, are represented in circumstances of extreme distress. Jabin, the Canaanite king of Hazor, has sent an army to afflict Israel. Hanniel presents a defeatist oration, rehearsing the Israelites' misery, the impossibility of their success because of the strength, skill, and numerous allies of their enemy's armies. Even if they are able to conquer Canaan they will be ruined in the process.

Joshua tries to reply that Providence is with them, but is interrupted by Hanniel who openly accuses Joshua of trying to usurp kingly authority. However, Joshua's rebuttal carries the hour. He points out the misery of their experience under the King of Egypt (that is, King George of England), and declares the certainty of their success, the favor and revealed designs of Heaven, and he exults in the future glory of their own kingdom.

This epic is as full of noble speech and deeds on the one hand, and yet gore and savage battle on the other, as any reader of the Hebrew scriptures could ever want.

> Now where the Chief terrific swept the field,
> And, cloth'd in terror, ranks on ranks repell'd;
> Whilst a red deluge o'er his footsteps spread,
> And countless torrents sprouted from the dead.[56]

Ultimately, Joshua and Israel's armies are successful. As the poem ends, Israel expresses gratitude to God, the Great Being who gave them both victory *and* their great mortal leader, Joshua.

> The storm retir'd; the ensigns gave command,
> And round their Leader throng'd the conquer-
>   ing band. . . .
> While Joshua's thoughts mount upward to
>   the skies,
> And fear, and wonder, in his bosom rise.[57]

It takes no great imagination to see, throughout the poem, the connection between ancient Israel's situation and the new American nation, which, having just defeated the British, owes it gratitude to God and to General Washington, a leader in the mold of Joshua. In fact, the work is explicitly dedicated to

> George Washington, Esquire,
> Commander in Chief of the American Armies
> The Savior of his Country,
> The Supporter of Freedom,
> And Benefactor of Mankind.[58]

The Conquest of Canaan is an epic of considerable emotion and power, and made more poignant by an appreciation for the original story in the Hebrew scriptures. It undoubtedly had an impact on contemporary times, as did other symbolic presentations connecting the new nation with events described in the Hebrew Bible. For the first president's inaugural in 1789, a Hebrew prayer was written in which the name of Washington appears as an acrostic. The prayer invokes God's blessing on the father of the country as well as the vice president, senators, and representatives of the United States.[59]

CONCLUSION

Truly, the Hebrew scriptures influenced American colonial life in so many and profound ways that it is as difficult to take note of them as it is to be cognizant of the air we breathe. Of this period Perry Miller has said, "The remarkable aspect about . . . such daily conversation as we find reliably recorded, is that the Biblical vision out of which these particular examples come was so predominantly, almost exclusively, confined to the Old Testament."[60] This Hebraic influence on the found*ers* and found*ing* of the American Republic is especially keen. Though we may think of the American Revolution as being under the direct influence of rationalists and rationalism, the images, even the language, from the pages of the Hebrew Bible were at least as powerful a force in shaping the new nation as Locke and Paine.

Ironically, in the early decades of the nineteenth century, when Protestant piety was turning away from the Old Testament towards the New (as Jefferson seems to have done in his later life), there was a cultural flowering or efflorescence of Hebraic feeling and imagery in art and popular literature. It came from the political sphere; it continues to infuse our national ethos today. Echoes of the words of Herman Melville, written in 1850, seem to continue to reverberate in the collective unconscious of the American nation, and they seem particularly poignant at this time in our nation's history. "We Americans are the peculiar, chosen people—the Israel of our time; we bear the ark of the liberties of the world."[61]

This article is adapted from a lecture presented at Creighton University and an article by the author, entitled "The Influence of the Hebrew Bible on the Founders of the American Republic," in Sacred Text, Secular Times: The Hebrew Bible in the Modern World, *ed. Leonard. J. Greenspon (Omaha: Creighton University Press, 2000), 13–34.*

Notes

1. Cecil Roth, *The Jewish Contribution to Civilization* (New York: Harper and Brothers, 1940), 16. For a picture of a Hebrew text, see a Sefardi Torah scroll [eighteenth century] in James H. Hutson, *Religion and the Founding of the American Republic* (Washington D.C.: Library of Congress, 1998), 9.

2. See the partial but extensive list of colonial Hebraists in Robert H. Pfeiffer, "The Teaching of Hebrew in Colonial America," *Jewish Quarterly Review* 45 (1955): 365–66.

3. David de Sola Pool, *Hebrew Learning among the Puritans of New England Prior to 1700* (Baltimore: n.p., 1911), 32, quoted in William Chomsky, *Hebrew: The Eternal Language*

(Philadelphia: Jewish Publication Society of America, 1975), 249.

4. "William Bradford," in *Dictionary of American Biography*, ed. Allen Johnson, 10 vols. (New York: Charles Scribner's Sons, 1937), 1:562.

5. Perry Miller, "The Garden of Eden and the Deacon's Meadow," *American Heritage* 7 (December 1955), 59.

6. Miller, "Garden of Eden and the Deacon's Meadow," 59.

7. Chomsky, *Hebrew: The Eternal Language*, 248.

8. Pfeiffer, "Teaching of Hebrew," 369.

9. Chomsky, *Hebrew: The Eternal Language*, 248.

10. Chomsky, *Hebrew: The Eternal Language*, 247.

11. Joshua Trachtenberg, *The Devil and the Jews* (Philadelphia: Jewish Publication Society of America, 1983), 61–63.

12. Randall Stewart, *American Literature and Christian Doctrine* (Baton Rouge: Louisiana State University Press, 1958), 3.

13. Carlos Baker, "The Place of the Bible in American Fiction," in *Religious Perspectives in American Culture*, ed. James Smith Ward and A. Leland Jamison (Princeton: Princeton University Press, 1961), 247, quoting Miller, "Garden of Eden and the Deacon's Meadow," 55. Baker adds, "The very probable reason [was] that these [New Testament] images smacked of popery." Baker, "Place of the Bible in American Fiction," 247.

14. Howard A. Bridgman, *New England in the Life of the World: A Record of Adventure and Achievement* (Boston: Pilgrim, 1920), 5.

15. Gabriel Sivan, *The Bible and Civilization* (Jerusalem: Keter, 1973), 236.

16. William H. Wilbur, *The Making of George Washington* (Deland, Fla.: Patriotic Education, 1970), 126.

17. Wilbur, *Making of George Washington*, 125.

18. *Ha-Doar*, January 17, 1941, quoted in Chomsky, *Hebrew: The Eternal Language*, 248.

19. Chomsky, *Hebrew: The Eternal Language*, 249, quoting Miller.

20. Miller, "Garden of Eden and the Deacon's Meadow," 60.

21. Miller, "Garden of Eden and the Deacon's Meadow," 60.

22. Sivan, *Bible and Civilization*, 236.

23. Timothy P. Weber, "Mapping the American Zion," *Textures: Hadassah National Jewish Studies Bulletin* 13, no. 2 (1995), 3.

24. The place name Nazareth is to be found eight times in countries around the world; four of those are in the United States: Colorado, Kentucky, Pennsylvania, and Texas.

25. Quoted in Bernard Bailyn, *The Ideological Origins of the American Revolution* (Cambridge: Belnap Press of Harvard University Press, 1967), 126.

26. Quoted in Bailyn, *Ideological Origins*, 126.

27. Quoted in Bailyn, *Ideological Origins*, 127, emphasis in original.

28. Quoted in Milton Klein, "Prelude to Revolution in New York: Jury Trials and Judicial Tenure," *William and Mary Quarterly*, 3d series, 17 (1960), 445.

29. Bruce I. Granger, *Political Satire in the American Revolution, 1763–1783* (Ithaca, N.Y.: Cornell University Press, 1960), 70.

30. Granger, *Political Satire*, 68–69, quoting Samuel Adams, *The First Book of the American Chronicles of the Times* (Philadelphia: B. Town, 1774–75), 1–70.

31. Granger, *Political Satire*, 69 n.

32. Roth, *Jewish Contribution to Civilization*, 15.

33. *(Boston) Gazette*, May 6, 1782, quoted in Miller, "Garden of Eden and the Deacon's Meadow," 58.

34. Richard S. Patterson and Richardson Dougall, *The Eagle and the Shield: A History of the Great Seal of the United States* (Washington, D.C.: U.S. Government Printing Office, 1978), 6. For Jefferson's and Franklin's written proposals for the Great Seal, see Hutson, *Religion and the Founding*, 50. For an artist's rendition of the descriptions, see *Rebellion to Tyrants Is Obedience to God*, drawing by Benson J. Lossing, 1856, in Hutson, *Religion and the Founding*, 51.

35. W. Cleon Skousen, *The Making of America* (Washington, D.C.: National Center for Constitutional Studies, 1985), 32.

36. Thomas Jefferson, *The Papers of Thomas Jefferson*, ed. Julian B. Boyd, 30 vols. to date (Princeton: Princeton University Press, 1950–), 1:494, emphasis in original.

37. Jefferson, *Papers of Thomas Jefferson*, 1:495.

38. Jefferson, *Papers of Thomas Jefferson*, 1:495.

39. Skousen, *Making of America*, 32.

40. Benjamin Franklin, *The Writings of Benjamin Franklin*, ed. Albert Henry Smyth, 10 vols. (New York: Haskell House, 1970), 8:257 n.

41. Franklin, *Writings of Benjamin Franklin*, 9:699, emphasis in original.

42. Franklin, *Writings of Benjamin Franklin*, 9:702–3.

43. Edwin Gaustad, *Sworn on the Altar of God: A Religious Biography of Thomas Jefferson* (Grand Rapids, Mich.: Eerdmans, 1996), 28. Skepticism over the Bible's infallibility persisted in American culture as represented by a statement by the founder of The Church of Jesus Christ of Latter-day Saints, Joseph Smith: "Ignorant translators, careless transcribers, or designing and corrupt priests have committed many errors" in the transmission of the biblical text. Joseph Smith Jr., *Teachings of the Prophet Joseph Smith*, ed. Joseph Fielding Smith (Salt Lake City: Deseret Book, 1970), 327.

44. Thomas Jefferson, *The Writings of Thomas Jefferson*, ed. Andrew A. Lipscomb, Monticello ed., 20 vols. (Washington: Thomas Jefferson Memorial Association, 1903–4), 6:258–60.

45. Quoted in Gaustad, *Sworn on the Altar of God*, 29.

46. Gaustad, *Sworn on the Altar of God*, 38.

47. Pauline Maier, *American Scripture: Making the Declaration of Independence* (New York: Alfred A. Knopf, 1997), 134.

48. Thomas Jefferson, *Writings*, ed. Merrill D. Peterson, (New York: Viking, 1984), 523.

49. Gaustad, *Sworn on the Altar of God*, 100.

50. Jefferson, *Writings of Thomas Jefferson*, 14:75.

51. Quoted in Gaustad, *Sworn on the Altar of God*, 29.

52. Alexander Hamilton, *The Papers of Alexander Hamilton*, ed. Harold C. Syrett, 26 vols. (New York: Columbia University Press, 1961–79), 26:774, emphasis in original.

53. Gaustad, *Sworn on the Altar of God*, 108.

54. "Timothy Dwight," in *Dictionary of American Biography*, 1:576.

55. Timothy Dwight, *The Conquest of Canaan; A Poem, in Eleven Books* (1788; reprint, Westport, Conn.: Greenwood, 1970): 3.

56. Dwight, *Conquest of Canaan*, 354–55.

57. Dwight, *Conquest of Canaan*, 362–63.

58. Dwight, *Conquest of Canaan*, iii.

59. Jacob Kabakoff, "The Use of Hebrew by American Jews During the Colonial Period," in *Hebrew and the Bible in America: The First Two Centuries*, ed. Shalom Goldman (Hanover, N.H.: University Press of New England, 1993), 193.

60. Miller, "Garden of Eden and the Deacon's Meadow," 55.

61. Quoted in Miller, "Garden of Eden and the Deacon's Meadow," 61.

BIBLICAL LAW IN AMERICA
HISTORICAL PERSPECTIVES AND POTENTIALS FOR REFORM

John W. Welch

This article presents a sort of *apologia,* an apology for greater awareness of biblical law in connection with the study of American legal history and the underlying fabric of the common law. Following a brief introduction to the modern study and broad relevance of biblical law, I review the prevalence and importance of biblical law in American colonial law, consider the influence of these biblical foundations on American law in general, and finally draw attention to some of the ways in which biblical law generates prospects for legal reforms alleviating some of the problems and challenges faced by the American legal system as it continues on into the twenty-first century. This article strives to show that the study of biblical law has much to offer to anyone interested not only in the history of American law but also in its future.

I. THE RELEVANCE OF BIBLICAL LAW

The study of legal materials in the Bible has changed dramatically in recent years. With these changes should come a shift in the way legal scholars view the current significance of biblical law. No longer do careful scholars view the Bible merely from parochial or inspirational points of view. Although most readers in the past have used the Bible simply as a repository of divinely revealed dicta, modern students bring greater sophistication to the understanding of this complex collection of ancient writings. Not only serving as the religious foundation of biblical society, the texts of the Bible also functioned, as it were, as the constitution, the codes of civil and criminal procedure, as well as the handbooks of public and private law for the Israelite world of its day. Therefore, to see the Bible as relevant only to religious as opposed to legal interests or political applications is to fundamentally misunderstand major portions of this text.

The Bible is indeed a rich source of a variety of legal materials.[1] It comprises so-called law codes, including the Code of the Covenant (Ex. 21:1–23:19), the Holiness Code (Lev. 19–26), and the laws in Deuteronomy (Deut. 12–26). It also features law lists, such as the Ten Commandments in Exodus (Ex. 20) and Deuteronomy (Deut. 5), or the cultic code in Exodus (Ex. 34:17–28). Actual lawsuits or legal proceedings are reported, namely the trial of the blasphemer (Lev. 24:10–23), the trial of the

Sabbath breaker (Num. 15:32–36), the resolution of the petitions of the daughters of Zelophehad (Num. 27:1–11; Num. 36:1–11), the detection and trial of Achan (Josh. 7:1–26), the trial of Ahimelech (1 Sam. 22:6–23), as well as the trials of Naboth (1 Kgs. 21:1–16), of Micah (Jer. 26:18–19; Micah 13), of Uriah ben Shemaiah (Jer. 26:20–23), and of Jeremiah himself (Jer. 26:1–24). Embedded in almost every narrative story in the Bible are legal assumptions and cultural expectations. Examples include the marriages of Abraham and the dealings of Jacob with Laban in Genesis (Gen. 31:25–55), the proceedings of Boaz before the elders at the town gate in the book of Ruth (Ruth 4:1–12), the killing of the rebel Sheba (2 Sam. 20), and the land transaction reported in Jeremiah (Jer. 32:10–14), to mention only a few. Prophetic speech forms (particularly the so-called prophetic lawsuit)[2] and proverbial wisdom sayings of the Bible also reflect the legal values and norms that stand at the root of the Judeo-Christian world. Nevertheless, despite the ubiquity of the Bible in the history of Western civilization, the breadth of legal subjects addressed in its law codes and legal sections is not widely understood or generally appreciated today. Indeed, biblical laws deal with topics ranging from criminal and penal law to judicial procedure and the administration of justice, commercial law, torts and injuries, family law, property law, estate planning, martial law, and social welfare, in addition to the laws concerning divine sanctity, cultic sacrifice, and religious taboos that usually come to mind when people first think of law in the Bible.

Due to its role as a vast repository of legal wisdom and social justice, the Bible has long been valued as a source of basic norms and rubrics. Thus, legal provisions in the Bible drew the attention of religious reformers and legal advocates, as well as clergymen and devotional readers, in the seventeenth and eighteenth centuries. Illustrative of this point, as will be discussed in detail below, American colonial legislators were no exception in this regard.[3] Particularly in New England, lawgivers drew heavily on isolated biblical provisions—which were, of course, taken out of context—in formulating their laws, especially their capital laws. This eclectic use of biblical law was consistent with the prevailing proof-text approach to the Bible employed generally by readers, preachers, and scholars in that day.

In the nineteenth and early twentieth centuries, books written about biblical law became more interested in compiling, classifying, and internally harmonizing the various legal provisions in the law of Moses, often in an effort simply to comprehend systematically this substantial and complex body of legal materials.[4] This approach, however, tended to marginalize biblical law from mainstream Anglo-American legal concerns by giving biblical law the appearance of a rigid, closed system of positive laws promulgated by a lawgiver far removed from contemporary society.

In the first half of the twentieth century, text critical scholars dominated the field of biblical law, hoping to discern clues about the authorship and dating of individual legal texts. These scholars, mostly inspired by German academicians but consonant with the enterprise of American legal realism, applied the techniques of higher criticism and the documentary hypothesis to segregate from each other the stylistically divergent bodies of law in the Bible.[5] At that time, the study of biblical law was mostly practiced by theologians as a limited subdiscipline within biblical studies. Driving their methodology was an unstated Darwinian model that all institutions evolve from simple to complex organisms as accretions occur in response to external stimuli and internal pressures.[6] While these efforts focused productive attention on the verbal particulars of biblical legal texts, the examination of the minutiae of the Hebrew text has, in many cases, proved to be a relatively sterile jurisprudential exercise, has raised as many questions as it has answered, and has probably left many legal historians or lawyers wondering if the study of biblical law is accessible to them and, if it is, whether the pursuit is worth the effort. During this period of biblical scholarship, interest in biblical law consequently almost disappeared in most circles.

A new discipline of biblical law, however—a discrete field of legal scholarship which attempts to understand the legal institutions and main juridical norms that comprised the legal system that operated in ancient Israel—has emerged mainly in the last fifty years. Owing largely to the contributions of scholars such as legal scholar David Daube,[7] law professor Ze'ev W. Falk,[8] barrister Bernard S. Jackson, and many others,[9] great strides have been made in reconstructing the legal system of ancient Israel and in understanding the fundamental values embedded in that justice system. This work by biblical scholars, many of whom are equally trained in the law, allows modern readers to undertake an examination of the main institutions of biblical law through techniques similar to those applied in any normal comparative or analytical law study. Accordingly, biblical legal texts have been examined through the tools of economics, semiotics,[10] feminine studies,[11] literature,[12] historical comparative studies,[13] anthropology, and many other modern methodologies. The extent of recent interest in the biblical law field can be measured, in part, by the *Biblical Law Bibliography* published initially in 1990, listing several thousand entries, to which another two thousand entries were added in an update published in a new journal dedicated solely to the study of law in the Bible and ancient Near East.[14] The overview of the discipline of biblical law by Raymond Westbrook, a lawyer and scholar of the ancient Near East, which appears in Oxford's *Introduction to the History and Sources of Jewish Law,* provides an excellent point of entry for any scholar wishing to learn the latest thinking on the backgrounds, sources, and main institutions pertinent to this field.[15] With this significant transformation in the scholarly understanding of biblical law, contemporary jurisprudence must once again redefine its attitudes toward the sources of law in the Bible and their relevance to current American law and society. It is even somewhat ironic that this new turn toward secular approaches in the study of legal materials in the ancient scriptures has opened the door for sacred writings to become applicable and useful in the modern world.

Nevertheless, twenty-first-century jurists may still be reluctant to entertain the need for, or to see any value in, studying biblical law. Such reluctance, however, will jeopardize one's ability to understand the broad legal elements in Western civilization and the American experience. As discussed below, several factors may contribute to this reluctance, but they are not insurmountable.

A. Tension Between Law and Religion

One may be hesitant to deal with the Bible because of its religious character in general. Tensions between law and religion, however, come from both sides.[16] Moreover, in a world in which religious motivations are increasingly significant in driving world politics, even those most squeamish about giving to anything religious even the slightest presence in the secular liberal state must pay attention to how law and religion have always interacted.[17] It also promotes a higher comfort level in dealing with this intersection in the sphere of biblical law in particular to realize that the bible not only regulated religious practices but also functioned in the ancient Israelite state much as did the laws in the lands of its surrounding neighbors. It is a mistake to view biblical law simply as ecclesiastical law or merely as an outgrowth of religious impulses.

B. Claims of Divine Origins

Others may dismiss the Bible out of hand because it claims divine origins for some of its precepts. Biblical law can be studied, however, as a practical legal system, quite independent of its truth claims or assertions of divine origins. Hammurabi and other lawgivers in antiquity regularly claimed divine origins for their laws,[18] but that does not deter modern minds from recognizing the significance of those laws in world history.

C. Separation of Church and State

Modern scholarship, along with secular politics, typically maintains a strict separation of church and state, religion and law. But this is strictly a post-enlightenment phenomenon. Even Thomas Jefferson crossed out the preceding word "eternal" in the draft of his Danbury letter when he coined the phrase "wall of separation."[19] The current categorical constructs of "church" and "state" did not exist two hundred years ago, let alone in any ancient society.[20] Thus, as the modern liberal world becomes more and more removed from its historical and biblical or religious roots, people will have a harder and harder time understanding the past in which religion and the Bible played an enormously significant and influential role. Nevertheless, as Harold Berman and others have extensively demonstrated, religion, Christianity, and the Bible have had a great impact on the development of American laws and legal systems.[21]

D. Arcane Nature of Biblical Text

Other barriers may exist because of the technical and foreign nature of biblical and ancient Near Eastern legal studies. In some respects, the sources are esoteric and arcane. But modern translations and commentaries now exist that make this body of scholarship less remote and much more accessible.

E. Relevance of Biblical Law

Moreover, one needs not worry that biblical law will be found to be irrelevant. In teaching biblical law to law students for twenty years, I have noticed that its topics and underlying policies have always proved to be surprisingly relevant and stimulating to me and to my students. Not only do Israelite and other Near Eastern texts promulgate rules that deal with problems and address legal issues that still arise in society today, but comparison and analysis is also illuminating and profitable for American law students precisely because the roots of the legal system in the United States are so deeply intertwined with biblical law. Thus, the study of its solutions and value structures helps to illuminate the issues and elements that both shaped the origins of American law and also remain relevant in modern times.

With these ideas as a prologue, one can recognize and appreciate the dominant role of biblical law in colonial America. Especially in New England, the Bible served as the bedrock of most principles of early American jurisprudence.

II. BIBLICAL LAW IN COLONIAL AMERICA

The first step in approaching biblical law in America is to become aware of the prevalence of the Bible in early American history. The Bible was nothing short of the underlying fabric upon which American society was founded. Most people are surprised to learn, however, how large a role the Bible played in the formulation of the earliest laws of several of the American colonies. Indeed, it has rightly been concluded that "the ideal polity of early Puritan New England was thought to comprehend divine intentions as revealed in Mosaic law."[22] The rule of law began not with the rules of man but with the rules of God. One Puritan document directly states, "The more any law smells of man, the more unprofitable," and thus, it asserts, the only proper laws were in fact "divine ordinances, revealed in the pages of Holy Writ and administered according to deductions and rules gathered from the Word of God."[23]

While the profound influence of biblical law on early American colonial law is obvious to those who have studied seventeenth-century law in America, few publications have actually examined such things as the way in which Calvin's experiment in theocracy at Geneva influenced the Puritans' view of law (who believed that the judicial language in the law of Moses was binding on all people and should be incorporated into the laws of the land), and how these attitudes were then put into practice in drafting early colonial laws and permeated the whole mode of Puritan life and thought.[24] Few people may be aware of this phenomenon partly because so few copies of these early laws have survived, some being completely lost to scholars for many years. Thus, the recently published encyclopedia *Religion and American Law* laments, "The role of the Bible in influencing American constitutional thought has only recently begun to attract significant scholarly attention," even though the influence of the Bible on American thought in general has long been widely recognized.[25] A recent Brandeis University Press publication on Hebrew and the Bible in America in its first two hundred years makes no mention whatever of law or the influence of the Bible on the early American legal experience.[26]

Without wishing to overstate the influence of biblical thought in the history of early American law,[27] the full extent of the influence of the Bible on colonial law has never been adequately assessed or appreciated. One could quote several scholars such as Patrick O'Neil, who concludes, "In the early era of the formation of American law the Bible acted as an important source of law,"[28] but conclusory statements such as these are no substitute for looking at the documents themselves. The following amassing of evidence offers a window into the quantity and the quality of biblical law that was used in early colonial American law.

A. Explicit Use of Biblical Law

A broadside entitled "The Capital Laws of New England as They Stand Now in Force in the Commonwealth, 1641, 1642" was printed in England in 1643 (near the beginning of the Cromwellian era).[29] This document appears to be the earliest publication of American law. It was based on a now-lost document called the "judicials of Moses," prepared as early as 1636 by John Cotton and Nathaniel Ward, only sixteen years after the landing of the Pilgrims at Plymouth Rock.[30] The obvious biblical content and source attributions in this early publication may well come as a surprise to most modern readers:

Capitall Lawes, Established within the Jurisdiction of Massachusets

1. If any man after legall conviction, shall have or worship any other God, but the Lord God, he shall be put to death. *Deut.* 13. 6, &c. and 17. 2. &c. *Exodus* 22. 20.

2. If any man or woman be a Witch, that is, hath or consulteth with a familiar spirit, they shall be put to death. *Exod.* 22. 18. *Lev.* 20. 27. *Deut.* 18. 10, 11.

3. If any person shall blaspheme the Name of God the Father, Sonne, or Holy Ghost, with direct, expresse, presumptuous, or high-handed blasphemy, or shall curse God in the like manner, he shall be put to death. *Lev.* 24. 15, 16.

4. If any person shall commit any wilfull murther, which is manslaughter, committed upon premeditate malice, hatred, or cruelty, not in a mans necessary and just defence, nor by meer

casulatie, against his will; he shall be put to death. *Exod.* 21. 12, 13, 14. *Num.* 35. 30, 31.

5. If any person slayeth another suddenly in his anger, or cruelty of passion, he shall be put to death. *Num.* 35. 20, 21. *Lev.* 24. 17.

6. If any person shall slay another through guile, either by poysonings, or other such divilish practice; he shall be put to death. *Exod.* 21. 14.

7. If a man or woman shall lye with any beast, or bruit creature, by carnall copulation, they shall surely be put to death; and the beast shall be slaine, and buried. *Lev.* 20. 15, 16.

8. If a man lyeth with mankinde, as he lyeth with a woman, both of them have committed abomination, they both shall surely be put to death. *Lev.* 20. 13.

9. If any person committeth adultery with a maried, or espoused wife, the Adulterer, and the Adulteresse, shall surely be put to death. *Lev.* 20. 10. *and* 16. 20. *Deut.* 22. 23, 24.

10. If any man shall unlawfully have carnall copulation with any woman-childe under ten yeares old, either with, or without her consent, he shall be put to death.

11. If any man shall forcibly, and without consent, ravish any maid or woman that is lawfully married or contracted, he shall be put to death. *Deut.* 22. 25. &c.

12. If any man shall ravish any maid or single woman (committing carnall copulation with her by force, against her will) that is above the age of ten yeares; he shall be either punished with death, or with some other grievous punishment, according to circumstances, at the discretion of the Judges: and this Law to continue till the Court take further order.

13. If any man stealeth a man, or man-kinde, he shall surely be put to death. *Exod.* 21. 16.

14. If any man rise up by false witnesse wittingly, and of purpose to take away any mans life, he shall be put to death. *Deut.* 19. 16. 18, 19.

15. If any man shall conspire, or attempt any invasion, insurrection, or publick rebellion against our Common-wealth, or shall indeavour to surprize any Towne or Townes, Fort or Forts therein: or shall treacherously, or perfidiously attempt the alteration and subversion of our frame of pollity, or government fundamentally, he shall be put to death. *Num.* 16. 2. *Sam.* 3. & 18. & 20.[31]

In skillful fashion, the 1641 capital laws of New England were collected and crafted from the texts of the Bible. These capital offenses included three affronts against God (idolatry, witchcraft [an offense that presumed loyalty to some other spiritual power besides the true God], and blasphemy), three kinds of manslaughter (premeditated murder, crimes of cruel passion, and killing by stealth), six types of sexual offenses (bestiality, homosexuality, adultery, child abuse, statutory rape, and forcible rape), and three crimes against other people (kidnapping, perjury in a capital case, and treasonous sedition). Nor is the biblical influence unacknowledged—scripture references are supplied as authority for each of these capital laws in much the same fashion as other laws of this period cited previous legislative sessions for the legal imprimature behind each provision. The legal craftsmen of these provisions clearly knew their Bible well. Indeed, the idea that a man or a woman could be a "witch" comes directly from the Bible. Exodus 22:18 was understood to include both men and women in the Talmud, which is emphatically consistent with explicit language in Leviticus 20:27. A careful check of the biblical references cited, however, will readily show that the Puritan legislators were not slavishly tied to the biblical text.[32] They stood ready and willing to paraphrase, restate, combine, and modify biblical laws to suit the current sensibilities and needs of their colony. For example, in the first provision in this 1641 declaration, the lawgiver begins with the provision that a person is

A page from *General Laws and Liberties of Massachusetts Colony: Revised and Reprinted* (Cambridge, Mass., 1672). These capital laws demonstrate the degree to which the law of colonial Massachusetts was based on biblical law.

subject to the death penalty for idolatry or heresy only "after legal conviction" as a first time offender. No such provisions for due process and judicial warning are found anywhere in the Bible. Likewise, these laws only went so far with biblical mandates. Thus stoning, which is the proper form of punishment for blasphemy as prescribed in Leviticus 20, was not to be used in Boston.

B. Expansion and Development of Biblical Law

This utilization of biblical law was not a passing fancy in colonial America. Slightly modified forms of the 1641 Capital Laws persisted in colonial law throughout the seventeenth century. A collection of laws dated 1647 (and printed in Cambridge, England, in 1648) restates and codifies the same list of capital offenses. At this time, some of its provisions were expanded and developed. For example, section 3 on blasphemy was greatly enlarged to read (new words are shown here in italics):

> 3. If any person *within this Jurisdiction whether Christian or Pagan* shall *wittingly and willingly presume to* blaspheme the *holy* Name of God, Father, Son or Holy Ghost, with direct, expresse, presumptuous, or high-handed blasphemy, *either by willfull or obstinate denying the true God, or his Creation, or Government of the world:* or shall curse God in the like manner, *or reproach the holy Religion of God as if it were but a politick device to keep ignorant men in awe; or shall utter any other kinde of Blasphemy of the like nature & degree they* shall be put to death. *Levit.* 24. 15, 16.[33]

Going well beyond the biblical source, the law of blasphemy now more severely included denying, cursing, or reproaching the true God, his creation or government of the world, or the holy religion of God. At the same time, the biblical requirement that the same law shall apply to foreigners as well as citizens, "as well for the stranger, as for one of your own country," (Lev. 24:16–22) seems to stand behind the express application of this section to Christians as well as pagans, keeping the new legislation in this respect in harmony with scriptural law. As a mitigating factor, the new law softened the harsh result of the trial of the blasphemer in Leviticus 24, which sentenced to death a man who spoke the name of God in a fit of anger in the midst of a fight, and now called for the punishment only of those who debase God "wittingly and willingly" in a "wilfull or obstinate" frame of mind. Thus the American tradition of modifying, amending, revising, and constantly tinkering with legislation, even if its root lies in holy writ, was born at an early stage in colonial legal history.

Elsewhere in the 1648 publication, biblical law was also used as the basis for noncriminal law. For example, it lists the civil remedies for fornication, as adopted in 1642, as follows: "If any man shall commit Fornication with any single woman, they shall be punished either by enjoyning to Marriage, or Fine, or coporall punishment, or all or any of these as the Judges in the courts of Assistants shall appoint most agreeable to the word of God."[34] Indeed, the "word of God" calls for similar outcomes, although at the hands of the female's father, namely a fine of fifty shekels and the requirement of marriage without any right of divorce (Deut. 22:29), culpable with the generic possibility of flogging (Deut. 25:1–3).

Eight years later, virtually the same list of capital laws, again with interesting modifications and additions, appeared in 1656 in the laws of New Haven, a neighboring colony that was closely connected with Massachusetts.[35] Interestingly, in New Haven, in order to be convicted of blasphemy a person was required to blaspheme while "professing the true God," which effectively transformed the crime from blasphemy to leading others into apostasy.[36] Most noticeably, the brief prohibition against male homosexuality was greatly expanded, complete with scripture references to Romans 1:26, Jude 1:7, and Genesis 38:9 to include lesbianism, child abuse, sodomy, and male masturbation in the presence of others.[37]

C. Guiding Principles from Biblical Law

As was the case in Massachusetts, the New Haven legislature also turned to the Bible for guiding principles in drafting its civil laws. Thus, "to prevent or suppresse other thefts, and pilfrings," any person who had "stollen, assisted, or any way have been accessary to the stealing of any Cattel of what sort soever, or Swine" was required to "make such restitution to the owner, as the Court considering all circumstances, shall judge most agreeable to the word of God." By specific reference, the provisions of Exodus 22:1–5, regarding the theft of oxen, sheep, or donkeys, were to be applied in such cases.[38]

The pervasive use of the Bible as the undergirding spirit of the laws of New Haven is most clearly manifested in the opening charge given to the court as it was organized and instructed according to these "Lawes for Government." The following directives are quoted at some length to convey a clear idea of the dominant role that biblical precepts played in the foundations of the legal system in New Haven. At the head of several enumerated duties of the court, its first priority was to affirmatively maintain the "purity of Religion," and the second priority was to humbly acknowledge that legal authority ultimately emanates from God:

> This Court thus framed, shall first with all care, and diligence from time to time provide for the maintenance of the purity of Religion, and suppresse the contrary, according to their best Light, and directions from the word of God [citing *Psalms* 2:10–12 and *1 Timothy* 2:2].
>
> Secondly, though they humbly acknowledge, that the Supreame power of making Lawes, and of repealing them, belongs to God only, and that by him this power is given to Jesus Christ as Mediator, *Math*. 28. 19. *Joh*. 5. 22. And that the Lawes for holinesse, and Righteousnesse, are already made, and given us in the Scriptures, which in matters morall, or of morall equity, may not be altered by humane power, or authority, *Moses* only shewed *Israel* the Lawes, and Statutes of God,

and the *Sanedrim* the highest Court, among the *Jewes,* must attend those Lawes. Yet Civill Rulers, and Courts, and this Generall Court in particular . . . are the Ministers of God, for the good of the people; And have power to declare, publish, and establish, for the plantations within their Jurisdictions, the Lawes he hath made, and to make, and repeale Orders for smaller matters, not particularly determined in Scripture, according to the more Generall Rules of Righteousnesse.[39]

Significantly, in all major matters, the legal outcome was "determined in Scripture," and the jurisdiction of the court resided solely in the "smaller matters" of mundane enforcement of general law for the "good of the people."

D. Adaptive Persistence of Biblical Law

Back in Massachusetts, a revised and updated collection of the General Laws and Liberties of that colony was issued in 1660.[40] Once again, most of the Capital Lawes from 1641 were included (sections 10 and 11, regarding sex with a girl under the age of ten and rape, were deleted, probably as already covered by other sections), and two new sections that had been adopted in 1649 were added:

> 13. If any Child, or Children, above sixteen years old, and of sufficient understanding, shall CURSE, or SMITE their natural FATHER or MOTHER, he or they shall be putt to death, unles it can be sufficiently testifyed, that the Parents have been very unChristianly negligent in the education of such children: or so provoked them by extream & cruel correction, that they have been forced thereunto, to preserve themselves from death or maiming: *Exod.* 21. 17, *Lev.* 20. 9. *Exod.* 21. 15.

> 14. If a man have a STUBBORNE or REBELLIOUS SON of sufficient yeares and understanding (viz) sixteen yeares of age, which will not obey the voice of his Father, or the voyce of his Mother, and that when they have chastned him, will not hearken unto them, then shall his Father and Mother, being his natural Parents lay hold on him, and bring him to the Magistrates assembled in Court, and testifie unto them, that their Son is stubborn and rebellious, and will not obey their voyce and chastisement, but lives in sundry notorious crimes: Such a Son shall be put to death. *Deut:* 22 [21]. 20, 21.[41]

These provisions regarding insolent and rebellious children come, in principle, directly from the Bible, although once again with ample adaptation. The ancient law regarding a child who struck or cursed his father or mother literally applied only to a son and presumably not to a daughter, and no exculpation due to parental neglect or cruelty was stated (Ex. 21:15–17). Likewise, to the ancient law regarding a rebellious son has been added the age of accountability at sixteen and the requirement that the parents must both be his natural parents, not stepparents or adoptive parents (Deut. 21:15–21).

Essentially the same list of capital statutes is perpetuated in the laws of Massachusetts published in 1672,[42] with the reappearance of the prohibition against "*Carnal Copulation with a Woman Childe under the age of ten years,*" which originally appeared on the 1641 list but had been dropped in 1648. Now this offense was reinstated with emphasis, "as being more inhumane and unnatural in it self, and more perrilous to the life and well-being of the Childe."[43]

In the same year, 1672, laws promulgated in the Connecticut Colony reiterated the traditional Capital Laws, with the unique addition of a prohibition against arson:

> 13. If any person of the age of sixteen years and upward, shall wilfully and of purpose fire any Dwelling-House, Barn or out House, he shall be put to death, or suffer such other severe punishment as the Court of Assistants shall determine; if no prejudice or hazard to the life of any person come thereby, and also satisfie all damages to the wronger or agrieved party.[44]

Thus, throughout the seventeenth century, the traditional list of capital laws concisely defined the cases under which a person could be put to death within the jurisdiction of Massachusetts and the surrounding colonies. These provisions raise many intriguing questions about the selection and modification of these biblical provisions. But more than looking at the details of these individual provisions, if one wants to know what a particular legal system values most, it is generally best to look first to its use of capital punishment, especially in premodern societies. Here one finds what these systems considered crucial to the social order. As is readily apparent, the Bible played a crucial role in the legal fabric of community life in early America.

While the capital laws in their traditional form with biblical references drop out of the Acts and Laws of the king's province in the Massachusetts Bay in 1699, the influence of the Bible and religion was still prominently visible in these regulations printed in Boston. For example, a new section regarding "the better observation and keeping the Lords-Day" provided:

> All and every person and persons whatsoever, shall on that Day carefully apply themselves to Duties of Religion and Piety, publickly and privately; and that no Tradesman, Artificer, Labourer or other person whatsoever, shall upon the Land or Water, do or exercise any Labour, Business, or Work of their ordinary Callings; nor use any Game, Sport, Play or Recreation on the Lords-Day, or any part thereof; (works of necessity and charity only excepted) upon pain that every person so offending shall forfeit *Five Shillings*.[45]

Likewise, in New Haven, debt slavery resulted when a thief who could not make restitution received whippings of no more than forty stripes, which reflected biblical provisions (Ex. 22:3; Deut. 25:3). In Connecticut, two or three witnesses were required in capital cases.[46] In Quaker Pennsylvania, cursing, swearing, or blasphemy were against the law; debt servitude was limited to seven years (five for a married man); two-fold restitution was exacted for stealing an animal, with four-fold restitution if the stolen cattle could not be returned.[47] All of these provisions are familiar to biblicists.

III. THE IMPACT OF BIBLICAL LAW ON AMERICAN LAW

Naturally, one must not overstate the influence of the Bible on the development of law in America. Nevertheless, by one count, eleven percent of colonial laws were directly based on biblical texts, ranging from zero percent in Virginia to forty percent in New England.[48] And even these impressive statistics do not tell the whole story. From decade to decade,

the story changes within individual colonies, and many more provisions were indirectly based on the Bible. As the *Encyclopedia of Religion and American Law* states, "It is impossible to list all these indirect influences which Scripture has had on the minds of judges, lawmakers, and the electorate," for many aspects of American law were "strongly shaped by the popular understanding of biblical morality."[49]

From this strong use of the Bible in colonial American law, one may detect several important attitudes or ways in which biblical law has contributed to the fundamental development of American legal thought.

A. Seeing Church and State as Hand-in-Hand Partners

Embedded deep in the American legal system is an expectation or presumption of the concurrent validity, if not necessity, of basic religious or moral virtues thriving in the heart of the American state. It may have originally been an accident of history, but the use of biblical law filled an important gap in the life of the pioneer pilgrims who first came to America.[50] Their charters did not allow them to enact law as such, and yet they needed to regulate their community. As the preface to the *Book of the General Laws and Liberties of Massachusetts,* adopted in 1644 and published in 1648, makes clear, the colonists began with a strong assumption that a society must have laws: "For a Common-wealth without lawes is like a Ship without rigging and steeradge."[51] To find such social sails and helm, these Americans turned first to the Bible. Its rules were not adopted or officially "voted in Court."[52] They could not be adopted without exceeding the scope of the colony's authority, but then, brilliantly, neither did they need to be, for they were accepted as transcending any human authority. Moreover, the New Testament epistle to the Romans specifically sanctioned the cooperation of religious believers and secular institutions (Rom. 13:1–7). The emergent collaboration between church and state (even if these two arms remain separate while at the same time working together) has remained a fundamental axiom embedded in the nature of American polity ever since.[53]

B. Appealing to Citations of Authority

From the beginning in American legal thinking, jurists were assiduous about citing legal authority for principles they espoused. The force of the authority, rather than the mechanics of the law, became an essential ingredient in the American sense of justice. This particular approach to authority and precedent is fundamental to American jurisprudence, but it is not intuitively present in all legal systems. Thus, the laws of 1648 began with a recognition of authority in God's establishment of the law of Moses and its political institutions: "So soon as God had set up Politicall Government among his people Israel hee gave them a body of lawes for judgement both in civil and criminal causes."[54] One sees the appeal to specific justifying authority in numerous biblical citations throughout these early laws, not only regarding serious capital matters but even in regard to mundane matters, such as regulation concerning the weights and measures used by bakers, which followed the biblical pro-

hibitions against deceptive or fraudulent weights and measures.[55]

C. Emphasizing Codification, Publication, and Public Education

Law needs to be set forth, proclaimed, and published. In order to be bound, the public must know and accept the law. These principles are in operation from the beginning of American law, necessitated in part by the complexity of the Bible and its susceptibility to various divisive interpretations. Thus, codification was necessary. "Often acclaimed as the first English-language codification of laws, the 1648 book exists in only one copy," found today in the Huntington Library in San Marino, California.[56] Just as the Bible required the law to be proclaimed and taught among the people so that they might hear and fear (Deut. 19:20, 31:11–12), the Colonialists went to great lengths to have their laws published and taught. Even when no printing presses existed in the New World in the earliest years, the settlers returned to London or Cambridge to have their laws printed.[57]

Codification, collection, and articulation were perceived as necessary because it is not sufficient to

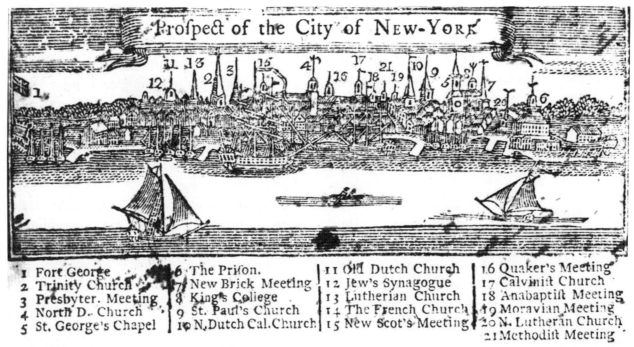

Prospect of New York City. Woodcut from Hugh Gaine, *New York Almanac*, 1771. This image demonstrates how churches dominated the New York City skyline on the eve of the American Revolution and demonstrates the preponderance of religion in America's national life generally.

give people principles alone: "It is very unsafe & injurious to the body of the people to put them [to require them] to learn their duty and libertie from general rules."[58] Someone must organize and set forth the requirements. Conceptually, this is an important point in legal history, constituting the beginnings of much larger collections of laws in America, such as the United States Code.

Growing out of this emphasis on publishing and promulgating the law, the sense of embracing the law was seen in America as a matter of personal commitment, as much it had once been a matter of individual covenant in Deuteronomy 27. As the preface to the 1648 publication states, each person has a personal duty to embrace and obey the law for the common welfare, even to "thy [personal] disadvantage: so another must observe some other law for thy good, though to his own damage; thus must we be content to bear [one] anothers burden and so fullfill the Law of Christ."[59]

D. Seeing Laws as Principles, Subject to Restatement and Adaptation

Americans typically understand law as a body of rules that are distilled from principles, capable of and in need of periodic restatement and adaptation to meet current circumstances. This understanding was at work from the beginning in these early laws, and it grew out of the way in which these people interpreted and applied biblical principles, restating them and deducing from them rules for their use. This procedure was articulated expressly as early as 1648: "These [the biblical rules] were brief and fundamental principles, yet withall so full and comprehensive as out of them clear deductions were to be drawn to all particular cases in future times."[60] This principle is inherently at work throughout the colonies. In 1647, a Rhode Island law resulted from a restatement of the law of accidental slaying, as set forth by the honorable judge of Israel "in the 19th [chapter] of his 5th book [Deuteronomy]."[61] This provision even included a modified concept of asylum: an inadvertent slayer must forfeit his property, but by submitting to trial he will be pardoned.[62] In

1656, the laws of New Haven tried to respect the "double portion" afforded to the eldest son, as required in Deuteronomy 21:17, but they also allowed the court discretion to give more to the widow and less to the son.[63] Similarly, in 1714, the Pennsylvania legislature drew on the principle of punitive damages in Exodus 22:1, 4, which required double restitution of a stolen sheep or ox if the animal is found still alive, while four- or five-fold punitive damages are imposed if the animal has been killed or sold. The same rule was adapted for use in Pennsylvania, but now it was extended to cover goods (not only animals); double satisfaction was required in addition to the return of the stolen property, with four-fold satisfaction if the goods or cattle are not found. In addition, a public whipping of twenty-one lashes and the wearing of a "T" for six months (for Thief) were added beyond anything the Bible would require.[64]

E. Producing a Basis for Unification and Efficient Implementation of the Law

Of the many further similar examples that might be offered, one other major contribution that biblical law made in shaping American jurisprudence was its sense of unification and equality. Mark DeWolfe Howe has identified the successful unification of "law" into one common domain as one of the great achievements of American colonial law.[65] Consider the legal world out of which the colonialists had come.[66] In it, the great English judge Edward Coke had recognized fifteen different brands of English law.[67] In it, different bodies of law, with idiosyncratic concepts, jurisdictions, and procedures, were each applied in numerous kinds of courts that proliferated in the King's realm. There were courts of common pleas, the Exchequer, and the Queen's Bench; there were laws of the Admiral, the Bishop, the Mayor, the local lord, the Star Chamber, the Court of Chivalry, the Court of Requests, and Court of Chancery, and so on.[68] Due to this multiplicity, it would have been almost impossible for a British subject to answer the question "Under what law are you living?"[69] In stark contrast to this cacophony of courts in the Old World, as Howe has argued, the colonialist could boast that he lived, for the first time, under a "unified judicial system."[70] In the New World, the fledgling colonies featured only one kind of court, a single court of general jurisdiction, applying all the law, equally in all kinds of cases.[71] This was an amazing step forward in legal history, probably more revolutionary than has been realized and recognized. But what Howe does not note is the undeniable role that the Bible played in this development. For the Bible transcended all these various brands of law. The Bible was the great unifying force that commanded ultimate loyalty and juridical respect. Ultimately, it was the harmony between the laws of God and the proper laws of any state that allowed the Americans to see every kind of law as belonging to a single order and system of law.

Returning to the preface to the 1648 General Laws and Liberties, one sees this unity clearly articulated in its concluding and undergirding declaration:

> That distinction which is put between the Lawes of God and the lawes of men, becomes a snare to many as is it mis-applied in the ordering of their obedience to civil Authoritie; for when the Authoritie is of God and that in way of an Ordinance *Rom.* 13. 1. and when the administration of it is according to deductions, and rules gathered from the word of God, and the clear light of nature in civil nations, surely there is no humane law that tendeth to [common] good (according to those principles) but the same is mediately a law of God, and that in way of an Ordinance which all are to submit unto and that for conscience sake. *Rom.* 13. 5.[72]

If, as this eloquent proposition insists, all law is ultimately "a law of God," then it readily follows that all law falls under a single category and unified hand of jurisdiction. The force of this revolutionary idea impelled directly forward the ideal of one nation, under God, and hence equality before that law for all.

F. A Lasting Legacy

Although it is no longer common to hear lawyers cite the Bible as legal authority in court, except perhaps when playing to the jury, the influence of biblical law continued to be felt in American jurisprudence well into the twentieth century.[73] It was accepted implicitly by legal historians as recently as 1943 that "many provisions of biblical law are still seen in American statutes and court decisions."[74] In 1923, a prominent legal publication asserted, "Allusions to the Bible are perhaps more frequent than to any book other than professional law treatises and previous decisions."[75] The Constitution of North Carolina in 1776 and other state constitutions excluded from office all nonbelievers in the Protestant religion or the divine authority of the Old or New Testament,[76] and many early American cases held that biblical law was a part and parcel of the common law. Thus, displaying a representation of the Ten Commandments on the wall of a courtroom or other public building is not, strictly speaking, simply a matter of church iconography; such a depiction simultaneously presents several underlying policies deeply ingrained in the character of American common law.[77]

IV. Prospects for Continuing Application and Reform

If biblical law has been a significant historical factor in the legal history of America, and if biblical principles and values are interwoven into the fabric of the legal system modern American lawyers have inherited, then studying the values operating in and behind the biblical legal system should offer insights into the nature of law in America today and, consequently, into possible solutions suitable to some of the problems now confronted in that legal world. For the law is a seamless web, and if the American legal system in actuality presupposes certain underlying values that were essential to the underpinnings of American society at the time that system was put in place, it is unlikely that the superstructure built on that foundation will continue to stand if that foundation is simply taken away. To the extent that a modern system is derived from biblical social precepts or even unwittingly presupposes that such precepts are operational in society, the lack of any of the essential elements of that constitutive system may give rise to serious problems in the resultant system. If an airplane is designed with the assumption that the plane will have a rudder, and then the rudder is taken away, the airplane cannot be expected to function properly.

In the study of biblical law, I have noted several values that were essential to the fabric and operation of that legal system. I will mention only a few of these policies here, suggesting ways in which strengthening or observing similar principles today could produce sound results in the legal well-being of America in the coming decades.

A. Commitment to Legal Order

Biblical law presupposed that individual members of the community would respect the law and were bound to obey the law out of inner devotion to a civil order that makes freedom possible. Law in the biblical period operated without police, investigators, paid prosecutors, or judges. Its rules and remedies were fashioned with a voluntary compliance system in mind. Largely grounded in the solemn making of personal and national covenants, the biblical law system presumed that people would be loyal to the lawgiver and have no other god before him, and would show respect to the lawgiver and to the name of the law.

Likewise, presupposed in the Preamble to the United States Constitution and in other works of the day (such as Adam Smith's *Theory of Moral Sentiments*) is the assumption that citizens will willingly respect and charitably obey the law.[78]

Democracy as a political *modus vivendi* presupposes a moral basis and background; it is moral before it is political. For a people to rule, there must prevail among them a hunger for justice and righteousness and a thirst for liberty, both for oneself and one's brother; without these fundamental virtues, a people, even if living under a form of democracy, will find itself in fact living under tyrannous masters.[79]

Democracy in America has succeeded because its society has possessed an underlying moral order, and historically that order has been informed largely by basic ideals supplied by the Bible, especially "in shaping popular social values in the early United States."[80]

In the American legal system today, one counts on this assumption even to the point of expecting individual citizens to report their taxes voluntarily and to comply with the law for the common good. Being free from government intervention and regulation assumes that each member of the society will voluntarily honor and respect the law without intrusive compulsion or governmental constraint. Of course, this objective will not always be realized in every case, but the system as a whole assumes that most people will honor and respect the law most of the time. Reforms aimed at encouraging voluntary compliance and, concurrently, more stringently punishing those who abuse this fundamentally essential value of American law should therefore be considered and implemented.

B. Knowledge of the Law

Biblical law assumed that every person was knowledgeable of the law. Parents were required to teach the law to their children, and rulers would read the law publicly to the entire community at least once every seven years. It would be impossible to read the United States Code Annotated to every American citizen, even if it were read constantly and streamed over the Internet continuously for seven years. But improvements in communication with television and electronic publication now make it possible for the laws of the United States and of the individual states to be published and made available and understandable to people much more widely than ever before, not only to the relatively exclusive group of lawyers who can afford to use Lexis and Westlaw. Public access to the law should be given higher priority in America. If programs make access to the law more user friendly, individual citizens will probably take a greater interest in researching and studying laws relevant to their own circumstances and keep up to date on amendments and changes in the law.

C. Duties and Social Justice

The biblical concept of justice has more to do with shaping and encouraging social duties in protecting the weak, the poor, the widows, and the orphans than it does with asserting and protecting individual rights or liberties. In other words, the underlying jurisprudence of the Bible is more based on principles of duty than on concepts of rights. Such duties include the duty not to kill, not to steal, and not to take sexual or economic advantage of others. While the vindication and protection of individual rights against government power has been the monumental achievement of the American experiment, the roots of that legal system should remind modern citizens that rights do not exist independent of duties. The biblical method of limiting governmental powers (as is found, for example, in the paragraph of the king in Deuteronomy 17:14–20) was not to grant to individuals enhanced rights against the king, but to impose higher levels of duties on people in power. Rulers are not ordinary people because they wield extraordinary powers. Reformers might well consider how all those who were entrusted or blessed with rights and privileges in the ancient world were held to higher standards of conduct and performance than were those who were without.

D. Accountability in Using the Judicial Process

Biblical law placed high entry barriers on those initiating lawsuits. In this system, which punished a losing litigant by doing to him "as he had thought to have done unto his brother" (Deut. 19:19), it is not surprising that few court cases are chronicled in the biblical narratives. Knowing the high stakes of failure, most litigants probably found other ways to negotiate, settle, resolve, mediate, or alternatively end their legal disputes. In a country that is becoming more and more litigious, and while the legal profession is seeking ways to encourage alternative dispute resolution, reformers might well recognize that the biblical system worked for hundreds of years, efficiently and successfully, in large part because significant responsibility was placed on litigants to be sure that the actions they brought were sincere and well founded. In eagerness to give every litigant a day in court, perhaps the American system has bent over too far in the direction of lowering the entry barriers to court. Of course, defendants need

to be given all of the protections of the Constitution, but with respect to civil law plaintiffs a legal system need not be and cannot be open to all comers, unless they are willing to bear more of the burden they may wrongly impose on others or on the society.

E. Honesty and Talionic Penalties for Perjury

One of the major problems creating backlogs in courts today is the pervasive problem of perjury. District attorneys and prosecutors with whom I have spoken report that perjury is rampant and that they assume that virtually every witness is lying to some degree. Yet perjury is hardly ever studied, let alone prosecuted. The stakes are too small, and the difficulty in getting a conviction is too high.

Yet here again, biblical law may provide some insight. The biblical legal system worked largely because it exacted high penalties for perjury (Deut. 19:15–19). The prohibition against bearing false witness was aimed not so much against lying in general but more particularly against committing perjury in a judicial proceeding, especially where the name of God was invoked in bearing testimony as a witness (and therefore offending God by such prevarication). Biblical law assumed that people would tell the truth, and oaths were taken very seriously. If they did not tell the truth, false witnesses were punished by suffering the consequences that would have befallen the person against whom they had falsely testified (Deut. 19:15–19).

While I would not advocate that particular remedy for perjury in the twenty-first century, biblical law points toward a crucial premise necessary to the proper functioning of any system of law that promotes limitations on governmental powers and the protection of individual freedoms. That important premise is the assumption that people will tell the truth. If people do not tell the truth, the system sputters.

The question is what to do about the rampant perjury in our courtrooms and depositions. Here again, biblical law may have some insights to offer. One of the underlying principles of biblical justice is the concept of talionic punishment, the idea that a punishment should suit the crime.[81] The biblical formulas of "an eye for an eye and a tooth for a tooth," have been grossly misunderstood. This rubric is not a principle of vengeance or retaliation, but an equitable principle of equivalence, and probably one of limitation and restraint. The text says, "an eye for an eye," and this would also mean no more than an eye. Many implementations of this principle in biblical narratives show that the talionic principle also appeared in a poetic sense. Proper justice returns to a person that which is deserved. So for example, when Ahab put Naboth to death through a miscarriage of justice, Ahab himself was soon killed in battle; and as the dogs had licked the blood of Naboth, so the dogs licked the blood of Ahab (1 Kgs. 21:19, 22:28). This is talionic justice.

Although the principle of having the punishment fit the crime has not been forgotten in British and American literature (as one of the songs in Gilbert and Sullivan's *Mikado* makes clear), the principle has been largely overlooked as a judicial tool in modern law. Occasionally judges will use this principle in fashioning creative remedies, such as requiring people to pick up trash on the highway instead of fining them for their littering, but for the most part we prefer to fine people or put them in prison than to exact such penalties.

Fines and prison terms are not, however, practicable deterrents in the case of perjury. But, with creative thought, the talionic principle may be especially helpful in punishing perjurers. If a person commits perjury, that person should not be trusted; and so, a punishment that would fit the crime of perjury would be one that would deny that person of the privileges of being trusted within the legal system from that point forward. For instance, biblical jurisprudence might deny perjurers the legal privilege of trust by disqualifying them from serving as a director of a corporation, a trustee of a trust, or to hold other fiduciary positions. For some people, especially those who serve as trustees of their own pension plans, this could be a serious deterrent. For rank and file members of society, most people cherish their credit rating. If people knew that judges had the power to report perjury in such a way as to enter it on a person's credit record, they might be less inclined to lie on the witness stand. And in drastic cases, the government might want to presume that such a person would also have likely lied on his or her tax returns. A modern application of the biblical talionic principle might be to punish the perjurer by requiring the Internal Revenue Service to audit the offender for all open years. One might rationally guess that a higher incidence of tax fraud would be found among perjurers than among the average body of citizens.

F. A Source of Insight

In ways such as these, the study of the use of the Bible in colonial and American law may open to modern legal thinkers insights and potentials for reform that will not only make sense but will have a high likelihood of success because they are consistent with the underlying character of the American legal system. Many other similar examples could be given; for example, biblical law was not administered impersonally; plaintiffs and defendants met in court personally, not through lawyers who denied them this important channel of remorse, repentance, and reconciliation. Biblical law assiduously guarded judicial integrity; taking gifts (even after a lawsuit was concluded) was not tolerated (Ex. 23:6–8). Returning to the roots of one's language or culture, customs or traditions, often produces important insights and possibilities for future success. The same result can be expected in returning to the roots of one's laws and system of justice. This is not to say that modern America should return to an understanding of law and the Bible as it was misunderstood by the Puritans, and this is not to argue for the return of biblical law as such. But if understanding the past will ever help one to understand the future, then understanding biblical law and its influence in getting us to where we now stand should also help in getting us on in the pursuit of justice and the future enjoyment of liberty in America under American law.

This lecture was based on a paper presented in Minneapolis on October 17, 1997, at the annual meeting of the American Society for Legal History and also appears in Brigham Young University Law Review *(2002): 611–42.*

Notes

1. On the influence of the Bible in American law and politics, see generally Edward McGleynn Gaffney Jr., "The Interaction of Biblical Religion and American Constitutional Law," in *The Bible in American Law, Politics, and Political Rhetoric,* ed. James Turner Johnson (Philadelphia: Fortress; Chico, Calif.: Scholars, 1985), 81–105; Wilcomb E. Washburn, "Law and Authority in Colonial Virginia," in *Law and Authority in Colonial America,* ed. George Athan Billias (New York: Dover, 1965), 116–35; Clifford K. Shipton, "The Locus of Authority in Colonial Massachusetts," in *Law and Authority in Colonial America,* 136–48; Andrew C. Skinner, "The Influence of the Hebrew Bible on the Founders of the American Republic," in *Sacred Text, Secular Times: The Hebrew Bible in the Modern World,* ed. Leonard Jay Greenspoon and Bryan F. LeBeau (Omaha: Creighton University Press, 2000), 13–34; Bernard Meislin, "The Role of the Ten Commandments in American Judicial Decisions," in *Jewish Law Association Studies III: The Oxford Conference Vollume,* ed. A. M. Fuss (Atlanta: Scholars, 1987), 187.

2. See Kirsten Nielsen, *Yahweh as Prosecutor and Judge: An Investigation of the Prophetic Lawsuit,* trans. Frederick Cryer (Sheffield: Department of Biblical Studies, University of Sheffield, 1978).

3. Andrew Skinner argues, "The further back one goes in American history, the more saturated with Hebraic references and allusions one finds American culture to be. Ironically, it is this Hebraic milieu rather than one grounded in the Christian New Testament, which most fueled the fires of motivation and imagination among American Christian colonists and founders of the Republic. Thus, Cecil Roth could write that were we to 'deprive modern Europe and America of [their] Hebraic heritage . . . the result would be barely recognizable.'" Skinner, "Influence of the Hebrew Bible," 13, quoting Cecil Roth, *The Jewish Contribution to Civilization* (New York: Harper and Brothers, 1940), 16.

Further, Clifford Shipton claims,

The century and a half during which the Colony and Province of Massachusetts Bay were trying to adjust law and authority in order to realize these principles [of biblical law] are critical ones in this long period of their evolution. But what went on in these years has been quite generally misunderstood by historians, particularly by those who have not realized that in the period and the group with which we are concerned, religious and civil life were an integrated whole. Shipton, "Locus of Authority in Colonial Massachusetts," 136.

Abraham I. Katsh further explains,

This Hebraic influence gradually deepened as the institutions of the diverse colonies evolved and eventually merged into the underlying framework of the American Republic. The natural channels of this influence were from the first spiritual leaders of the communities, who drew their very livelihood from these Scriptural sources. Due to the religious nature of the new society, it was the ministers and preachers who in effect molded the forms of polity through their influence and nurtured its spirit by the personal examples and exhortations. Abraham I. Katsh, *The Biblical Heritage of American Democracy* (New York: Ktav, 1977), 113.

Edward McGleynn Gaffney Jr. argues, "'The principal affirmation is that law and religion are two different but interrelated aspects of social experience—in all societies, but especially in Western society, and still more especially in American society today. Despite the tensions between them, one cannot flourish without the other.' Legal culture has shaped the form and content of major themes of biblical religion both in ancient and modern times." Gaffney, "Interaction of Biblical Religion," 81, quoting Harold J. Berman, *The Interaction of Law and Religion* (Nashville: Abingdon, 1965), 11.

4. See Joseph Blenkinsopp, *Wisdom and Law in the Old Testament: The Ordering of Life in Israel and Early Judaism* (London: Oxford University Press, 1983); H. B. Clark, *Biblical Law* (Portland: Binfords and Mort, 1948); Jacob W. Ehrlich, *The Holy Bible and the Law* (New York: Oceana, 1962); Roger S. Galer, *Old Testament Law for Bible Students: Classified and Arranged as in Modern Legal Systems* (New York: Macmillan, 1922); C. B. McAfie, *The Mosaic Law in Modern Life* (New York: F. H. Revell, 1906); H. Schmokel, *Das Angewandte Recht im Alten Testament* (Leipzig: Universitätsvertag von Robert Noske in Borng, 1930); Henry S. Simonis, *Some Aspects of the Ancient Jewish Civil Law* (1928); R. J. Thompson, *Moses and the Law in a Century of Criticism Since Graf* (Leiden: Brill, 1970); H. M. Wiener, *Studies in Biblical Law* (London: D. Nut, 1907).

5. See A. Alt, "The Origin of Israelite Law," in *Essays on Old Testament History and Religion,* trans. R. A. Wilson (Oxford: Blackwell, 1966).

6. See Ze'ev W. Falk, *Hebrew Law in Biblical Times,* 2d ed. (Provo, Utah: BYU Studies; Winona Lake, Ind.: Eisenbrauns, 2001), 1–3; Umberto Cassuto, *The Documentary Hypothesis and the Composition of the Pentateuch: Eight Lectures,* trans. Israel Abrahams (Jerusalem: Magnes Press, Hebrew University, 1983).

7. John W. Welch, *David Daube Bibliography* (n.p.: 2001).

8. See Falk, *Hebrew Law in Biblical Times,* 25.

9. Raymond Westbrook, "Biblical Law," in *An Introduction to the History and Sources of Jewish Law,* ed. Neil S. Hecht and others (Oxford: Clarendon, 1996), 15–17.

10. Bernard S. Jackson, *Studies in the Semiotics of Biblical Law* (Sheffield: Sheffield Academic Press, 2000).

11. Carolyn Pressler, *The View of Women Found in the Deuteronomic Family Laws* (Berlin: W. de Gruyter, 1993).

12. Joseph Sprinke, *The Book of the Covenant: A Literary Approach* (Sheffield: Journal for the Study of the Old Testament Press, 1995).

13. Moshe Weinfeld, *Social Justice in Ancient Israel and in the Ancient Near East* (Minneapolis: Fortress; Jerusalem: Magnes, 1995).

14. John W. Welch, *Biblical Law Bibliography: Arranged by Subject and Author* (Lewiston, N.Y.: E. Mellen, 1990), with supplements in Zeitschrift für die Biblische und Altorientalishe Rechtsgeschichte (1997 and 2003).

15. Westbrook, "Biblical Law," 1–17.

16. See Thomas L. Shaffer, "The Tensions Between Law in America and the Religious Tradition," in *The Weightier Matters of the Law: Essays on Law and Religion,* ed. John Witte Jr. and Frank S. Alexander (Atlanta: Scholars, 1988), 313–35.

17. See Stephen Botein, *Early American Law and Society* (New York: Knopf, 1983), 18; Shaffer, "Tensions Between Law in America and the Religious Tradition," 316–24. Harold J. Berman argues, "It is the religious and legal beliefs and practices of a particular society, and not some ideal religion and some ideal law, that give the members of that society their faith in the future, on the one hand, and their social cohesion, on the other. And the religious and legal beliefs and practices of a particular community are always intimately related to the unique experience of that community, its unique history." Berman, *Interaction of Law and Religion*, 50. Bernard Meislin explains,

> My search through American law reports for Ten Commandment references amply supports [this] contention that "no affinity is more strongly marked than that likeness in the strength and prominence of the moral fibre, which, notwithstanding immense elements of difference, knits in some special sort the genius and history of us English, and our American descendants across the Atlantic, to the genius and history of the Hebrew people." Meislin, "Role of the Ten Commandments," 187, 189–200.

According to Mark A. Noll, "It should not be surprising that even the least orthodox of the founders of the nation paid some attention to scripture, for they lived at a time when to be an educated member of the Atlantic community was to know the Bible." Further, Noll argues, "Important as the Bible was for political leaders in the generation that established independence, it was an even more significant force for the next generation, whose task was to work out the meaning of the Revolution for an emerging American culture." Lastly, "The conclusion to which this evidence points is that nearly everyone of consequence in America's early political history was, if not evangelically committed to scripture, at least conversant with its content. To one degree or another, the Bible was important for America's first great public representatives." Mark A. Noll, "The Bible in Revolutionary America," in *Bible in American Law*, 39–41. Harold J. Berman claims, "Religious factors were also at work. The creation of modern legal systems was, in the first instance, a response to a revolutionary change within the Church and in the relation of the Church to the secular authorities." Harold J. Berman, "The Origins of Western Legal Science," *Harvard Law Review* 90 (1976–77): 894, 897.

18. Martha T. Roth, *Law Collections from Mesopotamia and Asia Minor* (Atlanta: Scholars, 1995), 76–81.

19. James H. Hutson, *Religion and the Founding of the American Republic* (Washington, D.C.: Library of Congress, 1998), 85.

20. For the influence of the Bible on the Founding Fathers, see Noll, "Bible in Revolutionary America," 39–42.

21. Berman, *Interaction of Law and Religion*, 49.

22. See Botein, *Early American Law and Society*, 25.

23. This view is cited in John D. Cushing, ed., *The Laws and Liberties of Massachusetts, 1641–1691*, 3 vols. (Wilmington, Del.: Scholarly Resources, 1976), 1:xvi.

24. See George L. Haskins, "The Beginnings of Partible Inheritance in the American Colonies," in *Essays in the History of Early American Law*, ed. David H. Flaherty (Chapel Hill: University of North Carolina Press, 1969), 204, 236.

25. Patrick M. O'Neil, "Bible in American Constitutionalism," in *Religion and American Law: An Encyclopedia*, ed. Paul Finkelman (New York: Garland, 2000), 29.

26. Shalom Goldman, ed., *Hebrew and the Bible in America: The First Two Centuries* (Hanover, N.H.: Brandeis University Press and Dartmouth College, 1993).

27. See generally Flaherty, *Essays in the History of Early American Law.*

28. Patrick M. O'Neil, "Bible in American Law," in *Religion and American Law,* 30.

29. *The Capital Laws of New England as They Stand Now in Force in the Commonwealth, 1641, 1642,* reprinted in Cushing, *Laws and Liberties of Massachusetts,* 1:1.

30. According to Stephen Botein, "In 1636, at the request of legislators eager to lay the groundwork for an infant jurisdiction, John Cotton had drawn up a code known as 'Moses his Judicialls.' This was not adopted, but some of its Hebraic content resurfaced in the 'Body of Liberties' formulated in 1641 by another minister, Nathaniel Ward, who had also been trained as a lawyer in the mother country." Botein, *Early American Law and Society,* 25.

31. *Capital Laws of New England,* 1:1.

32. See Shipton, "Locus of Authority in Colonial Massachusetts," 140–43; Katsh, *Biblical Heritage of American Democracy,* 126–31; Peter Charles Hoffer, *Law and People in Colonial America* (Baltimore: Johns Hopkins University Press, 1992), 16–24.

33. *The Book of the General Lawes and Libertyes concerning the Inhabitants of the Massachusets . . . 1647* (Cambridge, Mass.: n.p., 1647), reprinted in Cushing, *Laws and Liberties of Massachusetts,* 1:11, emphasis in original.

34. *Book of the General Lawes, 1647,* 1:29.

35. *New-Haven's Settling in New England and Some Lawes for Government* (London: M. S., 1656), reprinted in John D. Cushing, ed., *The Earliest Laws of the New Haven and Connecticut Colonies, 1639–1673* (Wilmington, Del.: Michael Glazier, 1977), 1–58.

36. Further, the law states,

> If any person within this Jurisdiction, professing the true God, shall wittingly and willingly presume to blaspheme the holy name of God, Father, Son, or Holy Ghost, with direct, expresse, presumptuous, or high-handed blasphemy, either by willfull or obstinate denying the true God, or his Creation, or Government of the world, or shall curse God, father, Son, or Holy ghost, or reproach the holy Religion of God, as if it were but a politick device to keep ignorant men in awe; or shall utter any other kind of blasphemy of like nature, and degree, such person shall be put to death. Lev. 24.15, 16. (*New-Haven's Settling in New England,* 18.)

See also Deut. 13:6–11.

37. *New-Haven's Settling in New England.* 19.

38. *New-Haven's Settling in New England,* 17.

39. *New-Haven's Settling in New England,* 11, citing Deut. 5:8, 17:11, and Rom. 13:4, emphasis in original.

40. *The Book of the General Lawes and Libertyes concerning the Inhabitants of the Massachusets . . . 1649* (Cambridge, Mass.: n.p., 1660), reprinted in Cushing, *Laws and Liberties of Massachusetts,* 1:69.

41. *Book of the General Lawes, 1649,* 1:79.

42. *The General Laws and Liberties of the Massachusets Colony: Revised and Reprinted* (Cambridge Mass.: Samuel Green, 1672), reprinted in Cushing, *Laws and Liberties of Massachusetts,* 2:240.

43. *General Laws and Liberties of the Massachusets Colony,* 241, emphasis in original.

44. *The General Laws and Liberties of Conecticut Colonie: Revised and Published by Order of the General Court* (Cambridge, Mass.: Samuel Green, 1672), 9.

45. *Acts and Laws of His Majesties Province of the Massachusetts-Bay, in New England* (Boston: Bartholomew Green, 1699), 17, emphasis in original.

46. *General Laws and Liberties of Conecticut Colonie*, 9; see also Deut. 19:15.

47. *Laws of the Province of Pennsilvania* (Philadelphia: Bradford, 1714), reprinted in John D. Cushing, ed., *The Earliest Printed Laws of Pennsylvania, 1681–1713* (Wilmington, Del.: Michael Glazier, 1978), 13–14, 85, 36–37; see also Ex. 21:2, 22:1–5.

48. O'Neil, "Bible in American Law," 31.

49. O'Neil, "Bible in American Law," 30.

50. See Botein, *Early American Law and Society*, 18.

51. *Book of the General Lawes, 1647*, 1:5.

52. *Book of the General Lawes, 1647*, 1:5. See also Skinner, "Influence of the Hebrew Bible," 13–14; Katsh, *Biblical Heritage of American Democracy*, 91–102; and Mark DeWolfe Howe, "The Source and Nature of Law in Colonial Massachusetts," in *Law and Authority in Colonial America*, 1–16.

53. Gaffney, "Interaction of Biblical Religion," 88. Gaffney discusses the influence imposed by the Bible on several areas of Constitutional theories including the following: (1) the freedom of expression:

> Biblical religion, then, cannot be viewed simply as an ancient prototype of repression and uniformity that is contrary to the model of free expression so cherished in our liberal democracy. On the contrary, the bold speech and the variety of beliefs witnessed to in the biblical record makes the Bible one of the significant ancient sources of freedom of expression. Viewed in this way, the Bible can continue to serve modern American society by providing the motivation to believing members of that society to speak their minds courageously but without hubris on a variety of social issues concerning which the voice of religious conscience is entirely appropriate.

(2) freedom of association: "Although concerned intensely with persons, the Bible does not view them as isolated atoms, but as interrelated, socially connected parts of a whole, or as members of a community," and (3) limited government: "The biblical traditions on limited governmental authority cannot be used to support the particular allocations of powers made in the American constitution. But these traditions can serve as a powerful motivating force for persons to challenge such authority whenever it exceeds the bounds of legitimacy." Gaffney, "Interaction of Biblical Religion," 89, 92, 96.

54. *Book of the General Lawes, 1647*, 5.

55. *New-Haven's Settling in New England*, 12.

56. Cushing, *Laws and Liberties of Massachusetts*, xxi.

57. As discussed previously in Part II, the earliest of Massachusetts's laws were printed in Cambridge and New Haven's laws were printed in London.

58. *Book of the General Lawes, 1647*, 1:5.

59. *Book of the General Lawes, 1647*, 1:6.

60. *Book of the General Lawes, 1647*, 1:6.

61. *Proceedings of the First General Assembly of "The Incorporation of Providence Plantations," and the Code of Laws Adopted by That Assembly in 1647*, reprinted in John D. Cushing, ed., *The Earliest Acts and Laws of the Colony of Rhode Island and Providence Plantations, 1647–1719* (Wilmington, Del.: Michael Glazier, 1977), 20.

62. *Proceedings of the First General Assembly*, 20.

63. *New-Haven's Settling in New England*, 12.

64. *Laws of the Province of Pennsilvania*, 36–37.

65. See Howe, "Nature of Law in Colonial Massachusetts," 1–2.

66. See Howe, "Nature of Law in Colonial Massachusetts," 1–2.

67. See Howe, "Nature of Law in Colonial Massachusetts," 2, citing Sir Edward Coke on Littleton.

68. See Howe, "Nature of Law in Colonial Massachusetts," 2.

69. See Howe, "Nature of Law in Colonial Massachusetts," 3.

70. See Howe, "Nature of Law in Colonial Massachusetts," 4.

71. See Howe, "Nature of Law in Colonial Massachusetts," 4.

72. *Book of the General Lawes, 1647*, 1:6.

73. Meislin, "Role of the Ten Commandments."

74. Clark, *Biblical Law*, 37.

75. Clark, *Biblical Law*, 37.

76. Clark, *Biblical Law*, 38.

77. Amy Green, "Sides Going Toe-to-Toe on 10 Commandments," *Deseret News*, Apr. 13, 2002, E1, referencing the decision in *Am. Civil Liberties Union of Tenn. v. Hamilton County, Tenn.*, 202 F. Supp. 2d 757 (2002).

78. U.S. Const. Preamble; Adam Smith, *The Theory of Moral Sentiments*, ed. Knud Haakonssen (Cambridge: Cambridge University Press, 2002).

79. Katsh, *Biblical Heritage of American Democracy*, 138.

80. Noll, "Bible in Revolutionary America," 48.

81. See Falk, *Hebrew Law in Biblical Times*, 6; Jackson, *Studies in the Semiotics of Biblical Law*, chapter 10.

VIRGINIA FOUNDERS AND THE BIRTH OF RELIGIOUS FREEDOM

W. Cole Durham Jr. and Elizabeth A. Sewell

The Library of Congress exhibition *Religion and the Founding of the American Republic* was displayed at BYU at the same time that Salt Lake City was hosting the 2002 Winter Olympic games. Media coverage, of course, focused on the games and the ensuing award ceremonies, but far more enduring public trophies of the human spirit were housed in the exhibition. Among those treasures were several key documents and original publications written by the Founding Fathers from Virginia, whose stand on religious freedom indelibly changed the face of law and society in America.

The views and writings of early Virginian leaders such as Thomas Jefferson, James Madison, and George Mason have had a tremendous impact on the subsequent understanding and protections of religious freedom in the United States. Indeed, much of the language and interpretation of the First Amendment to the United States Constitution has been derived over the years from writings of these Virginia Founders. This impact is not surprising, given the importance of Virginia at the time of the founding and the stature of these remarkable men, who were truly Olympians of the spirit.

Virginia, the largest and most populous state in the new union, was also one of the states where the Church of England was most fully established, resulting in significant church-state challenges after the American Revolution.[1] The debates over establishment of religion brought out Virginia's best talent and resulted in deeply thoughtful documents and legal solutions that have continued to influence American understandings of freedom of religion. Much truth still remains in what John Adams wrote to Patrick Henry in 1776: "We all look up to Virginia for examples."[2]

The most powerful examples from Virginia are a handful of documents that continue to have lasting effect on our understanding of religious freedom, such as the Virginia Declaration of Rights, James Madison's Memorial and Remonstrance, Jefferson's Statute on Religious Freedom, and his Danbury letter. For us as specialists in this area of constitutional law, looking over the originals of these documents and other similar ones contained in the Library of Congress exhibition was reminiscent of looking at certain treasured items each of us has in our homes, such as gifts from close friends and family, pictures, or other items linked to important life events. If an outsider came to our homes, they would not see the significance of the items, but members of our households know what these things mean. In the household of our heritage as Americans and as human beings, many of the items in the Library of Congress exhibition are infused with meaning of far greater magnitude. They look like little things, simple books or parchments, but these objects represent some of the greatest achievements and deepest sacrifices of the American people. They lie at the foundations of the society in which we now live. In this article, an outgrowth of the lecture delivered by Professor Durham in connection with the Library of Congress exhibition, we hope to share some insight into the reasons why certain key documents from Virginia are particularly charged with meaning for us as modern Americans and as inheritors of their legacy.

Examining Virginia's struggle for religious freedom demonstrates just how tenuous the quest for that freedom was in the era of the early republic.[3] Even when the First Amendment was ultimately ratified in 1791, the United States Constitution only barred *Congress* from establishing religion; states were free as a matter of constitutional law to continue the establishment and funding of churches that existed prior to the Revolutionary War.[4] Many states felt that an established church was vital to the promotion of public virtue—deemed an essential element of republican government. In fact, several states did continue to support one or a range of established churches until 1833, when Massachusetts became the last state to disestablish its state church.[5] While Virginia was not the first state to end the establishment of religion, its decision and the documents arising in the course of developments there have had a unique influence in the history of the United States. This influence ultimately led to the adoption of the First Amendment and eventually to the system of benevolent separation of church and state that has emerged in the years since.

Before we turn our attention to some key documents from Virginia, we would like to mention in passing one non-Virginian work displayed in the exhibition: Roger Williams's *Bloody Tenet of Persecution.*[6] Roger Williams, one of the great figures in the struggle for religious freedom, was driven out of intolerant Puritan Massachusetts to found Rhode Island, the state with the longest history of protecting religious freedom. Roger Williams and the *Bloody Tenet of Persecution* stand for a certain heritage that is sometimes missed in the focus on the Virginia Founders. Today we talk glibly of the separation of church and state, but often overlook the fact that this idea has two poles. All too often, the focus is on protecting the state from overly powerful religion, with the result that the importance of protecting religion recedes from view. Roger Williams is the great apostle of the countervailing value that holds that a primary aim of separation is to protect religion from the state. His book, a key contribution to the seventeenth-century debate, is the fountainhead of this vital stream in our constitutional tradition.[7] In contrast, the great Virginians—Jefferson, Madison, and others—tend to be associated with the other pole in the tradition of separation, which emphasizes the need for equality and for protecting the state from the excessive power that had too often accrued to organized religion in the history of Europe. Though we will not address Roger Williams in this article further, it is worth noting at the outset that in some ways the quieter, less visible strand of separationism associated with Roger Williams may be the more critical one, particularly in our secular age.

"FREE EXERCISE": THE VIRGINIA DECLARATION OF RIGHTS

A key early document on religious freedom was the Virginia Declaration of Rights, authored primarily by George Mason in June 1776. Article 16, the final article, addresses religious freedom:

> Religion, or the duty which we owe to our CREATOR and the manner of discharging it, can be directed only by reason and conviction, not by force or violence; and therefore, all men

George Mason's draft of his Virginia Declaration of Rights. This draft had two fewer articles than the final one; here article fourteen dealt with religious freedom. From Kate Mason Rowland, *The Life of George Mason, 1725–1792* (New York: G. P. Putman's Sons, 1892).

are equally entitled to the free exercise of religion according to the dictates of conscience; and that it is the mutual duty of all to practice Christian forbearance, love, and charity, toward each other.[8]

This provision articulates a number of significant points. First, it is a key early source of the language of the Free Exercise Clause of the First Amendment. Another aspect that is less obvious is the somewhat paradoxical phrase "Entitled to the free exercise of religion according to the *dictates* of conscience." Freedom and "dictates" are generally considered opposites. However, their placement together is not an accident and it is, in our view, something that is often forgotten about religious freedom. In our time, we tend to think of religious freedom as of one of many liberties that we have, as though religion is like a club one chooses to join. What that idea overlooks is a fundamental aspect of the nature of religion and why religious freedom is so important. This concept varies according to religious tradition, but certainly for most of the traditions we think of in America, religion is more than simply something that one chooses;

the voice of conscience dictates and commands. It is at least in part because of that deep compulsion of conscience and respect for the human response to this call that the law protects religious freedom.

The Virginia Declaration of Rights has significance that goes beyond being the verbal source for the phrase "free exercise." The clauses originally drafted by Mason read, "All Men shou'd enjoy the fullest Toleration in the Exercise of Religion."[9] The phrase ultimately adopted represented a significant shift from thinking solely in terms of religious toleration to thinking about full free exercise of religion. In the European states that were forward-looking enough to already have some notion of religious toleration, toleration meant that there was an established or dominant religion that would tolerate, or put up with some of these dissenters.[10] Significantly, James Madison along with Edmond Pendleton suggested changing the phrase to "all men are equally entitled to the free exercise of religion."[11] This phrase articulated a significant paradigm shift in the way people think of religious liberty. Less obvious, perhaps, but still significant here, is the sense that freedom of belief is a natural right—an idea of great significance for subsequent documents.

James Madison also wanted to add the following phrase at the end of the Declaration of Rights: "And therefore that no man or class of men ought, on account of religion to be invested with peculiar emoluments or privileges; nor subjected to any penalties or disabilities."[12] This amendment failed. Already in 1776, Madison was pressing for a view that would suggest a stricter separation of church and state that would cut off the established church and end the pattern of state financial support of the church. But Virginia had not yet come that far. As of 1776 and the adoption of the Virginia Declaration of Rights, freedom of conscience was affirmed, but Virginians were not ready to take on the task of disestablishing the church.

At this time, Thomas Jefferson, ideologically sympathetic to Madison's position, was doing some fairly extensive studies of the legal background of various statutes relevant to the relationship of church and state. Based on this research, Jefferson campaigned in 1776 for the repeal of all the laws passed during the colonial period that restricted religious freedom.[13] As indicated, however, the legislature did not do that. Indeed, the legislature wanted to retain what by today's standards was as a fairly strict control over religion generally.[14]

By 1777, Jefferson drafted what was to become the statute on religious liberty, but by that time, the colonists were in the throes of the Revolutionary War.[15] Understandably, issues of church and state were pushed to the back seat.

ATTEMPTS AT DISESTABLISHMENT: THE MEMORIAL AND REMONSTRANCE

After the Revolutionary War, the leading revolutionaries were acutely conscious that they were engaged in a radical experiment in nation building. They realized that the success of this venture was anything but a foregone conclusion. There was no real historical experience with the kind of government that was being considered. One of the issues in particular running through the pamphlet literature, the sermons, and the thought of the Revolutionary period was the importance and vulnerability of the republican order.[16] The leading political figures were all convinced that for the experiment in democracy to work, there had to be a heavy dose of "public virtue," which the Founders understood as the willingness to sacrifice private interests in the interest of the common good.[17]

After the war, however, there was a widespread perception that people started relaxing and returning to their more material pursuits. Religious devotion, assumed to be critical to the cultivation of public virtue, appeared to be declining.[18] As a result, the leading thinkers began to worry that there was too much luxury and decadence, that American society was rapidly disintegrating, and that the experiment was at risk. This concern was particularly evident in Virginia. People seemed to be losing interest in religion, working instead on their farms and trying to get gain to be able to buy material things. Religious leaders and those committed to the democratic experience were concerned, particularly since the republic was thought to be at a very vulnerable point.[19]

In the eyes of many, the weakened status of the traditional Church of England (now the Episcopalian Church) and of other religions constituted an ominous threat to the success of the republican experiment. Clergy salaries had gone unpaid during the war, and the clergy were dependent on subscriptions by local members to pay their bills. The dismal financial state and insecure position of the clergy provided a strong disincentive for candidates for the priesthood.

It was natural in that setting that powerful political leaders such as Patrick Henry should view state financial support for religion as crucial to the success of the republican venture. This was a natural response to questions about how the state could best help religion to flourish and inculcate the civic virtues that the state needed in order to survive. Because religion was thought to be crucial to the survival of the republic, and both religion and the republic were in danger, many citizens sought a way to rehabilitate the forces of religion.

Patrick Henry turned out to be a strong advocate for shoring up support for the established church in his state, and he proposed a general assessment to give financial support to religion in Virginia.[20] His bill, eventually titled "Bill Establishing a Provision for Teachers of the Christian Religion," enjoyed wide support.[21] The bill sought to tax Virginians to support churches, but allowed individuals to specify the church to which their tax moneys would go. Those who wished to support no church at all would be able to earmark their funds for their local schools.[22] Many petitions began circulating in support of the bill, resting on the need to promote civic virtue and the bill's even-handed approach.[23]

Patrick Henry was an extremely influential politician, and it appeared that as long as Henry was in the Virginia state legislature, he would be able to outflank Madison and the rest of the opposition to his plan for a general assessment. In one of the many small miracles that led to modern American protections of religious freedom, Patrick Henry was elected governor in November 1784.[24] Once he became governor, he was no longer a direct participant in legislative leadership, and his influence on the general assessment bill was reduced, with the result that it was never acted upon.[25]

Having succeeded in delaying action on the general assessment legislation in late 1784, the bill's opponents started a broad public campaign.[26] The most memorable and influential document to come out of that controversy was James Madison's Memorial and Remonstrance.[27] This memorial, or petition, was circulated across Virginia for signature and submission to the Virginia General Assembly.[28] Of all the documents on religious freedom drafted by the Virginia Founders, the Memorial and Remonstrance is the most profound. For a short document originally written as a political pamphlet, it constitutes a remarkable collection of arguments that remain current and persuasive to this day. While a full study of the document is worthwhile, we highlight here only a few of its key statements.

The petition begins, "We hold it for a fundamental and undeniable truth, 'that Religion or the duty which we owe to our Creator and the manner of discharging it, can be directed only by reason and conviction, not by force or violence.'"[29] Madison and Jefferson agreed that government could not compel religion. While government can perhaps compel outward observance—the hypocrisy of outward performance—the inner life of the soul cannot be driven.

Madison continued, "This right is in its nature an unalienable right."[30] Drawing on the natural rights tradition, Madison underscored that religious freedom is not merely an accommodation granted by a permissive government. Governments often have a hard time reconciling themselves to that idea. In contemporary terms, this principle is usually expressed by the phrase "human rights"— there are inalienable rights that we have simply because we are human beings. As rights that belong to all humans, these have normative validity, even if they are violated in fact by governments.

"It is unalienable, because the opinions of men, depending only on evidence contemplated in their own minds cannot follow the dictates of other men."[31] The immensely personal and personally compelling nature of religious belief forms the core importance of the right. Ultimately, conscience is something that only one's own mind can respond to and to which individuals must answer for themselves. Later in the Memorial and Remonstrance, Madison connected this reality with a related insight that civil magistrates have no special capacity to judge rival conceptions of religious truth. The implication that they have such a capacity "is an arrogant pretension falsified by the contradictory opinions of Rulers in all ages, and throughout the world."[32] Attempts to use religion "as an engine of Civil policy" are, in Madison's words, "an unhallowed perversion of the means of salvation."[33]

"It is the duty of every man to render to the Creator such homage and such only, as he believes to be acceptable to him. This duty is precedent both in order of time and in degree of obligation, to the claims of Civil Society." Here one sees the natural rights and the natural law tradition at work. Madison distinguishes religious freedom from other rights, which are rights among other men, because religious rights arise from duties owed towards their Creator. Religion involves obligations that are "prior to" any social contract and higher than mere social obligations.[34] Since all obligations imposed by states are social obligations, those duties are necessarily subordinate to the natural right to freedom of religion.

Madison explained,

> Before any man can be considered a member of Civil Society, he must be considered as a subject of the Governor of the Universe: And if a member of Civil Society, who enters into any subordinate Association, must always do it with a reservation of his duty to the General Authority; much more must every man who becomes a member of any particular Civil Society, do it with the saving of his allegiance to the Universal Sovereign. We maintain therefore that in matters of Religion, no mans right is abridged by the institution of Civil Society and that Religion is wholly exempt from its cognizance.[35]

The central idea expressed here is that, just as associations within a particular society are governed by the laws of that society, the laws of society are subject to the higher order laws of the universal sovereign. In effect, freedom of religion is a kind of "reservation clause" on the "treaty" of the social contract. By its nature, freedom of religion is unalienable, and thus cannot be waived in the process of human beings creating and acceding to fundamental charters of government.

Madison not only makes natural law arguments for religious freedom, but offers pragmatic considerations as well. "Who does not see," he argues, "that the same authority which can establish Christianity, in exclusion of all other Religions, may establish with the same ease any particular sect of Christians, in exclusion of all other Sects?"[36] No denomination is safe when the government is entrusted with the power to determine preferred versions of religion. Madison draws upon a line of thought going back

to arguments in Locke's *Letter on Toleration*[37] to explain that, contrary to the common assumption that endorsing or supporting religion would give added stability to a country, a broad understanding of religious freedom that treats all citizens equally gives greater legitimacy and stability to a nation. Not only does such a nation gain a "lustre to [the] country" by taking in religious refugees, but the "moderation and harmony" gained will increase support for a government, promote health and prosperity, and prevent animosities and jealousies over government preference and support.[38]

DISESTABLISHMENT: THE STATUTE ON RELIGIOUS FREEDOM

Owing in no small part to the influence of the Memorial and Remonstrance, the general assessment bill was defeated. Shortly thereafter, Madison took the occasion to resurrect the bill Jefferson had drafted in 1777 concerning religious freedom. The bill was passed in January 16, 1786. It outlawed any government compulsion to support religious worship or teaching and barred any civil penalties for individuals' religious opinions or belief. The extensive introductory section of the bill reiterates many of the arguments for religious freedom that Madison raised in the Memorial and Remonstrance.[39] The opening is particularly stirring and well known:

> WHEREAS Almighty God hath created the mind free; that all attempts to influence it by temporal punishments or burthens, or by civil incapacitations, tend only to beget habits of hypocrisy and meanness, and are a departure from the plan of the Holy author of our religion, who being Lord both of body and mind, yet chose not to propagate it by coercions on either.[40]

Jefferson continued in the same vein, with such powerful phrases as "our civil rights, have no dependence on our religious opinions, any more than our opinions in physics or geometry."[41] In sum, "All men shall be free to profess, and by argument to maintain, their opinions in matters of religion, and that the same shall in no wise diminish, enlarge, or affect their civil capacities."[42]

Although the statute was simple legislation and these protections could thus be repealed by subsequent legislation, the statute, in its final paragraph, gives a powerful statement of the primacy of the rights addressed: "And though we well know that this assembly elected by the people . . . have no power to restrain the acts of succeeding assemblies, constituted with powers equal to our own, . . . yet we are free to declare and do declare, that the rights hereby asserted are the natural rights of mankind."[43]

In some ways, Virginia's 1786 Statute on Religious Freedom comes later than similar developments in other states. In the legislatures of many other colonies, a burst of activity disestablishing official churches had occurred in 1776 and 1777.[44] However, calling the Virginia statute a latecomer is misleading because a number of these other constitutions were not necessarily understood to embody the full strength of the Jeffersonian-type commitment to religious freedom. While many would argue that scholars and historians—particularly judicial historians—have overemphasized the Virginia model, there can be no doubt that the Virginia Statute on Religious Freedom was a vital starting point for many of the developments that have shaped American church-state tradition.

Even in its own day, the Virginia law received widespread publicity and enjoyed a good deal of influence. In a letter to Madison in 1786, Jefferson wrote from Paris:

> The Virginia act for religious freedom has been received with infinite approbation in Europe and propagated with enthusiasm. I do not mean by the governments, but by the individuals who compose them. It has been translated into French and Italian, has been the best evidence of the falsehood of those reports which stated us to be in anarchy. It is inserted in the new "Encyclopédie," and is appearing in most of the publications respecting America.[45]

Separation of church and state as contained in the Virginia bill was part of what Europeans came to understand as quintessentially American. Jefferson added,

> In fact, it is comfortable to see the standard of reason at length erected, after so many ages,

during which human mind has been held in vassalage by kings, priests and nobles; and it is honorable for us to have produced the first legislature who had the courage to declare, that the reason of man may be trusted with the formation of his own opinions.[46]

Jefferson's sense of the importance of the statute transcended the time of its enactment. Jefferson chose to have engraved on his gravestone the three things that he thought were his most important accomplishments. The first, not surprisingly, was the Declaration of Independence. The third was founding the University of Virginia. The second is authoring the Virginia Statute on Religious Freedom. The literal wording is "Here was buried Thomas Jefferson, author of the Declaration of American Independence, of the Statute of Virginia for religious freedom, and the father of the University of Virginia, born April 2nd, 1743."

"A WALL OF SEPARATION": THE DANBURY LETTER

While Jefferson may have seen the Virginia Statute on Religious Freedom as one of his most significant works, his church-state attitudes tend to be more closely associated with a phrase from a letter he wrote to the Danbury Baptist Association in Connecticut in 1802—"a wall of separation between church and state."[47] The Danbury letter was in fact one of the most famous documents in the Library of Congress exhibition. Building on Jefferson's support, through Madison, of the First Amendment, the Supreme Court has used this phrase from Jefferson's later letter as "an authoritative declaration of the scope and effect" of the First Amendment.[48] However questionable this interpretative strategy may be from the perspective of those who think experience from other states should be given greater attention, Jefferson's phrase has come to be closely associated with the First Amendment and with the ideological divide over the degree of government accommodation of religious organizations. Because of the contemporary significance of Jefferson's metaphorical wall, the Danbury letter has proved to be both tremendously significant and exceedingly controversial.[49]

Before the Library of Congress originally mounted this exhibition in 1998, it had the FBI Laboratory examine the holograph draft of the letter in order to decipher what Jefferson had blotted out immediately after the phrase "a wall of separation between church and state."[50] The resulting disclosures have led to considerable controversy over what the scratched-out portion can teach us about Jefferson's thought.

It appears that the inked-out lines referred to Jefferson's rejection of public days of thanksgiving and public fasts, describing these as "religious exercises" that were taken from the practice of English kings. In the margin, he noted that the "paragraph was omitted on the suggestion that it might give uneasiness to some of our republican friends in the eastern states where the proclamation of thanksgivings etc. by their Executives is an ancient habit & is respected."[51]

By itself, this omission and explanation does not seem unduly controversial, given Jefferson's general thought on the subject of government displays of religious devotion.[52] What proved controversial was the interpretation given by James H. Hutson, chief of the Manuscript Division at the Library of Congress, when he announced the FBI's findings.[53] He tried to put the letter in context, arguing that the letter was written to Jefferson's Federalist opponents to defend his policy of not declaring public days of thanksgiving and fasts.[54] The letter, a response to an address from the Danbury Baptist Association, was a typical venue for "dissemination of partisan views."[55] Hutson argued that the inked-out portion shows that Jefferson "expected the American public to conclude that he refused to proclaim thanksgivings and fasts, not because he was irreligious, but because he was an American patriot who would not genuflect at the altar of British monarchy as Federalist leaders had done."[56] Hutson then reasoned that, after eliminating the argument to avoid offending New England Republicans that supported thanksgivings

and fasts, Jefferson tried to rebut the contentions that he was an atheist through his public participation in worship services, including those held in the Capitol. This participation began within forty-eight hours after his issuance of the letter and lasted throughout his presidency; Jefferson also made available executive-branch buildings for church services.[57] Ultimately, Hutson took the position that Jefferson's letter and action combine to support an assumption that "in the relationship between religion and government, a distinction could be drawn between active and passive, which government, although it could not take coercive initiatives in the religious sphere, might serve as a passive, impartial venue for voluntary religious activities."[58]

Because Jefferson's theories and "wall of separation" have served as a touchstone for Supreme Court understandings of the First Amendment, Hutson's reinterpretation of Jefferson's thought carries enormous potential significance. For example, the extent to which the government can passively support voluntary religious activities has been the subject of several recent Supreme Court cases that permit government aid to flow to religious institutions if it is channeled via voluntary choices.[59] Many view these decisions as constituting a significant shift in establishment clause analysis. While some scholars have supported Hutson's arguments,[60] others have challenged him, asserting that the inked-out portions of the Danbury letter add little to what is already known of Jefferson's views and actions[61] and do not alter the core principles Jefferson stood for or the questions that modern courts must decide.[62] Most significantly perhaps, Hutson's work has performed a valuable service in bringing increased attention to the context of the famous "wall" metaphor and Jefferson's own public religious devotion. Perhaps the wall was intended to have a few doors and windows in it.

CONCLUSION

We live at a time when the principles of religious freedom enshrined in our founding documents have begun to find their way into a growing body of international documents, such as the Universal Declaration of Human Rights, the International Covenant on Civil and Political Rights, and the European Convention on Human Rights and Fundamental Freedoms, to name a few. While these documents do not use exactly the same wording that Jefferson, Madison, and the other framers used, these historic statements have become increasingly influential in much of the modern world, serving as crucial benchmarks as various countries strive to establish their own constitutional orders.

To us, the reality of this enduring influence has been brought home with particularly telling force as we have had opportunities to take visiting foreign government officials responsible for religious affairs in their countries to see Jefferson's grave or Jefferson Memorial. These modern leaders clearly understand that they serve roles in their countries that parallel those functions played by Jefferson in ours. They understand the fragility of religious freedom. Conscious of the unstable situations and uncertain futures of their own countries, and acutely aware of the many pressures that chip away at religious liberty, they understand in ways we often forget just how much courage and determination was required to stand for religious freedom in Jefferson's day, or in any other day. As we see their dedication and come to understand the tremendous challenges they face, we are renewed in our appreciation for the Olympians of every country and for the precious documents in all the households of human heritage that have built the grand edifice of religious freedom.

Notes

1. Thomas E. Buckley, *Church and State in Revolutionary Virginia, 1776–1787* (Charlottesville: University Press of Virginia, 1977), 5.

2. John Adams, *The Works of John Adams,* ed. Charles F. Adams (Boston: Little, Brown, 1850–56) 9:387.

3. See the discussion of fragility in Joseph J. Ellis, *Founding Brothers* (New York: Knopf, 2000).

4. Modern readers often overlook the obvious wording of the federal establishment clause: "Congress shall make no law respecting an establishment of religion." At the time of its adoption, this clause was designed both to prevent the federal government from establishing a church and to keep the federal government from interfering with existing church-state arrangements in the states. See Steven D. Smith, *Foreordained Failure: The Quest for a Constitutional Principle of Religious Freedom* (New York: Oxford University Press, 1995).

5. Leo Pfeffer, *Church, State, and Freedom* (Boston: Beacon, 1967), 139–49.

6. Roger Williams, *The Bloudy Tenent of Persecution, for Cause of Conscience, Discussed, in a Conference between Truth and Peace* (n.p.: 1644).

7. For an excellent exposition of Williams's views, see Mark DeWolf Howe, *The Garden and the Wilderness* (Chicago: University of Chicago Press, 1965).

8. *Virginia Gazette* (Williamsburg), June 14, 1776.

9. James Madison, *The Papers of James Madison,* ed. William T. Hutchinson and William M.E. Rachal, 27 vols. to date (Chicago: University of Chicago Press, 1962–), 1:173. See also Buckley, *Church and State in Revolutionary Virginia,* 18.

10. See the discussion of this progression in Malcolm Evans, "Historical Introduction to Freedom of Religion and Belief as a Technique for Avoiding Religious Conflict," in *Facilitating Freedom of Religion and Belief: A Deskbook,* ed. Tore Lindholm (Leiden: Martinus Nijhoff, 2004 forthcoming).

11. Madison, *Papers of James Madison,* 1:173, 175.

12. Madison, *Papers of James Madison,* 1:174. It is interesting that, given their later disagreements on this issue, Madison was able to persuade Patrick Henry to sponsor the amendment. At the time, Patrick Henry denied that the amendment would disestablish the Church of England in Virginia. Buckley, *Church and State in Revolutionary Virginia,* 18–19.

13. Buckley, *Church and State in Revolutionary Virginia,* 30–31.

14. At this time, the legislature was still dictating the contents of the liturgy. Buckley, *Church and State in Revolutionary Virginia,* 21.

15. Thomas Jefferson, *The Papers of Thomas Jefferson,* ed. Julian B. Boyd, 29 vols. to date (Princeton: Princeton University Press, 1950–), 2:545–47.

16. Buckley, *Church and State in Revolutionary Virginia,* 72–73.

17. Gordon S. Wood, *The Creation of the American Republic, 1776–1787* (Chapel Hill: University of North Carolina Press, 1969), 65–70. See also James H. Hutson, *Religion and the Founding of the American Republic* (Washington, D. C.: Library of Congress, 1998), 62.

18. Wood, *Creation of the American Republic,* 428–29.

19. See William Warren Sweet, *The Story of Religion in America,* 2d ed. (New York: Harper, 1950), 172–204.

20. Edwin S. Gaustad, *Neither King nor Prelate: Religion and the New Nation, 1776–1826* (Grand Rapids, Mich.: Wm. B. Eerdmans, 1993), 38–39.

21. For a picture of Henry's *A Bill Establishing a Provision for Teachers of the Christian Religion,* see Hutson, *Religion and the Founding,* 66.

22. Buckley, *Church and State in Revolutionary Virginia,* 108–9.

23. See William Wirt Henry, *Patrick Henry: Life, Correspondence, and Speeches,* 3 vols. (New York: Charles Scribner's Sons, 1891), 2:201–9.

24. Buckley, *Church and State in Revolutionary Virginia,* 100–101.

25. Henry, *Patrick Henry,* 2:206–9.

26. Gaustad, *Neither King nor Prelate,* 39–40.

27. Madison, *Papers of James Madison,* 8:295. For a picture of Madison's draft of *A Memorial and Remonstrance,* see Hutson, *Religion and the Founding,* 72.

28. Buckley, *Church and State in Revolutionary Virginia,* 135–37.

29. Madison, *Papers of James Madison,* 8:299.

30. Madison, *Papers of James Madison,* 8:299.

31. Madison, *Papers of James Madison,* 8:299.

32. Madison, *Papers of James Madison,* 8:301.

33. Madison, *Papers of James Madison,* 8:299.

34. Madison, *Papers of James Madison,* 8:299.

35. Madison, *Papers of James Madison,* 8:299.

36. Madison, *Papers of James Madison,* 8:300.

37. John Locke, *A Letter concerning Toleration* (Indianapolis: Bobbs-Merrill, 1955). See also John Locke, *Two Treatises of Civil Government* (London: Dent, 1953).

38. Madison, *Papers of James Madison,* 8:302.

39. William W. Hening, ed., *The Statutes at Large, Being a Collection of All the Laws of Virginia,* vol. 12, *1785–1788* (New York: Bartow, 1823), 84–85.

40. Hening, *Statutes at Large,* 84.

41. Hening, *Statutes at Large,* 85.

42. Hening, *Statutes at Large,* 86.

43. Hening, *Statutes at Large,* 86.

44. Pfeffer, *Church, State, and Freedom,* 115–18.

45. Thomas Jefferson, *The Best Letters of Thomas Jefferson,* ed. J. G. de Roulhac Hamilton (Boston: Houghton, Mifflin, 1926), 25.

46. Jefferson, *Best Letters of Thomas Jefferson,* 25.

47. Thomas Jefferson to Messrs. Nehemiah Dodge, Ephraim Robbins, and Stephen S. Nelson, a Committee of the Danbury Baptist Association in the State of Connecticut, Jan. 1, 1802, Thomas Jefferson Papers, Manuscript Division, Library of Congress. For a picture of Jefferson's "Danbury Baptist letter," see Hutson, *Religion and the Founding,* 85.

48. See Daniel L. Dreisbach, *Thomas Jefferson and the Wall of Separation between Church and State* (New York: New York University Press, 2002).

49. *Reynolds v United States,* 98 U.S. 145, 164 (1878); see also *Committee for Public Education v Nyquist,* 413 U.S. 756, 761.

50. James H. Hutson, "Thomas Jefferson's Letter to the Danbury Baptists: A Controversy Rejoined," *William and Mary Quarterly* 56 (October 1999): 776.

51. Jefferson to Dodge.

52. See Matthew S. Holland, "Thomas Jefferson: Religious Beliefs and Political Doctrines," in this book.

53. See Forum, *William and Mary Quarterly* 56 (October 1999): 775–824.

54. Hutson, "Jefferson's Letter to the Danbury Baptists," 776–81.

55. Hutson, "Jefferson's Letter to the Danbury Baptists," 782.

56. Hutson, "Jefferson's Letter to the Danbury Baptists," 783.

57. Hutson, "Jefferson's Letter to the Danbury Baptists," 784–86.

58. Hutson, "Jefferson's Letter to the Danbury Baptists," 789.

59. See, for example, *Zelman v Simmons-Harris,* 536 U.S. 639 (2002); *Good News Club v Milford Cent. School,* 533 U.S. 121 (2001); *Mitchell v Helms,* 530 U.S. 793 (2000).

60. See Thomas E. Buckley, "Reflections on a Wall," *William and Mary Quarterly* 56 (October 1999): 795–800.

61. See Robert M. O'Neil, "The 'Wall of Separation' and Thomas Jefferson's Views on Religious Liberty," *William and Mary Quarterly* 56 (October 1999): 793.

62. See Edwin S. Gaustad, "Thomas Jefferson, Danbury Baptists, and 'Eternal Hostility,'" *William and Mary Quarterly* 56 (October 1999): 801–4; Isaac Kramnick and R. Laurence Moore, "The Baptists, the Bureau, and the Case of the Missing Lines," *William and Mary Quarterly* 56 (October 1999): 817.

RELIGION AT WAR IN SUPPORT OF THE AMERICAN REVOLUTION

Milton V. Backman Jr.

The tension between American colonists and Great Britain that eventually led to the American Revolution is often characterized by a famous statement attributed to James Otis: "Taxation without representation is tyranny."[1] Colonists in the mainland English colonies declared that they were Englishmen, that they had the rights of Englishmen, and that among these rights was that of being taxed by their representatives. They further emphasized that they were not represented in the English Parliament, and, subsequently, Parliament had no right to levy taxes on colonists. At the same time that Otis was decrying Parliamentary taxation, Isaac Backus, a New England leader of the Baptist community, was denouncing ecclesiastical taxes levied by colonial governments as tyranny. In the American Revolution, political and religious elements combined to oppose the British but also critiqued many things that the colonists themselves were doing. Indeed, the American Revolution was one of the significant turning points in history. It served as a propelling catalyst, hastening the process of change. Many positive tendencies, forces, and developments that had long been gathering strength seemed to have burst forth during the late eighteenth century. The religious consequences of this war were in many respects greater than that which took place during any other secular event in American history.[2]

One of the main principles that I have learned as I have studied and taught history is that to simplify history is to falsify history. There is no simple explanation for any major event. One cannot accurately describe the background of the War for Independence by limiting the discussion to political or constitutional issues. One must also consider economic, social, and religious forces. In this lecture transcript (which has been footnoted and edited), I emphasize religion at war in support of the American Revolution. But remember, to simplify history is to falsify it. Perhaps, this emphasis may seem inappropriate because I shall not concentrate on attitudes of loyalists or neutrals, or on many of the political and economic issues that are generally considered the most significant forces in leading to the Revolution. My purpose is to examine incidents from history that will help us better understand the impact of religion on the causes and consequences of the American Revolution.

RELIGION IN THE SOUTHERN COLONIES

Prior to the American Revolution, the Church of England was a tax-supported faith in all southern English mainland colonies and in New York City. Settlers in these colonies were required by law to pay an ecclesiastical tax that was used to purchase property, build meetinghouses, and pay salaries of Anglican ministers. Religious establishments in various colonies were very different. For example, Virginia had over 90 ministers and parishes and possibly more than 160 churches or chapels. At the same time, there were only 2 Anglican meetinghouses in Georgia, a less-populated colony that had only about a dozen churches. The religious situation also varied between large settlements, plantations, and rural areas. Most people in the southern colonies attended church infrequently partly because they lived on isolated farms located miles from the nearest meetinghouse. In the South towards the end of the colonial period, no more than 10 percent, perhaps even 5 percent, of all people were active members of a church. And yet, colonists throughout the South were required by law to pay a tax that was used to support the Church of England.[3]

Although a high percent of colonists in the South either did not attend church regularly or did not consider themselves members of the state-supported religion, colonists could not disestablish the Anglican Church under the colonial political system. In order for laws to be enacted in royal colonies (all southern colonies were royal colonies), bills had to be endorsed by the assembly comprised of representatives of the people. This legislative body had the sole right of formulating revenue bills. Prior to passage, bills also had to be approved by the council that was usually made up of wealthy aristocrats generally loyal to the crown and to the state church. These members were usually appointed for life. To become law, bills also had to be approved by the governor, who had absolute veto power in royal colonies. If, by chance, a governor was persuaded to sign a disestablishment bill, the king would have disallowed it because the king was the nominal head of the Church of England. Subsequently, many Southern colonists were frustrated because they were required by law to pay an ecclesiastical tax, which they did not approve and could not repeal.[4]

Baptists, Presbyterians, and Deists

Shortly prior to the American Revolution, a number of developments occurred in the England mainland colonies that weakened the religious establishments. One was the growth of the Baptists. Few Baptists lived in most colonies before 1740, but following the Great Awakening (beginning about the 1730s), the Baptists increased significantly in numbers and influence. Baptists solved the problem of shortage of ministers by calling new converts to serve as part-time ministers. Most of these ministers were farmers who preached the gospel in their spare time. Baptist preachers generally did not rely on parishioners for their financial support. Between 1740 and 1776, Virginia and other colonies were flooded with itinerant ministers. Thousands were converted, and more united with the Baptists than any other religious persuasion. Members of this faith created hundreds of new congregations. Converts gathered in homes and other buildings and eventually built small meetinghouses. Importantly, Baptists emphasized as fundamental beliefs religious liberty and separation of church and state. They interpreted these beliefs as meaning that people should not be required to pay ecclesiastical taxes. Ecclesiastical taxation, they declared, was tyranny.[5]

Another development that took place during the pre-Revolutionary period was the growth of the Presbyterian faith. Early in the eighteenth century, after Indians threatened the lives of old settlers, Virginians decided to create a buffer zone on the frontier. They advertised that free land was available to anyone who would settle in the western wilderness and defend the colony. Prior to the Revolution, emigrants from Northern Ireland (Presbyterians) and Germany poured into western Pennsylvania, Maryland, Virginia, and the Carolinas. At the time of the American Revolution, a high percent of all people living in the western sections of the South,

The Mt. Shiloh Baptist Church, an early Baptist meetinghouse in Virginia.

including the Shenandoah Valley, were not members of the Church of England. Even though there were few Anglican ministers available to serve the people in the western sections of the South, by law, all settlers were supposed to pay an ecclesiastical tax that supported the state church.[6]

Simultaneous to the growth of the Baptists and influx of Presbyterians in the South and other colonies was the impact of the Enlightenment, or eighteenth-century rational thinking. Prior to the American Revolution, many colonial leaders were influenced by a new age of reason. Previously, people lived in what came to be called the Age of Authority, where individuals tended not to question the Bible or teachings of the clergy. In the Age of the Enlightenment, however, many influential leaders replaced elements of faith with axioms of reason. As many leaders in the colonies examined the tenets of traditional Christianity, they identified many beliefs that they considered unreasonable, such as a belief in hell fire and brimstone, original sin, and the Trinity (God being three persons of one essence).[7] Some of the better-educated Americans, such as

Thomas Jefferson, considered the Trinity as a mathematical inconsistency. Jefferson wrote in a letter to John Adams, "Three are one and one is three; and yet that the one is not three, and the three are not one. . . . This constitutes the craft, the power and the profit of the priests. Sweep away their gossamer fabrics of factitious religion, and they would catch no more flies."[8]

The Toleration Act passed by the English Parliament in 1689 (which applied to the colonies) extended toleration to Trinitarian Protestants. Although there were no organized Protestant societies that embraced creeds that differed from the traditional concept of the Trinity, in most mainland colonies in the eighteenth century, there was an increase in the number of Protestants who rejected that belief and fell outside the Act's protection. The Toleration Act of 1689 also did not extend toleration to Roman Catholics. In most English mainland colonies during most of the eighteenth century, Roman Catholics were not permitted legally to attend public masses, vote, or hold public office. During the years of increased political debates on the rights of colonists, opposition, often led by leaders of the Revolution who had been influenced by the Enlightenment, was mounting to replace toleration and religious restrictions with a new birth of religious freedom.[9]

The Parson's Cause Case

One of the major events that demonstrate the complex nature of the coming of the Revolution was the Parson's Cause Case. In Virginia, tobacco was the medium of exchange, and beginning in the 1690s ministers were paid an annual salary of 16,000 pounds of tobacco. Tobacco prices had remained level at about 2 pence a pound, but in the 1750s, there was a drought that caused a shortage of tobacco and an increase in the price. After the drought, tobacco sold for about 6 pence a pound. Because of this price increase, the Virginia assembly passed laws in 1755 and 1758 that provided that people could pay the ministers' salaries with a reduced amount of tobacco, thereby reducing the ministers' salaries by approximately two-thirds of the amount of tobacco they would have received. Ministers complained, arguing that when prices were low, they were not benefited with an increased amount of tobacco. It wasn't fair, they reasoned, to give them less when prices were high. Their complaints were submitted to the British government, and the king disallowed the controversial laws.[10]

Ministers were jubilant, but the people hesitated in paying the clergy their legal salaries. The laws had already been enacted and the tax had already been paid, but now colonists were told that the laws of 1755 and 1758 were of no effect. Since settlers hesitated in making proper payments, ministers decided to sue members of their parishes. One of these ministers was Rev. James Maury. A jury was summoned to determine the extent of damages. Technically, this was an easy task: just take the amount actually paid and multiply by three. The person being sued called on a new attorney, Patrick Henry, who had recently passed the bar.[11] During the trial, Henry denounced the clergy, saying that the clergy were in Virginia to bless the lives of the people and that by refusing to acquiesce to the laws that had been passed for the benefit of the people the clergy had degenerated into tyrants. Henry argued that instead of paying the ministers the additional amount of tobacco, the people should remove them from office; the clergy should be punished, he said, not paid. Henry further argued, "A king, by disallowing acts of this salutary nature . . . degenerated into a Tyrant, and forfeits all rights to his subjects' obedience." This attack was in 1763, before the passage of the Stamp and Townsend Acts. Many were shocked with Patrick Henry's denunciations, and, according to some reports, said, "Treason, treason!" "The gentleman has spoken treason."[12]

Patrick Henry stood his ground. He continued to denounce the clergy and the king. The jury finally deliberated and awarded the parson one penny, the least amount that they could determine. It was a jubilant victory for the people, and ministers decided not to sue additional members of their parishes.[13]

The Parson's Cause Case demonstrates that prior to the American Revolution, the clergy in Virginia were beginning to lose their influence and an anti-clerical attitude was developing, and that there was growing opposition to the ecclesiastical establishment in Virginia—the Church of England.

Disestablishment of Religion in the South

Shortly after the colonists declared independence, they began forming new governments. Representatives of the people gained political control and began writing constitutions and declarations of rights. In October 1776, Virginians began considering the fate of the Church of England. Baptists, Presbyterians, and leaders influenced by the Enlightenment (many being members of the Church of England) united in opposition against the established church. Before the end of that year, Virginia voted that citizens no longer were required to pay ecclesiastical taxes. Within months after Americans declared independence, citizens began the process of destroying the Anglican establishment. Within two years, every Anglican state religion in the new nation was disestablished, replacing the traditional public support of religion with an experiment of voluntary support. In Maryland, Virginia, North Carolina, South Carolina, Georgia, and New York City, the Anglican Church was nearly ruined economically. The Church of England was eventually replaced in the new nation by the Protestant Episcopal Church, but the Revolution was a major setback to this church.[14]

Thomas Jefferson was a member of the committee on religion in Virginia that was formed shortly following our declaring independence from England. To secure religious liberty, the committee reviewed acts which restricted toleration. Jefferson wrote a bill guaranteeing all people of all faiths, Christians and non-Christians, complete religious liberty.[15] The bill was finally passed in Virginia in 1785 and became law in 1786. For the first time through the legislative process, representatives of the people passed a law guaranteeing all people complete religious freedom. Jefferson regarded the writing and adoption of this bill as one of his greatest contributions. When he left instructions regarding the inscriptions on his tomb, he wanted people to remember him for being the author of the Declaration of Independence, the founder of the University of Virginia, and the author of the Statute of Religious Liberty. Prior to and during the conflict between the colonists and the British, religious matters were a major issue; when colonists created new governments, one of the important objectives of many legislators was the establishment of religious liberty.[16]

RELIGION IN NEW ENGLAND

New England's religious situation was very different from the South's. Except for Rhode Island, the Congregational Church was a tax-supported religion in that region, but, unlike the South, a high percent of church attendees in those colonies were members of the state religion. Whereas Jefferson could argue that two-thirds of the people of Virginia were opposed to the established church, he could not say that about the people in New England. Prior

to the 1680s, the Congregational Church was the only legal religion in most of New England, and some who opposed this faith were beaten, branded, clipped, imprisoned, and fined; Mary Dyer, a Quaker missionary, was hanged on Boston Common. Before the end of the seventeenth century, however, pressure from England forced the Puritans to grant toleration to Trinitarian Protestants. Although Anglicans, Baptists, and Quakers (members of the Society of Friends) were allowed to officially organize during the eighteenth century, the Congregational Church continued to be the state church or tax-supported religion.[17]

During the early decades of the eighteenth century, Anglicans, Baptists, and Quakers increased their objections to paying ecclesiastical rates. The legislature responded by establishing a program of exemptions through certificates. Although some Baptists insisted that they complied with the certification laws, they were nonetheless imprisoned. One Baptist farm preacher, Isaac Backus, emerged as the foremost spokesman of his faith.[18] This pioneer champion of liberty delivered sermons, published pamphlets, and wrote many articles that appeared in American newspapers exposing what he called the tyranny that was taking place, especially in Massachusetts where he lived. Backus persisted in identifying those who were imprisoned for failing to pay ecclesiastical taxes and describing groups who were enduring other forms of persecution.[19]

As the crisis between the colonists and the British intensified in the mid-1770s, Isaac Backus and other Baptists agreed that they would not comply with the certification laws nor would they pay ecclesiastical taxes. They estimated the amount of their assessed taxes that was used to support the state church and deducted that amount from the taxes they paid. This Baptist rebellion coincided with the outbreak of the Revolution. Members of this faith strongly supported the patriot cause, and many joined militias that were organized to force Britain to repeal what were considered intolerable laws. Since leaders of the American Revolution in

Massachusetts decided not to act against those who failed to pay their ecclesiastical taxes, the Baptist revolt proved successful.[20]

During the war, Congregational leaders remained in control of the state governments in Massachusetts, Connecticut, and New Hampshire. The new governments adopted different programs for the public support of religion that enabled many to secure exemptions from or to opt out of ecclesiastical assessments. Some people were instructed to pay the tax but were allowed to designate the local religious society that should receive such funds, and some groups who objected to such a program were not required to pay any ecclesiastical taxes.[21] Gradually, throughout New England the public support of religion was discontinued. The last vestige of a state religion finally disappeared in the United States in 1833 when Massachusetts replaced a partial religious establishment with a system of voluntary support of religion.[22]

Ministers not only played an important role in advancing toleration in New England, but they also helped prepare colonists for the rebellion.[23] Isaac Backus was one of the influential leaders of the patriot cause. For ten years prior to the Revolution, the minister from Middleboro, located south of Boston, discussed the nature of government in his sermons and publications. Governments were instituted, Backus reasoned, to protect the rights of people. When he identified these rights, he discussed the right to be taxed only by representatives of the people and emphasized the right of religious freedom. Meanwhile, he denounced many Parliamentary laws, such as the Stamp Act, the Townsend Act, the Tea Act, and the Quebec Act, as acts of tyranny.[24]

Following the first battles at Lexington and Concord in April 1775, Backus grabbed his pen and mounted his pulpit; in sermons and pamphlets, he urged others to support the patriot cause. He asked the question, "Are defensive wars in harmony with teachings found in our Scriptures?" "Yes," he replied, and said, in essence, the British have attacked. They are taking from us our liberty, our rights, and our

In this tract from 1778, Isaac Backus denounced tax-supported churches as tyranny.

lives. We must unite with the troops that are organizing. In harmony with many others, Backus also taught a principle emphasized in the Declaration of Independence. People, he explained, are justified in revolting when their rights are violated. And during the war, the minister from Middleboro periodically mounted his horse, rode to areas where troops were camped, and encouraged soldiers to continue fighting for a righteous cause.[25]

Throughout the war years, Backus urged others to support patriots in their struggle for increased liberty. One of the pamphlets published by this leader in 1778 that helps us better understand religion at war in support of that conflict was entitled *Government and Liberty Described; and Ecclesiastical Tyranny Exposed*. In this pamphlet, Backus continued to teach others political principles upon which the war was based. Backus argued that governments were instituted to preserve men's liberty, and he continued to identify the rights of men and to determine actions of the British that violated these rights. Freedom is not the privilege of acting at random, he reasoned, but the right to act by "reason and rule." Liberty is like the raging force of a mighty stream, he added, eventually eroding everything in its path and not resting until all obstacles are removed.[26]

Taking advantage of a new birth of political freedom, Backus also continued to emphasize the right of religious freedom. He declared in that 1778 treatise on liberty that one of the obstacles that needed to be removed was intolerance. The law of liberty is not yet a reality in Massachusetts, he added; tyranny is continuing. Baptists are still being persecuted, he explained. Mobs are interrupting baptismal services and are driving Baptists from their homes.[27]

Thus, Isaac Backus continued to fight for religious liberty. Nevertheless, Backus recognized the role that the American Revolution had played in increasing political and religious freedom. Particularly impressive is the statement he included in 1805 in one of his last publications: "We have cause to remember with thankfulness, that God has established a civil government over us, which allows equal liberty to all; so that each one may lead a quiet and peaceful life in all godliness and honesty. Such great, such unspeakable privileges demand proportional love and obedience."[28]

Conclusion

The American Revolution led to greater religious changes than any other secular event in American history. It led to the disestablishment of the Church of England and the weakening of the Congregational establishment, and it accelerated the movement to replace the public support of religion with the practice of voluntary support of religion. The American Revolution also advanced the movement of legal religious liberty. During this war for independence, America became a laboratory of creating governments and constitutions. Unlike any other group in the history of the world, representatives of the

people created new state and national governments. While involved in this great experiment, Americans concentrated on issues such as individual rights, sovereignty, separation and fusion of powers, representation, and religious freedom.[29] One of several remarkable accomplishments of the Revolutionary generation was the framing of laws and bills of rights guaranteeing religious freedom to people of all faiths, not just Trinitarian Protestants, but Catholics, Jews, and people of other religious persuasions.

The new birth of freedom in the new nation led to the organization of many new religious communities, such as the Methodist Church (which emerged in Britain but was officially organized in the United States), Unitarian and Universalist societies, various communal societies, and many restorationist groups. This multiplication of faiths united with other forces which accelerated the movement of religious freedom and helped precipitate the world's greatest religious revival.[30]

In the early nineteenth century, there was greater political and religious freedom in the young nation than in any other country.[31] Americans set an example that eventually influenced many other nations. Religion at war in support of the American Revolution helped precipitate a movement that changed the history of the world.

Notes

1. Whether Otis ever used these exact words is not known. See "James Otis," *Dictionary of American Biography,* ed. Dumas Malone, 22 vols. (New York: Charles Scribner's Sons, 1928–37), 14:102.

2. Milton V. Backman Jr., *American Religions and the Rise of Mormonism,* rev. ed. (Salt Lake City: Deseret Book, 1970), 183–85; Robert T. Handy, *A History of the Churches in the United States and Canada* (New York: Oxford University Press, 1977), 142-45; and Nathan O. Hatch, *The Democratization of American Christianity* (New Haven: Yale University Press), 3–15, 210.

3. Backman, *American Religions,* 254–63. The arm of the law was weak in the English colonies, especially in the frontier.

4. Lawrence Henry Gipson, *The Coming of the Revolution* (New York: Harper, 1954), 2–3. See also L. W. Labaree, *Royal Government in America* (New Haven: Yale University Press, 1930).

5. Milton V. Backman Jr., *Christian Churches of America: Origins and Beliefs,* rev. ed. (New York: Charles Scribner's Sons, 1983), 133–36. For a depiction of the persecution of Baptists in Virginia, see *The Dunking of David Barrow and Edward Mintz in the Nansemond River, 1778,* oil painting by Sidney E. King, 1990,

in James H. Hutson, *Religion and the Founding of the American Republic* (Washington, D.C.: Library of Congress, 1998), 71.

6. David Hackett Fischer, *Albion's Seed: Four British Folkways in America* (New York: Oxford University Press, 1989), 617–18, 633–34.

7. Backman, *American Religions*, 197–207.

8. Thomas Jefferson to John Adams, August 22, 1813, printed in *The Writings of Thomas Jefferson*, ed. Thomas A. Lipscomb, 20 vols. (Washington, D.C.: Thomas Jefferson Memorial Association, 1903–4), 13:350.

9. Sydney E. Ahlstrom, *A Religious History of the American People*, 2 vols., Image ed. (Garden City, N.Y.: Image, 1975), 1:413, 433–36.

10. Henry Mayer, *A Son of Thunder: Patrick Henry and the American Republic* (New York : Watts, 1986), 59–61.

11. For more on Henry, see Hutson, *Religion and the Founding*, 67.

12. Letters of James Maury printed in Ann Maury, *Memoirs of a Huguenot Family* (New York: George P. Putnam, 1853), 420–23; Sanford H. Cobb, *The Rise of Religious Liberty in America* (New York: Macmillan, 1902), 110–11. What Henry actually said is not fully known, but some accounts are just too interesting to be doubted, such as "Give me liberty or give me death." Portions of his remarks were recorded shortly following the trial.

13. Mayer, *Son of Thunder*, 65–66.

14. Backman, *American Religions*, 183; Handy, *A History of the Churches in the United States*, 144–46.

15. For a copy of Jefferson's *An Act for Establishing Religious Freedom*, see Hutson, *Religion and the Founding*, 73.

16. Backman, *American Religions*, 199–200; Dumas Malone, *Jefferson and His Times*, 6 vols. (Boston: Little, Brown, 1948–81), 1:276–80.

17. Backman, *American Religions*, 161–75. Partly because of the religious diversity that characterized the Middle Colonies and Rhode Island, there were no religious establishments in that area (except in New York City) in the eighteenth century. Prior to the American Revolution, by their examples and experiments, these colonies led a movement of voluntary support of religion and the securing of a policy of religious liberty. See Winthrop S. Hudson, *Religion in America*, 3d ed. (New York: Charles Scrinbers' Sons, 1983), 99–106.

18. For more on Backus, see in Hutson, *Religion and the Founding*, 69.

19. William G. McLoughlin, *Isaac Backus and the American Pietistic Tradition* (Boston: Little, Brown, 1967), 110–15.

20. McLoughlin, *Isaac Backus*, 59–60, 126–28, 134–35, 157–66.

21. For a legal analysis and full text of such a "protest" and opting out, see John W. Welch, "Jesse Smith's 1814 Protest," *BYU Studies* 33, no. 1 (1993): 131–44.

22. Backman, *American Religions*, 183–85.

23. Alice M. Baldwin, *New England Clergy and the American Revolution* (New York: Ungar, 1958).

24. Milton V. Backman Jr., "Isaac Backus: Pioneer Champion of Religious Liberty" (Ph.D. diss., University of Pennsylvania, 1969), chaps. 6–7. Between 1770 and 1787, Backus published thirty-two tracts (five of which were revised and republished). Ten tracts were written in an effort to secure religious freedom. He also wrote ten articles that were published in Boston newspapers. His political theories in support of the American Revolution were included in a number of these publications.

25. McLoughlin, *Isaac Backus*, 123–27, 134; Backman, "Isaac Backus," chap. 9. See Diaries of Isaac Backus, 8:145–51, Backus Collection, Andover Newton Theological Library, Newton Centre, Massachusetts; and Isaac Backus, *History of New England with Particular Reference to the Denomination of Christians Called Baptists*, 2d ed., 2 vols. (Newton, Mass.: Backus Historical Society, 1871), 1:529–30, 536–37; 2:192–96.

26. Isaac Backus, *Government and Liberty Described; and Ecclesiastical Tyranny Exposed* (Boston: Powars and Willis, 1778), 3–6, 11. This pamphlet was probably read by more Americans than any other tract written by Backus.

27. Backus, *Government and Liberty Described*, 15–20.

28. Isaac Backus, *A Great Faith Described and Inculcated* (Boston: Lincoln, 1805), 16.

29. For a discussion of major issues considered by founders of this nation, including the framers of the Constitution of 1787, see Jack N. Rakove, *Original Meanings: Politics and Ideas in the Making of the Constitution* (Ann Arbor: University of Michigan Press, 1998); J. Reuben Clark Jr., *Stand Fast by Our Constitution* (Salt Lake City: Deseret Book, 1965), 147–50, 187–88; and Edmund S. Morgan, *Inventing the People: The Rise of Popular Sovereignty in England and America* (New York: Norton, 1988).

30. Backman, *American Religions*, 283–309. Some of the new religious communities that were organized following the American Revolution did not embrace the traditional concept of God. Subsequently, some Christian faiths would not have been permitted legally to hold public meetings by the provisions of the Toleration Act of 1689.

31. Cobb, *Rise of Religious Liberty in America*, 2–6, 15–18, 509, 521–28; Richard L. Bushman, "1830: Pivotal Year in the Fulness of Times," *Ensign*, vol. 8 (September 1978), 9. For a discussion of the transformation of American Christianity following the American Revolution, see Hatch, *Democratization of American Christianity*, 3–15, 210.

THOMAS JEFFERSON
RELIGIOUS BELIEFS AND POLITICAL DOCTRINES

Matthew S. Holland

Given Thomas Jefferson's prominence in the fight to establish religious and political liberty in America, an examination of his personal religious beliefs and how those beliefs relate to his political doctrines is well warranted. This is no small task, however. Jefferson was, to put it simply, a very complicated man and thinker. For good reason, one of the best single-volume biographies of his life is titled *American Sphinx*.[1] Jefferson was especially laconic when the topic turned to his own theological views. As he once wrote in a letter to a correspondent seeking information for a biographical sketch, "Say nothing of my religion. . . . It is known to my god and myself alone."[2] Nevertheless, Jefferson left behind a voluminous collection of personal writings and public papers from which one can tease out the evolving general contours of his religious beliefs and their influence on his politics. Jefferson's attitudes toward Christianity—at least Christ's moral teachings—changed over time, and these changes appear to have prompted Jefferson to subtly modify his earlier political philosophy.

BACKGROUND: JOHN WINTHROP AND THE PURITAN HERITAGE IN AMERICA

Much of Jefferson's religious and political philosophies responded, in part, to a Puritan legacy delineated by the thought of an earlier figure in America's cultural history, John Winthrop. Winthrop, the first governor of Massachusetts, was singled out by Alexis de Tocqueville as a figure of founding importance for America.[3] As Tocqueville saw it, the most important cause of America's singular democratic success was not her fertile land kindly separated from aristocratic Europe or her ingenious constitutional and federal laws but her national character, defined by her ideas and ideals. Of course, the sources for these ideals were as varied as the different geographic regions that made up early America. However, for Tocqueville, the first and most significant influencers of these powerful American mores were the Puritans, among whom John Winthrop stood out above all others.

Perhaps the richest resource of the Puritan legacy comes from Winthrop's political sermon delivered on the deck of the *Arbella*, the lead ship of the 1630 Puritan migration. This sermon spelled out his vision of public life in New England and was titled "A Model of Christian Charity."[4] The speech contained five ideals that continue to have a profound impact on American culture and public life.

First, Winthrop taught that the settlement was to be a model society of Christian love, which meant that these New Englanders should care for each other as they cared for themselves, specifically that there should be no poor among them. One of Winthrop's chief criticisms of England and her Church was that not nearly enough was being done to help the poor.[5] Such was not the case in Winthrop's Boston, where a remarkably efficient system of welfare provided for those who could not provide for themselves.

Second, the colonists must learn to rule themselves. Winthrop himself was a trained lawyer and as governor saw that the fundamentals of the English legal tradition took root in Massachusetts. Both community and church business were conducted by consent. Though it was a hierarchical society by contemporary standards, the Massachusetts Bay Colony practiced an unusually advanced form of democracy. Almost forty years before John Locke published his *Second Treatise,* this hardy band of Puritans were making their own social contracts, holding regular elections, extending the franchise, and separating legislative and executive powers.

Third, these early New Englanders must be educated. Winthrop taught that to purify their faith and arm themselves against the influence of Anglican clerical powers, the Massachusetts Bay colonists must have highly educated preachers and parishioners. Thus, even in the very earliest and most challenging years of the colony, Winthrop and his fellow Puritan leaders set up Harvard College.

Fourth, they must be a "city on a hill." Borrowing this image from the book of Matthew, Winthrop taught that the charity they practiced must not just be to members of their own community, but to the rest of mankind. They were to be a people whose positive influence knew no boundaries. The sense that America has a special mission in the larger world is one of the most permanent and powerful ideals passed on by this visionary Puritan to succeeding generations of Americans.

Last, Winthrop taught they must persecute those who jeopardized the community's standing before God. Of course, Winthrop did not preach this explicitly, but the Puritan tendency to punish severely those who undermined prevailing orthodoxies was built into the very logic of Winthrop's view of Christian charity. According to Winthrop, charity was not just a matter of loving others but also of loving God. And the Puritans particularly believed that the love between God and man was of "a most strict and peculiar manner."

The Puritans saw themselves as a special, covenant people, not unlike the children of Israel—an allusion that crops up repeatedly in Winthrop's sermon. They believed that God loved them above all people, and therefore if they would love him above all other things and manifest their love through a strict and careful obedience to the covenant they established with him, they would prosper like no other plantation in the world. Alternatively, they believed if they stumbled in their collective covenant with God, he would, like a jealous and jilted lover, punish them severely. Specifically, Winthrop warned of shipwreck on the Atlantic crossing or perishing in the wilderness upon arrival. It thus was a matter of life and death to see that every colonist strictly adhered to the communal covenant with God.

The Library of Congress exhibition *Religion and the Founding of the American Republic* contained an etching of Mary Dyer, a Quaker, being led to her execution in Massachusetts in 1660.[6] As the exhibition explained, Mary was killed in part because she was a follower of Anne Hutchinson, a woman who espoused the "evil" doctrine of direct, personal revelation—a powerful threat to the orthodoxy Winthrop and others thought needed to prevail for Puritan survival. Something not seen in the exhibition, but which is almost as horrific as the etching of

Dyer's execution, is an account in Winthrop's own journal about how, in 1638, he had Mary Dyer's miscarried fetus disinterred from its grave so its reportedly monstrous deformities could be catalogued and used as evidence of God's punishment for Dyer's unorthodox and headstrong beliefs.[7]

This is the complicated, dual legacy of a figure like John Winthrop, and it underscores the complicated, dual legacy of religion in American political life. On one hand, a number of the religious influences and related social practices that Winthrop was instrumental in planting deeply in American soil provided a powerful foundation for the unique mores and positive national character that enabled America to scale so quickly and successfully the sunlit uplands of modern, republican democracy. On the other hand, Winthrop is also representative of America's legacy of a severe and awful spirit of religious persecution in the very name of religion.[8]

The persistence of this spirit of persecution in America was well manifest throughout the Library of Congress exhibition, which concluded with a sketch of the nineteenth-century martyrdom of Joseph Smith.[9] Such persecution is utterly tragic, but it is not cause for utter pessimism about our history or our future. The exhibition also showed that between Mary Dyer and Joseph Smith, much happened in America to combat the darker, persecuting side of religion's influence on American political life.

Thomas Jefferson's Early Political Philosophy—Secular Liberalism

Thomas Jefferson loathed man's inhumanity to man in the name of religion. Jefferson's stance was neatly and symbolically captured in the Library of Congress exhibition: directly underneath the etching of the execution of Mary Dyer sat a first edition copy of Thomas Jefferson's *Notes on the State of Virginia* opened to Query 17, where Jefferson laments the long history of religious persecution in this country.[10] Arguably, no one has done more to stem this tragic tendency in American political life than Jefferson.

In one of his earliest and most significant political accomplishments, the drafting of the Declaration of Independence, Jefferson steered America away from the Winthropian aspiration to be a "model of Christian charity." Jefferson began the Declaration by recasting the world in which politics took place. The opening line of Winthrop's "Model of Christian Charity" situated his constituents' departure from England in an environment where God's care and providence operated everywhere and at "all times." Jefferson's memorable first seven words, "When in the course of human events," conveyed that even earth-shattering political movements such as the American Revolution take place as part of a drama more mortal than divine. While Winthrop's speech endeavored to fully satisfy the demands of a jealous God, Jefferson only aimed to accommodate "a decent respect to the opinions of mankind."[11]

But what about those famous lines at the end of the Declaration that appealed to the "supreme judge of the world" and humbly acknowledged "a firm reliance on the protection of divine Providence"? Those passages were not written by Jefferson. They were added by his editors in the Continental Congress. Nor was Jefferson responsible for the famous "endowed by their Creator" line in the second sentence; this came from the drafting committee, which slightly revised Jefferson's original rough draft before forwarding it to the full Congress.[12]

Of course, God was not entirely missing from Jefferson's political cosmology. Jefferson claimed in his rough draft that the "laws of nature and of nature's god" "entitle" a people to throw off their subordinate status and acquire an "equal and independent station" in the universe of politics. To be *entitled* to something presupposes the existence of a standard of judgment by which one might ascertain whether one is or is not entitled. In politics, Jefferson's first sentence argued that such a standard exists: "nature's god" provides a norm by which key considerations of politics can be judged. While Jefferson sought to liberate America from the extensive demands of the punishing and providential

God of Winthrop, he stopped well short of an amoral Machiavellianism, which holds that politics is not subject to any moral requirements higher than getting and keeping power.

Because "nature's god" of Jefferson's politics was a barely visible and inactive presence—sustaining a morality by which to judge politics but neither punishing those who offend such a morality or blessing those who follow it—there was no need for Jefferson, or any statesman, to insist on a careful obedience to this god. In just the first sentence of the Declaration, Jefferson did much to relieve the pressure for Americans to persecute one's religious-minority neighbors to please a far-reaching God who demanded orthodoxy. Some may have found this view of God uninspiring if not blasphemous. For instance, it appears to greatly water down, if not eliminate, the political community's need to show their love for God and each other through obedience to God's commandments—a need which is a fundamental component of virtually any traditional understanding of Christian charity (Matt. 22:36–40). Nevertheless, the image of an inactive god did provide a number of salient political features based on what Jefferson believed were the fundamental rules, or self-evident truths, the god of nature sets for politics.

The first truth Jefferson tendered is that "all men are created equal." By this, Jefferson meant simply that no man has a God-given or natural claim to rule over another. One may possess superior physical, intellectual or spiritual talents—one may in fact be a potential member of what Jefferson hoped would be a "natural aristocracy . . . of virtue and talents"—but one is not, *ipso facto,* entitled to rule over another.[13] In other words, because no natural political authority exists, all men are naturally free to govern themselves.

Jefferson's claim about natural equality led to a claim about natural rights, namely that all are endowed with certain inalienable rights including life, liberty, and the pursuit of happiness. This troika of rights is tantamount to an inherent freedom from the rule of another. Consider how one scholar has characterized what Jefferson meant by the right to the pursuit of happiness:

> When Jefferson spoke of an inalienable right to the pursuit of happiness, he meant that men may act as they choose in their search for ease, comfort, felicity, and grace, either by owning property or not, by accumulating wealth or distributing it, by opting for material success or asceticism, in a word, by determining the path to their own earthly and heavenly salvation as they alone see fit.[14]

In a letter to Doctor John Manners written toward the end of his life, Jefferson confirmed this interpretation by stating that the same god who put it "in the nature of man to pursue happiness" had also left man "free in the choice of place as well as mode" of that happiness.[15]

From the first two assertions in the Declaration about equality and rights followed two concrete criteria for judging the moral legitimacy of government. One is that government must "secure" the free and safe exercise of these "inherent" rights, and two, the government that does so must derive its "just powers from the consent of the governed." The existence of a state of natural equality implies that no natural political authority exists. However, natural equals cannot individually secure, in the face of strong anthropological forces, the rights to which their equality entitles them. They mutually agree on a form of government that will effect the safe exercise of their rights to live their lives as they see fit. By design, this contractually created power will set some limits on the full and free exercise of individual rights, for rights must be limited to some degree in order to protect one person's rights from the unfettered practice of rights by another. This limitation does not signal a surrender of those rights. It only signals that natural equals have, of their own accord, agreed on a conventional form of authority to identify and enforce conventional limits to those rights.

We are left with a political paradigm often referred to as classical, or philosophical, liberalism (this is to distinguish Jefferson's form of liberalism from "modern" liberalism associated with today's welfare state). At the base of this paradigm is a rather bland, thin morality. It is the simple morality of natural rights. It does not ask much of us. We are not commanded to be fully committed practitioners of Christian charity, nor are we allowed to be Machiavelli's prince. And while this morality is thin, it is broad: it applies to all men everywhere, regardless of a particular religious or nonreligious orientation. This morality gives rise to a certain kind of government. The government, like the morality, is thin but broad in its scope. It creates only a wall of separation between itself and complex private moralities, as well as walls of protection between the private moralities themselves.

The government's range must extend to encompass the different kinds of private moralities that constitute a republic. The followers of these private moralities are free to reach the heights of Judeo-Christian righteousness or the self-satisfying pursuits of Epicureanism so long as in their quest they do not trouble the rights of those who subscribe to some other competing morality or try to undermine or hijack the foundational public morality.

Many religious believers today may find this broad, thin public morality too secular and insufficient to sustain a stable community of freedom. But consider for a moment what it might have meant to a Mary Dyer or a Joseph Smith had such a public morality widely prevailed in the America they inhabited.

JEFFERSON'S CHANGING VIEWS ON CHRISTIANITY

Jefferson's paradigm should be well regarded for the protections it offers religious believers (especially those outside of mainstream religious beliefs), but at the time of drafting the Declaration, Jefferson was not a promoter of organized religion. Though Jefferson was raised an Anglican, most historians agree that in his teens he experienced something of a "religious crisis." While more or less continuing a lifelong habit of attending the Anglican church, in the place of his former faith he appears to have adopted "a vaguely defined natural religion" based on reason and moral-sense philosophy.[16]

Jefferson's youthful rejection of the traditional Protestant Christianity of his day can be attributed to a budding preference for evidence and reason, as heavily underscored in his "Literary Commonplace Book," where Jefferson, in his teens and twenties, copied passages from his favorite poets, dramatists, and philosophers. The author Jefferson copied down most extensively is Lord Bolingbroke, an English Tory whose writings have been characterized by one scholar as "a veritable *summa* of rationalistic criticisms of revealed religion."[17] Jefferson copied, among other things, Bolingbroke's rejection of the Bible as an inspired text because inspiration cannot be proved by reason and evidence, of miracles as testimony of the divinity of Christ because they are found convincing only in an environment where "ignorance . . . abound[s]," and of the general gospel message as a comprehensive ethical guide because

> it is not true that Christ revealed an entire body of ethics, proved to be the law of nature from principles of reason, and reaching all the duties of life. if mankind wanted such [a] code, to which recourse might be had on every occasion, as to an unerring rule in every part of the moral duties, such a code is still wanting; for the gospel is not such a code.[18]

Not only did Jefferson find Christianity rationally unconvincing, he also saw it as the source of unacceptable tyranny and malice. In 1822, a minister sent Jefferson some pamphlets and asked for his opinion on them. Jefferson wrote in response, "I have never permitted myself to meditate a specified creed. These formulas have been the bane and ruin of the Christian church, its own fatal invention which, thro' so many ages, made of Christendom a slaughter house, and at this day divides it into Casts of inextinguishable hatred to one another."[19]

In an 1819 letter he sent to William Short—who had earlier written to Jefferson that Epicurus was the "wisest of the ancient philosophers" and the ultimate source of instruction for "the attainment of happiness in this poor world"—Jefferson flatly asserts, "I too am an Epicurean." However, a few lines later, Jefferson concludes, "But the greatest of all the Reformers . . . was Jesus of Nazareth. . . .

[From him] we have the outlines of a system of the most sublime morality which has ever fallen from the lips of man. . . . Epictetus and Epicurus give us laws for governing ourselves, Jesus a supplement of the duties and *charities* we owe to others."[20] This statement appears to virtually invert the Bolingbroke claim that Jefferson copied in his youth.

The intellectual and spiritual journey that led Jefferson to this new position is a well documented, if not often told, story. During the decade before Jefferson's ascension to the presidency, a series of experiences unquestionably altered Jefferson's view of the role that Christianity in general, and Christian charity in particular, should play in the public morality of the country over which he was destined to preside.

In December 1789, Jefferson reluctantly accepted George Washington's request to serve as secretary of state and returned home from France. It was not long before Jefferson locked horns with Washington's influential secretary of treasury, Alexander Hamilton. Jefferson felt that Hamilton and, later, Adams consistently favored centralized government over local control, manufacturing concerns over agrarian interests, regal pomp over democratic simplicity, and royal England over republican France. Jefferson saw in these choices courtly intentions designed to turn America from its democratic-republican moorings for which he had labored almost all his entire adult life. This split produced a decade-long political battle that would give rise to the United States' first political parties, the Federalist party of Hamilton and Adams and the Republican party of Jefferson and Madison, and would go down in history as one of the most acrimonious periods of American politics.[21]

From the start, Jefferson saw Federalist actions as grave threats to the sacred truths of human equality and liberty enshrined in the Declaration.[22] However, by the end of the campaign of 1800, the increasingly ugly fight between Federalists and Republicans gave Jefferson pause to consider a different threat to the full realization

and perpetuation of the verities of 1776. Undermining successful self-rule was what Jefferson considered a dangerous lack of love among American citizens of different political persuasions.[23] One of the very first letters Jefferson wrote after becoming president was to Elbridge Gerry, wherein he stated, "It will be a great blessing to our country if we can once more restore harmony and social love among its citizens. I confess, as to myself, it is almost the first object of my heart, and one to which I would sacrifice everything but principle."[24]

Jefferson's mounting alarm over the political dangers associated with a lack of "social love" in America coincided with a fairly dramatic transformation of his views on Christianity. In the mid-1790s, sometime after resigning from Washington's cabinet, Jefferson read *An History of the Corruptions of Christianity* by Joseph Priestly, the English chemist turned Unitarian theologian. In this book, Priestly argued that early church leaders corrupted original Christianity with esoteric and irrational doctrines like the Trinity, original sin, and the Atonement to appeal to intellectual pagans and to exercise control over commoners through mysteries only the church fathers could interpret.[25] Priestley's work cleared away much of what Jefferson found unacceptably mysterious and irrational in Christianity since his young days of reading Bolingbroke.

At roughly the same time that Jefferson's attitude toward Christianity was being reshaped by the arguments of Priestly, Jefferson was in Philadelphia serving as a bored, marginalized vice-president to Adams. He began visiting regularly with Benjamin Rush, his old friend from the Continental Congress who was prayerfully determined to see Jefferson come to believe in the divinity of Jesus Christ and the importance of Christianity for America's political well-being.[26]

Jefferson never came to share Rush's millennial vision for America, or accept the divinity of Christ or the seemingly irrational concepts of miracles and atonement. To the end, he remained more of an Enlightenment deist than a traditional Christian

Dear Sir

Washington April 21. 1803.

In some of the delightful conversations with you, in the evenings of 1798.99. & which served as an Anodyne to the afflictions of the crisis through which our country was then labouring, the Christian religion was sometimes our topic: and I then promised you that one day or other, I would give you my views of it. they are the result of a life of enquiry & reflection, & very different from that Anti-Christian system imputed to me by those who know nothing of my opinions. to the corruptions of Christianity I am indeed opposed; but not to the genuine precepts of Jesus himself. I am a Christian in the only sense in which he wished any one to be; sincerely attached to his doctrines, in preference to all others; ascribing to himself every human excellence; & believing he never claimed any other. at the short intervals since these conversations, when I could justifiably abstract my mind from public affairs, this subject has been under my contemplation. but the more I considered it, the more it expanded beyond the measure of either my time or information. in the moment of my late departure from Monticello, I recieved from Doctr. Priestley, his little treatise of "Socrates & Jesus compared." this being a section of the general view I had taken of the field, it became a subject of reflection while on the road, & unoccupied otherwise. the result was, to arrange in my mind a Syllabus, or Outline of such an Estimate of the comparative merits of Christianity, as I wished to see executed by some one of more leisure and information for the task than myself. this I now send you, as the only discharge of my promise I can probably ever execute. and in confiding it to you, I know it will not be exposed to the malignant perversions of those who make every word from me a text for new misrepresentations & calumnies. I am moreover averse to the communication of my religious tenets to the public; because it would countenance the presumption of those who have endeavored to draw them before that tribunal, & to seduce public opinion to erect itself into that inquisition over the rights of conscience, which the laws have so justly proscribed. it behoves every man, who values liberty of conscience for himself, to resist invasions of it in the case of others; or their case may, by change of circumstances, become his own. it behoves him too, in his own case, to give no example of concession, betraying the common right of independent opinion, by answering questions of faith which the laws have left between god & himself. accept my affectionate salutations.

Doctr. Benjamin Rush.

Th: Jefferson

Thomas Jefferson, letter to Benjamin Rush, April 21, 1803. In this letter, Jefferson expresses his views on Christianity, mentions Joseph Priestly's influence (line thirteen), and mentions his hesitation of making his religious sentiments known (line twenty-two).

believer. However, his conversations with Rush, combined with his readings of Priestly and growing concern over the social animosity that seemed to jeopardize the survival of the republic, appear to have significantly transformed his attitude about the general validity and political importance of Christian morality.[27] As Fred Luebke has shown, from 1786 (the year Jefferson secured enactment of his bill establishing religious freedom in Virginia) through the end of the eighteenth century, Jefferson wrote very little on religion. Yet, from January 1800 to August 1801 he "wrote more letters with religious content than during his entire life prior to that time."[28] On April 21, 1803, just two years into his presidency, Jefferson wrote to Rush that, "To the corruptions of Christianity, I am indeed opposed; but not the genuine precepts of Jesus himself. I am a Christian in the only sense in which he wished one to be; sincerely attached to his doctrines, in preference to all others."[29]

Both the strength and direction of Jefferson's new views are perhaps best illustrated by the fact that just two years into his presidency Jefferson spent what he later reported was "one or two evenings only, while I lived at Washington, overwhelmed with other business," cutting out what he believed were the unadulterated teachings of the New Testament and pasting them onto large sheets of folded paper, which he then had bound. He titled the book *The Philosophy of Jesus of Nazareth*.[30] The index of this collection is illuminating. Prominent are the more compassionate, mercy-oriented parables found in Luke, like the "Lost Sheep," the "Prodigal Son," and the "Good Samaritan," which Jefferson specifically characterized,

Draft of index to Thomas Jefferson, *The Life and Morals of Jesus of Nazareth Extracted Textually from the Gospels in Greek, Latin, French, and English* (Washington, D.C.: Government Printing Office, 1904). Original at the Smithsonian. Here Jefferson listed some of the passages he considered to be the "real" teachings of Jesus.

in his table of contents page, as "true benevolence."[31] One also finds the passages from Matthew (chapters 19 and 22) concerning the two great commandments of Christian love, which Jefferson categorized as Jesus's "general moral precepts." Jefferson did not include any passages concerning the divinity of Christ's birth, the miracles of his ministry, or, most notably, the atoning, sacrificial nature of his death. Jefferson included comparatively few passages from the more esoteric book of John.

INFLUENCE OF CHRISTIAN MORALITY ON JEFFERSON'S LATER POLITICAL PHILOSOPHY

The pressing question then is this: how did Jefferson's altered views on what he called true and charitable "doctrines of Jesus" affect his political philosophy? The timing and importance of Jefferson's First Inaugural make it an unmatched platform for understanding Jefferson's revised and most influential thoughts on charity and politics. This speech is significant because, unlike when he wrote the Declaration, Jefferson was speaking only for himself, unconstrained by writing for a committee and larger voting assembly. Additionally, at the delivery of his First Inaugural, Jefferson was a few weeks shy of his fifty-eighth birthday. When he drafted the Declaration, he was only thirty-three years old. The First Inaugural speech was Jefferson, pure and mature. It is also significant that this speech came immediately on the heels of the bruising election of 1800 and right in the heart of Jefferson's intense reflections on his views of Christian doctrine and belief, as prompted by Priestly and Rush.

Jefferson's opening paragraph introduced something of a controlling theme for the whole address. Jefferson spoke of "the *happiness,* and the hopes of this beloved country committed to the issue and the auspices of this day."[32] Peppered throughout the rest of the address were six more references to happiness or synonyms of happiness. From beginning to end, national happiness rang as the leitmotif of the First Inaugural. The speech then went on to connect, at least implicitly, his view of Christian charity (though he never used the terms *Christian* or *charity*) as essential to America's national happiness.

After the introductory paragraph, Jefferson's first move was to extend a charitable olive leaf of peace to his former Federalist enemies, saying, famously, "Every difference of opinion is not a difference of principle. We have called by different names brethren of the same principle. We are all Republicans, we are all Federalists."[33] John Marshall, one of Jefferson's most ardent Federalist foes, called the speech "well judged and conciliatory."[34] Benjamin Rush was delighted to discover that in response to the publication of the address in Philadelphia, "Old friends too long separated by party names were reunited."[35]

All this had to be gratifying for Jefferson, for such a reaction was his stated objective. Early in the second paragraph, Jefferson said, "Let us, then, fellow citizens, unite with one heart and one mind. Let us restore to social intercourse that harmony and affection without which liberty and even life itself are but dreary things. And let us . . . "[36] The full-throated power of this passage was that it rhetorically underscored its substantive message of national unity. Each line began with the phrase "let us," and this anaphora conveyed a tone of gentle persuasion, demonstrating respect, or care, for the will of all listening. Jefferson did not simply dictate his own will upon the country, but he petitioned for cooperative collaboration in a countrywide effort to be of "one heart." This passage was more than just a deferential and poetic plea that partisan citizens be kinder and more respectful toward each other. It contains within it a somewhat startling and important addendum to the self-evident truths of the Declaration.

Jefferson explained that without affection, "liberty and even life itself are but dreary things."[37] He linked dreariness,[38] a clear antonym of happiness, to the absence of affection, a concept closely related to, if not embodied in or synonymous to, love.[39] He used the term *dreariness* with the terms *life* and *liberty,* the other two prominent components of the Declaration's famous triad of rights. This rhetoric alerted his careful listeners to an insight concerning the Declaration's "pursuit of happiness" clause: the pursuit of human happiness would be a difficult, if not impossible, task in an atmosphere absent of love practiced as a milder, more humanistic form of Christian charity. Jefferson more explicitly connected human happiness and New Testament–grounded love in later private correspondence, in which he declared that the charitable "doctrines of Jesus" as he understood them "tend all to the happiness of man."[40]

Jefferson listed two "blessings" he thought were essential to national happiness. The first was allegiance to "republican principles," or, to adopt language used earlier, the principles of public morality and natural rights. The second was what he called a benign religion.

> Enlightened by a benign religion, professed, indeed, and practiced in various forms, yet all of them inculcating honesty, truth, temperance, gratitude, and the love of man; acknowledging and adoring an overruling Providence, which by all its dispensations proves that it delights in the happiness of man here and his greater happiness hereafter.[41]

Given Jefferson's early and sometimes visceral denouncements of religion, both private and public, this statement was remarkable. Jefferson was, for the first time, openly congratulating America for its widespread religiosity, especially because that religiosity generally promoted a "love of man" and adoration of God—two staples of traditional Christian charity. Of course, keeping consistent with his deistic leanings and his firm view that government should not endorse or be governed by specific religions, Jefferson was careful to present religion in the most pluralistic light possible. Thus, he chose the generic term "religion" over a general reference to Christianity. Similarly, Jefferson preferred a vague reference to "Providence" over a more anthropological sounding "God" as the stated object of religious devotion. However, given what Jefferson revealed in his private communications with Rush and Priestly behind the scenes of his ascension to the presidency, it seems reasonable that his reconsideration of Christianity was coloring much of his speech.

Jefferson asked and answered the question "What more is necessary to make us a happy and prosperous people?" Jefferson identified "one thing more" needed to "close the circle of our felicities": "a wise and frugal Government, which shall restrain men from injuring one another, shall leave them otherwise free to regulate their own pursuits of industry and improvement, and shall not take from the mouth of labor the bread it has earned." As Jefferson put it, these restraints are the "sum of good government" that round out America's circle of happiness.[42]

One should be cautious, however, of assuming from this speech that Jefferson was as extremely libertarian as many claim today. Jefferson's First Inaugural defense of the night-watchman state must be contextualized. First, the speech clearly reflected Jefferson's sense of federalism, which held that most governance should be carried on at the state and local levels, basically limiting the federal government to "the defense of the nation, and its foreign and federal relations."[43] And there is clear evidence that Jefferson did see a role for local governments to play in actively caring for the poor.[44] Furthermore, Jefferson's sense was that vast income inequalities did not exist in America to the extent they did in Europe at that time, or in America today.[45] One should be wary of presuming that Jefferson would advocate the night-watchman state of his day for the America of our day. Nevertheless, Jefferson's theoretical point remains clear; the demands of love do not radically alter his overall commitment to a form of classically liberal government.

At first blush, it would seem Jefferson's revised thoughts on religion produced a theory of government little different than the one strictly coming out of his original public morality of natural rights; government remains, by and large, limited and individualistic, protecting wide swaths of human freedom. But Jefferson's phrase "the circle of our felicities" suggested a different conceptual framework than first mapped out by the Declaration. Rather than foundations and walls of separation, we now might see private moralities as separate arcs on the same circle, where some of the powers and virtues of private religion feed into and off of a public morality of natural rights ensured by a wise and frugal government unmistakably devoted to protecting individual rights. This is not quite as theoretically tidy as the first conceptual framework of the Declaration of Independence. But when has the practice of politics, especially democratic politics, ever been tidy?

By publicly teaching that the practice of some form of charity is essential to national happiness and helps ensure the stable perpetuation of democratic, rights-protecting government, and by privately teaching that the best resource for an understanding of charity is located in the New Testament, President Jefferson signaled the political importance and legitimacy of a specifically Christian concept of charity as he would not have done in his early career. While the public morality of natural rights would continue to properly limit the statesman from deploying discriminating and coercive legal sanctions to support Christian charity, Jefferson appears to have believed that a wise statesman would readily use the non-coercive, but nonetheless political, powers of his office to carefully advance charity. The more mature framework of Jefferson's thought, therefore, continues to effectively war against the unfortunate American tendency to persecute religious and other minorities even as it positively harnesses key components of one narrow but complex private morality whose finest expression is found in the teachings of Jesus Christ.

Notes

1. Joseph J. Ellis, *American Sphinx: The Character of Thomas Jefferson* (New York: Alfred A. Knopf, 1996).

2. Thomas Jefferson to Joseph Delaplaine, December 25, 1816, in Thomas Jefferson, *Jefferson's Extracts from the Gospels: "The Philosophy of Jesus" and "The Life and Morals of Jesus,"* ed. Dickinson W. Adams and Ruth W. Lester (Princeton, N.J.: Princeton University Press, 1983), 4.

3. Alexis de Tocqueville, *Democracy in America,* ed. Harvey Mansfield and Delba Winthrop (Chicago: University of Chicago, 2000), xvii.

4. John Winthrop and others, *The Winthrop Papers,* 5 vols. (Boston: Massachusetts Historical Society, 1929–47), 2:282–95.

5. Winthrop, *Winthrop Papers,* 1:302–3.

6. To view *Mary Dyer Led to Execution on Boston Common, 1 June 1660,* see the Library of Congress on-line exhibition at lcweb.loc.gov/exhibits/religion/rel01-2.html.

7. John Winthrop, *The [Abridged] Journal of John Winthrop, 1630–1649,* ed. Richard S. Dunn and Laetitia Yeandle (Cambridge: Belknap Press of Harvard University Press, 1996), 140–42.

8. It is important to qualify here that not all early Christian settlers in America demonstrated the kind of persecuting zeal associated with Winthrop and other Puritan figures. Roger Williams and the Baptists of Rhode Island, and William Penn and the Quakers of Pennsylvania, also exerted strong influences on America's cultural development and were far more accommodating to those of differing religious persuasions.

9. For the depiction of Joseph Smith's martyrdom, see *Martyrdom of Joseph and Hiram Smith in Carthage Jail, June 27, 1844,* in James H. Hutson, *Religion and the Founding of the American Republic* (Washington, D.C.: Library of Congress, 1998), 110, or see lcweb.loc.gov/exhibits/religion/re107.html.

10. For Jefferson's *Notes on the State of Virginia,* see the Library of Congress on-line exhibition at lcweb.loc.gov/exhibits/religion/rel01-2.html.

11. The most authoritative documentation of the Declaration of Independence and its preceding drafts is located in Thomas Jefferson, *The Papers of Thomas Jefferson,* ed. Julian P. Boyd, 30 vols. to date (Princeton, N.J.: Princeton University Press, 1950–), 2:420.

12. Pauline Maier, *American Scripture: Making the Declaration of Independence* (New York: Knopf, 1997), 148–49.

13. Thomas Jefferson, *Writings,* ed. Merrill D. Peterson (New York: Viking Press, 1984), 1305.

14. Ronald Hamowy, "Jefferson and the Scottish Enlightenment: A Critique of Gary Wills's *Inventing America: Jefferson's Declaration of Independence,*" *William and Mary Quarterly* 36, no. 4 (1979): 519.

15. Thomas Jefferson, *The Writings of Thomas Jefferson,* ed. Andrew A. Lipscomb, 20 vols. (Washington, D.C.: Thomas Jefferson Memorial Foundation, 1903–4), 15:124.

16. Jefferson, *Jefferson's Extracts from the Gospels,* 5.

17. Jefferson, *Jefferson's Extracts from the Gospels,* 5–6. For Jefferson's notations on Bolingbrooke in Jefferson's "Literary Commonplace Book," see the Library of Congress on-line exhibition at lcweb.loc.gov/exhibits/religion/rel02.html.

18. Thomas Jefferson, *Jefferson's Literary Commonplace Book,* ed. Douglas L. Wilson (Princeton, N.J.: Princeton University Press, 1989), 25, 33, 35.

19. Jefferson, *Jefferson's Extracts from the Gospels,* 404.

20. Jefferson, *Jefferson's Extracts from the Gospels,* 390, 388, emphasis added.

21. See John Herbert Aldrich, *Why Parties? The Origin and Transformation of Political Parties in America* (Chicago: University of Chicago Press, 1995), 68–69. For a political cartoon attacking Jefferson during the 1800 election, see *The Providential Detection,* 1800, in Hutson, *Religion and the Founding,* 81, or see lcweb.loc.gov/exhibits/religion/re106-2.html.

22. Ellis, *American Sphinx,* 210.

23. Jefferson, *Jefferson's Extracts from the Gospels,* 14–15.

24. Jefferson, *Writings,* 1089.

25. Jefferson, *Jefferson's Extracts from the Gospels,* 14.

26. Donald J. D'Elia, "Jefferson, Rush and the Limits of Philosophical Friendship," *Proceedings of the American Philosophical Society* 117, no. 5 (October 25, 1973): 336–37.

27. Jefferson, *Jefferson's Extracts from the Gospels,* 19.

28. Fred C. Luebke, "The Origins of Thomas Jefferson's Anti-Clericalism," *Church History* 32, no 3 (1963): 352.

29. Jefferson, *Jefferson's Extracts from the Gospels,* 331.

30. Jefferson, *Jefferson's Extract from the Gospels,* 27, 369.

31. Jefferson, *Jefferson's Extract from the Gospels,* 59.

32. Jefferson, *Writings,* 492, emphasis added.

33. Jefferson, *Writings,* 493.

34. Merrill D. Peterson, *Thomas Jefferson and the New Nation: A Biography* (New York: Oxford University Press, 1970), 659.

35. Peterson, *Jefferson and the New Nation,* 659.

36. Jefferson, *Writings,* 493.

37. Jefferson, *Writings,* 493.

38. Noah Webster's 1828 American Dictionary of the English

Language defines *dreary* as meaning "gloomy" and "sorrowful." *Noah Webster's First Edition of an American Dictionary of the English Language* (1828; reprint, San Francisco: Foundation for American Christian Education, 1987).

39. Webster's 1828 Dictionary defines *love* as "kindness, benevolence, charity, and . . . the qualities which render social intercourse agreeable."

40. Jefferson, *Jefferson's Extracts from the Gospels*, 405.

41. Jefferson, *Writings*, 494.

42. Jefferson, *Writings*, 494.

43. Jefferson, *Writings*, 1380.

44. As Jefferson explains in his *Notes on Virginia,*

> The poor who have neither property, friends, nor strength to labour, are boarded in the houses of good farmers, to whom a stipulated sum is annually paid. To those who are able to help themselves a little, or have friends from whom they derive some succours, inadequate however to their full maintenance, supplementary aids are given, which enable them to live comfortably in their own houses, or in houses of their friends. Vagabonds, without visible property or vocation, are placed in workhouses, where they are well clothed, fed, lodged, and made to labour. Nearly the same method of providing for the poor prevails through all our states; and from Savannah to Portsmouth you will seldom meet a beggar. (Jefferson, *Writings*, 259.)

At the time Jefferson gave this report, Virginia's care of the poor was being carried out according to a law passed in 1775. This law was revised—largely through the efforts of Thomas Jefferson—in 1785, when the Virginia legislature passed a "Bill for Support of the Poor" designed to render aid and care to the "poor, lame, impotent, blind, and other inhabitants of the county as are not able to maintain themselves." Jefferson, *Papers of Thomas Jefferson*, 2:420. The major change between the policies of 1775 and 1785 was that, in keeping with Jefferson's desire for a stronger separation of church and state, the care for the poor was transferred from Anglican vestrymen to "aldermen" of the county. Manifesting, well after his presidency, an enthusiasm for his early Virginia program of local care of the poor, Jefferson wrote to Adams in 1813, "My proposition had for further object to impart to these wards those portions of self-government for which they were best qualified, confiding to them *the care of the poor,* their roads, their police . . . in short to have made them little republics." Jefferson, *Writings*, 1308.

45. Jefferson, *Writings*, 841–42.

"AWASH IN A SEA OF FAITH"
AMERICA AND THE SECOND GREAT AWAKENING

Grant Underwood

At the outset, I wish to credit distinguished Yale historian Jon Butler for the colorful phrase that makes up the forepart of my title.[1] Though my approach will diverge somewhat from Butler's fascinating and significant revisionist study of American religious history, I find his phrase felicitous for capturing an image of waves of religious fervor washing over the American cultural landscape between the Revolution and the Civil War.

RELIGION AND THE AMERICAN REVOLUTION

The Revolutionary era is widely considered to have been a watershed moment in American history, but exactly how it was so varies from observer to observer. In terms of American Christianity, some historians stress its negative impact.[2] Because of the war, they point out, churches were disorganized and some destroyed; Loyalist ministers fled and Patriot preachers left their locales to act as chaplains in the army. Moreover, the Revolution's leaders tended to be drawn from a group of men who had been influenced by the Enlightenment to favor "natural religion" or deism over scripture-based, denominationally organized religion.

The Revolution in its aftermath also gave considerable impetus to the tendency to move further west, where links with established Eastern churches were difficult to maintain and where, as one visiting cleric noted, the people acted "like freed prisoners," engaging in all sort of "barbarous" activity.[3] What all this meant was that the period immediately following the Revolution marked a low point in church attendance in United States history.[4]

And yet the Revolutionary era bequeathed to American Christianity its greatest gift—disestablishment.[5] No longer would particular churches be officially and financially fostered by the government. Church and state were to be separated and full liberty of conscience was to prevail. With disestablishment, each denomination had to make its way by the sheer force of its persuasive powers, and by that alone. Henceforth, religion would be conducted on the "voluntary principle," where the nature and degree of religious affiliation was left to personal choice without interference from the state. For some, this prospect was frightening. They believed that without state support of religion the very moral fabric of the Republic would unravel. Yet, as we shall see, the very opposite occurred. By the mid nineteenth century, America was to become the most "Christian" nation in the industrialized world, with its roots firmly planted in the rich soil of religious disestablishment.

REPUBLICANISM AND AMERICAN RELIGION

One of the most significant and salutary results of the American Revolution was that traditional authorities of all kinds, religious ones included, began to be questioned and reconsidered. If America and Americans could fend for themselves in matters political, why not in matters religious?[6] Though Elias Smith has largely slipped from history, in the early 1800s, he was one of the great champions of "republican" or populist religion. He charged that religion had too long been controlled by the ministerial guild with their college degrees, broadcloth attire, and fancy carriages. Smith and others rebelled against the need for mediating elites. "Many are republicans as to government, and yet are but half republicans," wrote Smith, "being in matters of religion still bound to a catechism, creed, covenant or a superstitious priest. Venture to be as independent in things of religion," he urged, "as those which respect the government in which you live."[7] Elias Smith was not the only one to apply political republicanism to religion. Lorenzo Dow, a popular Methodist preacher, declared, "If all men are 'BORN EQUAL,' and endowed with unalienable rights by their CREATOR, in the blessings of life, liberty, and the pursuit of happiness"—an obvious tie to the Declaration of Independence—"then there can be no just reason, as a cause, why he may or should not think, and judge, and act for himself in matters of religion, opinion, and private judgment."[8] Such statements as these epitomize the democratizing attitude toward religion that developed in America in the years following the Revolution.

Concurrently, religious journalism flowered in America. Many of these newspapers were edited by religious "republicans," and the press became one of their most effective means to challenge the established religious order. Elias Smith, whose *Herald of Gospel Liberty* (notice the link between Christianity and freedom) was the first religious newspaper in the United States, called the press "a short and cheap way" to present "a general knowledge" of his ideals.[9] At the forefront of the populist Christian agenda was the destruction of "priestcraft," their term of choice to derogate the ministerial guild. Several lines from Rogerene Baptist Timothy Waterous's "Priestcraft Float Away" typify the animosity religious republicans felt toward the established clergy:

> Why are we in such slavery, to men of that degree; Bound to support their knavery when we might all be free; They'r nothing but a canker, we can with boldness say; So let us hoist the anchor, let Priestcraft float away.[10]

Such sentiments both reflected and reinforced the broader democratization of Protestant Christianity then underway in the United States. By the mid-1830s, Alexis de Tocqueville would be able to generalize that religion in America was "republican religion."[11]

PRIMITIVISM

To some people the word "primitive" means "crude, backward, or undeveloped." As used in religious discussions of early nineteenth-century America, however, it carried a different connotation. Primitive drew directly from its Latin root *primus* to mean "first" and was related to other English words like "prime," "primary," and "primordial." In religious conversation, it was often used, like Joseph Smith used it, to describe the New Testament church. The "prime-itive" or "first" church was the one Jesus organized in the first century A.D. In the early 1800s, there was considerable interest in America in the primitive church. Aware of the spiritual barnacles that over the centuries had attached themselves to existing Christian traditions, religious souls in a variety of denominations sought to re-form their churches in the primitive mold. Historians refer to this quest for the primitive church as "Christian primitivism" or simply "primitivism." Many of those who joined The Church of

Jesus Christ of Latter-day Saints in its early years were primitivists who found Mormonism to be the restoration of New Testament Christianity.[12]

Primitivism provided a popular antidote to the perennial problem of priestcraft. Alexander Campbell, one of the leading primitivists of the early 1800s, described the problem succinctly: "The stream of Christianity has become polluted," and "all the reformations that have occurred . . . have failed to purify it."[13] The answer, explained Alexander's father, Thomas, was to return "to the original standard of Christianity, the profession and practice of the primitive Church, as expressly exhibited upon the sacred page of the New Testament scripture."[14] Nothing since then was of any value. Elias Smith "protest[ed] against that unrighteous and ungodly pretense of making the writings of the fathers [Catholic ecclesiastics of the first centuries A.D.], the decrees of counsels, and synods, or the sense of the church, the rule and standard of judging of the sense of Scriptures, as Popish, Anti-Christian, and dangerous to the church of God."[15] Primitivists sought to cast away nearly two thousand years of Christian theology as obfuscatory accretions of the ages. Only by engaging the New Testament directly and taking it alone for their sure guide could truth seekers return to pure Christian beginnings and completely bypass the clerical corruption of the intervening centuries.

To be sure, such an enterprise was limited by human bias. Primitivists looked down the tunnel of time hoping to perceive the timeless primordium of truth. What, for the most part, they actually saw was their own reflection. Unaware of such cultural conditioning, though, seekers proclaimed that scripture was perspicuous, transparent even to the lowliest plowboy. The only requisite aid to understanding it was a sincere and open mind. In the end, primitivism tended to produce a proliferation of competing Christianities. As John W. Nevin, prominent mid-nineteenth-century theologian, noted, the belief was widespread that "every congregation has power to originate a new Christianity for its own use."[16] Richard McNemar, a Methodist-turned-Presbyterian-turned-Christian-turned-Shaker, spoke from experience when he penned these lines:

> Ten thousand Reformewrs like so many moles
> Have plowed all the Bible and cut it [in] holes
> And each has his church at the end of his trace
> Built up as he thinks of the subjects of grace.[17]

If ordinary folk embraced such visions, so, too, did Enlightenment-influenced elites like Thomas Jefferson. Sounding quite primitivist, he wrote, "To the corruptions of Christianity, I am indeed opposed, but not the genuine precepts of Jesus himself. I am a Christian in the only sense in which he wished one to be; sincerely attached to his doctrines, in preference to all others."[18] Moreover, Jefferson linked his concept of primitive Christianity to his republican ideals: "Christian religion," he declared, "when divested of the rags in which they [the established clergy] have enveloped it, and brought to the original purity and simplicity of its benevolent institutor, is a religion of all others most friendly to liberty, science, and the freest expansion of the human mind."[19] Thomas Jefferson spent a number years going through his Bible and excising passages that in his view evidenced priestly corruptions. What was left—Jefferson's choices for the authentic teachings of Jesus—became known as the Jefferson Bible. Thus, even Jefferson created "a new Christianity for [his] own use."

The creation of such renewed Christianities had millennial overtones. Alexander Campbell claimed, "Just in so far as the ancient order of things, or the religion of the New Testament, is restored, just so far has the Millennium commenced."[20] This sort of millennial optimism was common in the era of the Second Great Awakening where revivals and camp meetings seemed to be bringing about a spiritual prelibation of paradise.

METHODISM

With the disestablishment of religion in the final quarter of the eighteenth century (Massachusetts and Connecticut held on into the nineteenth century), ministers had to compete with each other for adherents. Having previously relied on the state for support, the old established churches like the Anglicans (now Episcopalians) and Congregationalists were often ill-equipped to participate in the religious "free market" that emerged in the early Republic. Other denominations, especially the newer "upstart" religions, quickly adapted to this environment, however. As a result, religion in the new Republic "flourished in response to religious deregulation."[21] In the words of historian Martin Marty, "The evangelizers started a Soul Rush that soon outpaced the Gold Rush. Here was a textbook example of free enterprise in the marketplace of religion."[22]

No religion was more successful in the era's Soul Rush than the Methodists. Methodism began in England not as a break-away sect but as a movement within the Anglican Church.[23] John Wesley and his associates felt that Anglicanism had grown overly formal and cold. Nicknamed "methodists," they sought in small-group gatherings known as "classes" to recapture a vital, spirit-empowered religiosity, pursuing devotional exercises designed to invite the Spirit and reinvigorate the national church. This effort was similar in intent to the later, larger "revivals" that would sweep the transatlantic world. Revivals of whatever size or form were designed to "revive" the flickering flame of faith. A revival was not so much a venue where ministers tried to convert the unconverted, though that was an element of it. More than anything, it was an event at which backsliders could be reclaimed and lukewarm Christians "reheated."

Because of its connection to Church of England, Methodism had a slow start in America, but after the war, under the leadership of Francis Asbury, a man of patriotic loyalties and boundless energy, the group mushroomed.[24] This "Father of American

The Circuit Preacher. Copyprint of wood engraving, after drawing by Alfred R. Ward. *Harper's Weekly,* October 12, 1867. Such depictions illustrate the itinerant preachers' dedication in the face of hardships.

Methodism" was an extraordinarily spiritual man among a group already noted for their religious rigorism. Here is a sampling of entries from his faithfully-kept journal, compiled by Martin E. Marty:

> "My heart is still depressed for want of more religion." On another day, "I must lament that I am not perfectly crucified with God." And again: "A cloud rested on my mind, which was occasioned by talking and jesting. I also feel at times tempted to impatience and pride of heart." When someone tried to compliment him, Asbury suspected them of flattery inspired of Satan. No one ever caught a glimpse of his furrowed face smiling over innocent pleasantries.[25]

For Methodists, logging seat time in a chapel on Sunday was far from salvifically sufficient; spiritual virtuosity was demanded.

So was evangelism. Methodism played a prominent role in helping to "church" the West. Asbury and his itinerant preachers did not shy away from the challenge of reaching the tiny hamlets and backwoods huts of expanding America. Early on, Asbury expressed disdain for ministers "who had manifested a desire to abide in the cities and live like gentlemen . . . [they] seem unwilling to leave the cities . . . but I think that I shall show them the way."[26] Asbury spent the remainder of his life riding the circuit. He never married, never owned a home, and could carry the bulk of his possessions on horseback. Before dismounting for the last time, this spiritual Spartan described himself as "an old worn out old man of about sixty years, who has the power given him of riding five thousand miles a year, at a salary of eighty dollars, through summer heat and winter's cold, traveling in all weather, preaching in all places; his best covering from rain often but a blanket."[27]

Asbury not only set the standard for ministers of other faiths in reaching outlying and isolated areas, but he inspired his own army of itinerants who helped him take Methodism to every corner of the new republic. As superintending "bishop," Asbury assigned each of his preachers a circuit or particular geographic area in which to minister. Circuit riders would organize converts into classes and appoint a class leader to watch over them while the traveling preacher was away. Asbury constantly rotated his ministers and worked them very hard, but "never asked a preacher to endure that which he did not undertake regularly."[28] The "worn out" circuit rider, or the itinerant preacher whose poor health finally forced him to retire, was not an uncommon phenomenon in the early days of American Methodism. Still, some were smitten by a different "disease"—marriage. According to Marty, as Asbury's preachers accepted the hospitality of families on their circuits,

> they observed the cozy life and met attractive and nubile women. . . . Because the Bible called marriage honorable, Asbury had to show grudging respect for its status before God, but this assent never helped him enjoy marriage, the "ceremony awful as death." Asbury cried that he thus lost two hundred of his best traveling men

in the world and feared that "the devil and the women" would eventually get all his preachers.[29]

In the end, his fears were unwarranted. Methodism grew in a dramatic fashion despite the fact that many of his preachers had to "run to their dears almost every night."[30] In 1780, American Methodists numbered less than ten thousand. By 1830 they had reached half a million—nearly a third, by some counts, of all U.S. citizens formally affiliated with a church.[31] Not surprisingly, historians have labeled the early 1800s "the Age of Methodism," a fitting title not only because of the Methodists' numerical predominance but also because their evangelical techniques and spiritual emphases were contagious and spread to other denominations. Nathan Hatch has called it "the most powerful religious movement in American history, its growth a central feature in the emergence of the United States as a republic."[32]

REVIVALISM

To quote Mark Noll,

> The Second Great Awakening was the most influential revival of Christianity in the history of the United States. Its very size and its many expressions have led some historians to question whether a single Second Great Awakening can be identified as such. Yet from about 1795 to about 1810 there was a broad and general rekindling of interest in Christianity throughout the country. This renewal, in turn, provided a pattern and an impetus for similar waves of revival that continued throughout the nation until after the Civil War.[33]

Prominent among the settings for the Second Great Awakening were "camp meetings," multi-day, and sometimes multi-denominational, outdoor religious gatherings that attracted large crowds to "hear the word."[34] Alexis de Tocqueville offered this description of camp meetings:

> Almost every summer, it is true, some Methodist preachers come to make a tour of the new settlements. The noise of their arrival spreads with unbelievable rapidity from cabin to cabin: it's the great news of the day . . . people show themselves almost starved for religion. . . . They come from fifty miles around. It's not in a church that the

faithful gather, but in the open air under the forest foliage. A pulpit of badly squared logs, great trees felled for seats, such are the ornaments of this rustic temple. . . . It's there that, during three days and three nights, the crowd gives itself over to almost uninterrupted religious exercises.[35]

Though Methodists made widespread use of the camp meeting, so did the Baptists and even the Presbyterians. The most prominent camp meeting of the early Second Great Awakening, a massive convocation in Cane Ridge, Kentucky, was essentially a Presbyterian event led by James McGready.[36] McGready, however, invited the participation of Baptists and Methodists. "In that awful day, when the universe assembled must appear before the quick and the dead, the question brethren, will not be, were you a Presbyterian—a Seceeder—a Covenanter—a Baptist—or a Methodist; but, did you experience a new birth? Did you accept of Christ and his salvation as set forth in the Gospel?"[37] Spiritual rebirth rather than denominational recruitment was the focus of most camp meetings and revivals.

To bring about such a dramatic consequence required both a dramatic setting and dramatic preaching. "Father McGready would so describe Heaven," reported one participant in the Cane Ridge revival, "that you would almost see its glories, and long to be there, and he would so array hell and its horrors before the wicked, that they would tremble and quake, imagining a lake of fire and brimstone yawning to overwhelm them, and the wrath of God thrusting them down the horrible abyss."[38] As for the setting, another eyewitness reported:

At night, the whole scene was awfully sublime. The ranges of tents, the fires, reflecting light amidst the branches of the towering trees; the candles and lamps illuminating the encampment; hundreds moving to and fro, with lights or torches, like Gideon's army; the preaching, praying, singing and shouting, all heard at once, rushing from different parts of the ground, like the sound of many waters, was enough to swallow up all the powers of contemplation. Sinners falling, and shrieks and cries of mercy awakened in the mind a lively apprehension of the scene, when the awful sound will be heard, 'arise ye dead and come to Judgement [sic].[39]

Of course, extraordinary behavior had also characterized the First Great Awakening, but it was the "innovations" of the Second Great Awakening that caught people's attention. These included

the rolling exercise, the "barking" exercise, in which new converts, like coon dogs, "treed" the devil; and the "jerks," during which, the heads of participants "would jerk back suddenly, frequently causing them to yelp or make some other involuntary noise" . . . Heads often moved back and forth so fast 'that the hair of females would be made to crack like a carriage whip," showering bystanders with hair pins.[40]

Not all was white-hot spirituality at camp meetings. Participants also partook of a kind of festival atmosphere and camp meetings became major

Courtesy Library of Congress

Lorenzo Dow and the Jerking Exercise. Copyprint of engraving by Losing-Barritt, c. 1840. An artist's redition of the intense nature of camp-meeting revivalism.

social events in their locales. On the isolated frontier, entertainment was at a premium. One contemporary observer claimed that the purpose of camp meetings was often to "engage our affections to the novelties of the scenes, and the greetings of new faces, and the hospitality of reciprocal visits, the exemption from the usual labours and cares."[41] A good deal of socializing and even courting took place at camp meetings. This mixture of pleasure and piety, religion and recreation evoked criticism. "All these things may give pleasing agitations to the mind," wrote one critic, "but are they holy? . . . Take away the worship, and there would remain sufficient gratifications to allure most of the young people, and thousands if equally fed and freed from labour would follow."[42] Often there was the allegation of rampant sexual impropriety. At camp meetings "more souls were begot than saved," wrote one wag.[43] Converts, however, sought to counteract such caricature. After the "Great Revival" swept through western Virginia in the early 1800s, one commentator noted, "Formerly, when [people] collected together, drinking, swearing, horseracing, fighting, and such like practices, were common among them—But now . . . you will seldom see one pursuing any of these practices."[44]

Oberlin College Archives, Oberlin, Ohio

Charles Grandison Finney and his wife, photograph taken during their visit to England. Finney developed a system of "producing" revivals that was highly successful in the United States during the 1820s and 1830s.

Not all revivals occurred in camp meetings and not all took place on the frontier. The revival, for instance, that broke out contemporaneously at Yale College under President Timothy Dwight, grandson of First Great Awakening luminary Jonathan Edwards, was a good deal more subdued than the Cane Ridge exuberance.[45] Indeed, both the appropriate character and the proper theology of revivals continued to be debated among Presbyterians for years and was major cause of the New School/Old School schism of 1837.[46] The traditional idea had been that while revivals could be prayed for, they were unpredictable, divinely-orchestrated outpourings that would occur only when and where God designed.

Reflecting the changed tenor of the times in the early 1800s, Charles Grandison Finney embraced "new measures" and became the great architect of revivals on demand. In his famous *Lectures on Revivals of Religion,* he laid out his philosophy logically and boldly, like the former lawyer that he was:

> There has long been an idea prevalent that promoting religion has something very peculiar in it, not to be judged of by the ordinary rules of cause and effect; in short, that there is no connection of the means with the result, and no tendency in the means to produce the effect. No doctrine is more dangerous than this to the prosperity of the church, and nothing more absurd.

Suppose a man were to go and preach this doctrine among the farmers, about their sowing grain. Let him tell them that God is a sovereign, and will give them a crop only when it pleases him, and that for them to plow and plant and labor as if they expected to raise a crop is very wrong, and taking the work out of the hands of God, that it interferes with his sovereignty, and is going on in there own strength; and that there is no connection between the means and the result on which they can depend.[47]

For Finney, revivals were not a mystery; there was a science to them which, once learned, could be applied over and over again with predictable success. A revival of religion, he wrote,

is not a miracle, or dependent on a miracle, in any sense. It is a purely philosophical [scientific] result of the right use of the constituted means. . . . I said that a revival is the result of the right use of the appropriate means. . . . But means will not produce a revival, we all know, without the blessing of God. No more will grain, when it is sowed, produce a crop without the blessing of God.

Still, he argued, though God's influence was indisputable, "I fully believe that could facts be known" in all previous instances of religious revival, "it would be found that when the appointed means have been rightly used, spiritual blessings have been obtained with greater uniformity than temporal ones."[48]

Theologically speaking, Finney's philosophy was a kind of "Arminianized Calvinism," the view that humans could choose to believe, to positively act for their salvation, rather than passively wait to be acted upon by God. As historian William McLoughlin has noted, such a perspective came to represent "a new ideological consensus after 1830."[49] Historian Timothy Smith explained that "the new evangelical synthesis required frank abandonment of the Old Calvinism," and noted "the appeal in a Christian democratic society of the Arminian doctrines of free will, free grace, and unlimited hope for the conversion of all men." In short, the Calvinist "idea of personal predestination could hardly survive amidst the evangelists' earnest entreaties to 'come unto Jesus.'"[50] However revivals were envisioned— as unexpected rain from God or the right use of constituted means—and however they were experienced—as subdued inner stirrings of the soul while one was seated in a stately urban chapel or as physical and emotional ecstasy in a sprawling, raucous camp meeting—revivals played a profound role in the creation of the myth, if not the reality, of a "Christian America."

REVIVALISM AND SOCIAL REFORM

Social reform efforts had been undertaken before, and would continue to be pursued after, the Second Great Awakening, but the revivals of the early 1800s provided a major impetus to such activities.[51] Those converted to Christ were to consecrate their lives to him and serve their fellow man as he did. It was the natural consequence of a changed heart. As Finney explained, Christians "will be filled with a tender and burning love for souls. They will have a longing desire for the salvation of the whole world. They will be in agony for individuals whom they want to have saved; their friends, relations, enemies."[52] Not surprisingly, as the Awakening spread so did missionary and tract societies. The executive committee of the American Tract Society founded in 1825 offered this justification for the society's existence: "A Minister may distribute Tracts among his people, and thus impress and extend his public instructions where the impressions of his official duty would otherwise be lost, or never extended; and in this way he may double his usefulness, and devote two lives to his Master's glory instead of one."[53]

Revivalism, however, generated more than just a concern for conversion. It raised questions about long-term religious obligations. What kind of Christian life should follow the "quickly achieved step of conversion? How would one live, by what signposts, in a world that supplied an ever-changing and evanescent offering of wants and needs? . . . Reform began to answer such questions."[54] The consecrated Christian was to carry the gospel into every walk of life, and reborn believers banded together in a great variety of societies intent on Christianizing the social and political fabric of America. Temperance, sabbatarian, and antislavery societies labored to eradicate their designated evils. Organizations to help the poor, the insane, the blind worked to alleviate suffering.[55] Such societies reflected the contemporary "perfectionist" emphasis that sin, both personal and societal, could be totally eradicated. It was the obligation of every true Christian to help bring it about.

This "Benevolent Empire" of interdenominational associations and reform societies that arose in the years following the Revolutionary War exerted a significant moral influence in antebellum America. Writes Timothy Smith, "The churches were making a far greater impact upon American society than their numbers or separation from the state would imply."[56] Much of this success can be credited to the enthusiastic and sustained involvement of women in the societies of the Benevolent Empire, as well as to their heightened role, in the nineteenth-century world of "separate spheres" for men and women, as moral guardians of their own homes.[57] This, Alexis de Tocqueville claimed, enabled men to better perform their public roles: when "the American [male] retires from the turmoil of public life to the bosom of his family, he finds in it the image of order and of peace. . . . While the European endeavors to forget his domestic troubles by agitating society, the American derives from his own home that love of order which he afterwards carries with him into public affairs."[58]

Some evangelists and reformers, as did their primitivist contemporaries, thought they saw in all of this the dawning of a new age. In 1835, Charles Finney predicted, "If the church will do all her duty, the millennium may come in this country in three years."[59] No effort was to be spared when such a magnificent prize was in view. According to John L. Thomas, this "romantic faith in perfectibility, originally confined by religious institutions, overflow[ed] these barriers and [spread] across the surface of society, seeping into politics and culture."[60] Yet, the hoped-for millennium was not to

be realized. In the words of James D. Bratt, "The three years Finney had targeted for the millennial dawn brought twilight instead."[61] Not only did Finney himself eventually retire from the fray but evangelical attention generally shifted to the massive influx of Irish Catholics into the country and to the nation's growing sectional tension. By 1845 both the Baptist and the Methodist churches had split along the Mason-Dixon line.[62] During and after the Civil War, the ebullient, perfectionist optimism of an earlier generation gave way to an acute awareness of the intransigence of many contemporary problems caused by industrialization, immigration, and urbanization.[63]

CONCLUSION

Looking back over the period between the American Revolution and the Civil War, it is clear that in the United States disestablishment did not, as some feared, sound the death knell of Christianity. Rather, it unleashed the "voluntary principle," which created the necessary climate for healthy and pervasive growth. Republicanism became a distinguishing characteristic of religion as well as government. Primitivism, with its faith in the fresh start and its manifestation of creative vitality, insured that "the American religious tradition was born and reborn."[64] The Second Great Awakening, despite its exotic excesses, rejuvenated the spiritual life of many otherwise "formal" Christians and compelled them to carry their principles into social, economic, and political arenas.[65] In sum, the circumstances and events of this era combined to make America, more than ever before, "awash in a sea of faith." Thus, that astute foreign observer Alexis de Tocqueville could proclaim in the mid-1830s that "there is no country in the world where the Christian religion retains a greater influence over the souls of men than in America." For de Tocqueville, America's religiosity was proof that "if the human mind be left to follow its own bent, it will regulate the temporal and spiritual institutions of society in a uniform manner, and man will endeavor, if I may so speak, to harmonize earth with heaven."[66]

Notes

1. Jon Butler, *Awash in a Sea of Faith: Christianizing the American People* (Cambridge: Harvard University Press, 1990).

2. Reviewed and assessed in Douglas H. Sweet, "Church Vitality and the American Revolution: Historiographical Consensus and Thoughts towards a New Perspective," *Church History* 45 (1976): 341–57. For a sampling of writing on religion and the Revolution, see William Warren Sweet, *The Story of Religion in America,* 2d ed. (New York: Harper, 1950), 172–204; and Mark A. Noll, *Christians in the American Revolution* (Grand Rapids, Mich.: Christian University Press, 1977).

3. Isaac D. Denman, letter, January 7, 1826, quoted in William Warren Sweet, "The Churches as Moral Courts of the Frontier," *Church History* 2 (March 1933): 8.

4. Butler, *Awash in a Sea of Faith,* 213.

5. For what follows in this paragraph, see William Lee Miller, *The First Liberty: Religion and the American Republic* (New York: Knopf, 1985); and Ronald Hoffman and Peter Albert, eds., *Religion in a Revolutionary Age* (Charlottesville: University Press of Virginia, 1994).

6. The discussion that follows relies on Nathan O. Hatch, *The Democratization of American Christianity* (New Haven: Yale University Press, 1989).

7. Elias Smith, *The Loving Kindness of God Displayed in the Triumph of Republicanism in America* (n.p., 1809), 32, quoted in Hatch, *The Democratization of American Christianity,* 69–70.

8. Lorenzo Dow, *History of Cosmopolite; Or, the Four Volumes of Lorenzo Dow's Journal* (Wheeling, Va.: Joshua Martin, 1814), 356–57, quoted in Hatch, *Democratization of American Christianity,* 37.

9. Elias Smith, *Herald of Gospel Liberty,* September 1, 1808, p. 1, quoted in Hatch, *Democratization of American Christianity,* 70, 73. Hatch, *Democratization of American Christianity,* 70, claims Smith's paper was the first of its kind in the United States.

10. Timothy Waterous, *The Battle-Axe and Weapons of War: . . . Aimed at the Final Destruction of Priestcraft* (Groton, Conn.: n.p., 1811), quoted in Hatch, *Democratization of American Christianity,* 45.

11. Alexis de Tocqueville, *Democracy in America,* trans. Henry Reeve, ed. Phillips Bradley, 2 vols. (New York: Alfred A. Knopf, 1945), 1:300.

12. On primitivism, see Richard T. Hughes, ed., *The American Quest for the Primitive Church* (Urbana: University of Illinois Press, 1988); and Richard T. Hughes and C. Leonard Allen, *Illusions of Innocence: Protestant Primitivism in America, 1630–1875* (Chicago: University of Chicago Press, 1988). Regarding Mormons and Primitivism, see Marvin S. Hill, "The Role of Christian Primitivism in the Origin and Development of the Mormon Kingdom, 1830–1844" (Ph.D. diss., University of Chicago, 1968).

13. Alexander Campbell, *Millennial Harbinger,* 1832, p. 13, quoted in Hatch, *Democratization of American Christianity,* 167.

14. Bill J. Humble, "The Restoration Ideal in the Churches of Christ," in *American Quest for the Primitive Church,* 222.

15. Elias Smith, *The Life, Conversion, Preaching, Travels and Sufferings of Elias Smith* (Portsmouth, N.H.: n.p., 1816), 352–53, quoted in Nathan O. Hatch, "*Sola Scriptura* and *Novus Ordo Seclorum,*" in *The Bible in America: Essays in Cultural History,* ed. Nathan O. Hatch and Mark A. Noll (New York and Oxford: Oxford University Press, 1982), 67.

16. John W. Nevin, "The Antichrist and the Sect System," cited in *The Mercersburg Theology,* ed. James Hastings Nichols (New York: Oxford University Press, 1966), 104, 111.

17. Richard McNemar, "The Moles Little Pathways," quoted in Hatch, *Democratization of American Christianity,* 81.

18. Thomas Jefferson, *Jefferson's Extracts from the Gospels: "The Philosophy of Jesus" and "The Life and Morals of Jesus,"* ed. Dickinson W. Adams and Ruth W. Lester (Princeton, N.J.: Princeton University Press, 1983), 331.

19. Thomas Jefferson, *Writings,* ed. Merrill D. Peterson (New York: Viking Press, 1984), 1087–88.

20. Alexander Campbell, in *The Christian Baptist* 2 (February 7, 1825): 136, quoted in Hughes and Allen, *Illusions of Innocence,* 173.

21. Roger Finke and Laurence R. Iannaccone, "Supply-Side Explanations for Religious Change," *The Annals of the American Academy of Political and Social Science* 527 (May 1993): 29. See also Roger Finke and Rodney Stark, "How the Upstart Sects Won America: 1776–1850," *Journal for the Scientific Study of Religion* 28 (March 1989): 27–44.

22. Martin E. Marty, *Pilgrims in Their Own Land: 500 Years in America* (Boston: Little, Brown, 1984), 169.

23. On the origins and growth of Methodism, see Richard P. Heitzenrater, *Wesley and a People Called Methodists* (Nashville: Abingdon Press, 1995).

24. Two indispensable recent studies of early American Methodism and Francis Asbury's role in its growth are John H. Wigger, *Taking Heaven by Storm: Methodism and the Rise of Popular Christianity in America* (Urbana: University of Illinois Press, 2001); and Dee E. Andrews, *The Methodists and Revolutionary America, 1760–1800* (Princeton: Princeton University Press, 2002).

25. Marty, *Pilgrims in Their Own Land,* 172.

26. Asbury, *Journal and Letters,* 1:10, 85, quoted in Hatch, *Democratization of American Christianity,* 85.

27. Asbury, *Journal and Letters,* 2:417, quoted in Hatch, *Democratization of American Christianity,* 86.

28. Hatch, *Democratization of American Christianity,* 86.

29. Marty, *Pilgrims in Their Own Land,* 173.

30. Quoted in Marty, *Pilgrims in Their Own Land,* 173.

31. Edwin Gaustad and Philip Barlow, *New Historical Atlas of Religion in America* (Oxford: Oxford University Press, 2001), 219–28, 374; and Finke and Iannaccone, "Supply-Side Explanations," 33.

32. Nathan O. Hatch, "The Puzzle of American Methodism," *Church History* 63 (June 1994): 177.

33. Mark A. Noll, *A History of Christianity in the United States and Canada* (Grand Rapids, Mich.: Eerdmans, 1992), 166. A convenient overview of the Second Great Awakening can be found in William G. McLoughlin, *Revivals, Awakenings, and Reform: An Essay on Religion and Social Change in America, 1607–1977* (Chicago: University of Chicago Press, 1978).

34. On camp meetings specifically, see Charles A. Johnson, *The Frontier Camp Meeting: Religion's Harvest Time* (Dallas: Southern Methodist University Press, 1955); and Dickson D. Bruce, *And They All Sang Hallelujah: Plain-Folk Camp-Meeting Religion, 1800–1845* (Knoxville: University of Tennessee Press, 1974). Kenneth O. Brown, *Holy Ground: A Study of the American Camp Meeting* (New York: Garland, 1992) emphasizes Methodist origins and prominence in the camp-meeting phenomenon.

35. George W. Pierson, *Tocqueville and Beaumont in America* (New York: Oxford University Press, 1938), 249, quoted in Johnson, *The Frontier Camp Meeting,* 232.

36. See Paul K. Conkin, *Cane Ridge: America's Pentecost* (Madison: University of Wisconsin Press, 1990).

37. James McGready, *The Posthumous Works of the Reverend and Pious James M'Gready,* ed. James Smith, 2 vols. (Louisville: W. W. Worsley, 1931–33), 2:71, quoted in John B. Boles, *The Great*

Revival, 1787–1805: The Origins of the Southern Evangelical Mind (Lexington: University Press of Kentucky, 1972), 40.

38. F. R. Cossitt, *The Life and Times of Rev. Finis Ewing* (Louisville: L. R. Woods, 1853), 43, quoted in Boles, *Great Revival*, 40.

39. Theophilus Armenius [psued.], "Account of the Rise and Progress of the Work of God in the Western Country," *Methodist Magazine* 2 (1819): 273, quoted in Boles, *Great Revival*, 67.

40. Daniel Cohen, *The Spirit of the Lord: Revivalism in America* (New York: Four Winds, 1975), 19, quoted in James H. Hutson, *Religion and the Founding of the American Republic* (Washington, D.C.: Library of Congress, 1998), 104.

41. "Scurator," 1822, quoted in Johnson, *Frontier Camp Meeting*, 208.

42. "Scurator," quoted in Johnson, *Frontier Camp Meeting*, 208.

43. Cohen, *The Spirit of the Lord*, 22, quoted in Hutson, *Religion and the Founding of the American Republic*, 105.

44. "Extract from a Letter from a Missionary to His Friend in Rockbridge County," *Virginia Religious Magazine* 1 (July 1805): 232, quoted in Boles, *Great Revival*, 187.

45. See Charles Roy Keller, *The Second Great Awakening in Connecticut* (1942; reprint, Hamden, Conn.: Archon Books, 1968).

46. See George M. Marsden, *The Evangelical Mind and the New School Presbyterian Experience: A Case Study of Thought and Theology in Nineteenth-Century America* (New Haven: Yale University Press, 1970).

47. Charles Grandison Finney, *Lectures on Revivals of Religion*, ed. William G. McLoughlin (Cambridge: Belknap Press of Harvard University Press, 1960), 14.

48. Finney, *Lectures on Revivals of Religion*, 13, 15.

49. McLoughlin, *Revivals, Awakenings, and Reform*, 138.

50. Timothy L. Smith, *Revivalism and Social Reform: American Protestantism on the Eve of the Civil War* (1957; reprint, Baltimore: Johns Hopkins University Press, 1980), 88–89.

51. See Smith, *Revivalism and Social Reform*; and Leonard I. Sweet, *The Evangelical Tradition in America* (Macon, Ga.: Mercer University Press, 1984).

52. Finney, *Lectures on Revivals of Religion*, 16.

53. Quoted in Edwin S. Gaustad, *A Documentary History of Religion in America to the Civil War* (Grand Rapids, Mich.: Eerdmans, 1982), 333.

54. Robert H. Abzug, *Cosmos Crumbling: American Reform and the Religious Imagination* (New York: Oxford University Press, 1994), 80.

55. See Clifford S. Griffin, *Their Brothers' Keepers: Moral Stewardship in the United States, 1800–1865* (New Brunswick, N.J.: Rutgers University Press, 1960); and Charles I. Foster, *An Errand of Mercy: The Evangelical United Front, 1790–1837* (Chapel Hill: University of North Carolina Press, 1960).

56. Smith, *Revivalism and Social Reform*, 44.

57. See A. Gregory Schneider, *The Way of the Cross Leads Home: The Domestication of American Methodism* (Bloomington: Indiana University Press, 1993); and Colleen McDannell, *The Christian Home in Victorian America, 1840–1900* (Bloomington: Indiana University Press, 1986).

58. Tocqueville, *Democracy in America*, 1:304.

59. Finney, *Lectures on Revivals of Religion*, 306.

60. John L. Thomas, "Romantic Reform in America, 1815–1865," *American Quarterly* 17, no. 4 (winter 1965): 656.

61. James D. Bratt, "The Reorientation of American Protestantism, 1835–1845," *Church History* 67 (March 1998): 61.

62. See C. C. Goen, *Broken Churches, Broken Nation: Denominational Schisms and the Coming of the American Civil War* (Macon, Ga.: Mercer University Press, 1985).

63. James Moorhead, "The Erosion of Postmillennialism in American Religious Thought, 1865–1925," *Church History* 53 (March 1984): 61–77.

64. Butler, *Awash in a Sea of Faith*, 291.

65. See Richard Carwardine, *Evangelicals and Politics in Antebellum America* (New Haven: Yale University Press, 1993).

66. Tocqueville, *Democracy in America*, 1:303, 300.

COULD A CATHOLIC BECOME AN AMERICAN?

THE CATHOLIC EXPERIENCE IN THE EARLY YEARS OF THE COUNTRY

Bishop George Niederauer

Could a Catholic become an American? The short answer is, Yes, with difficulty. This struggle was somewhat ironic because, as historian Sydney Ahlstrom points out, "The Roman Catholic church has a longer history in America—even in the United States—than any other Christian denomination."[1] What follows is a longer, detailed answer to this question, focusing on the colonial period and the early years of the republic until the Civil War.

James Hutson, at the beginning of *Religion and the Founding of the American Republic*, observes that European countries sought religious uniformity, either Protestant or Catholic: within almost every nation-state, only one profession and observance of religion was acceptable, and the Catholics and Protestants who settled the New World generally brought their intolerance with them.[2]

Catholics had a presence in North America from the beginning of colonization. North of the English colonies along the Atlantic seaboard, there was Catholic New France (present-day Canada). The French spread throughout North America, giving names to various American places. To the south there was New Spain, also

Catholic, and, like the French, the Spanish had a presence in the region that is now the United States, in Florida and in the West.

The colonies settled by the English, which eventually became the original thirteen states, were almost entirely Protestant. John Adams wrote of New England in 1765, "Roman Catholics are as scarce as a comet or an earthquake."[3] One exception to the generally Protestant colonies was Maryland. In 1632, George Calvert (Lord Baltimore), a convert to Catholicism in 1624, obtained a charter from Charles I, and in 1634 the *Ark* and the *Dove* sailed for Maryland. During the next twenty-five years the fortunes of religious toleration within Maryland waxed and waned with the religious passions characteristic of the English Civil War. Maryland enacted a "General Toleration" so that "all sorts who profess Christianity . . . might be at Liberty to worship God in such manner as was most agreeable with their Judgments and Consciences,"[4] but the Catholic establishment in Maryland was in continual conflict with the Protestants in that colony as well as with those from Virginia. Religious liberty for Catholics in Maryland died out after the "Glorious

Courtesy Historic St. Mary's City, Maryland

Chapel Interior, by Leslie Barker. Gouache on paper, 1997. The Catholic Church at St. Mary's City, Maryland, built ca. 1670, was the first free-standing Roman Catholic Church in British North America.

in positions of power in the colonies (seventeenth-century Maryland and New York), Catholics promoted the principle of religious toleration; (4) In the absence of one overwhelming Protestant denomination, Catholics benefited from some resultant, if grudging, toleration.[5] To quote Ahlstrom, "The period from 1692 to the American Revolution justifiably became known as the Penal Period, during which the church subsisted on a private, almost clandestine basis, while individual Catholics constantly were threatened or visited with legal actions."[6]

The American Revolution brought together citizens from colonies with varying traditions of religious tolerance. In his recent popular biography of John Adams, David McCullough tells a revealing story about Adams during a session of the Continental Congress in Philadelphia.[7] "Led by curiosity and good company," Adams wrote to his wife, he went with George Washington and others to an afternoon mass at St. Mary's Catholic Church on Fifth Street. Adams was greatly intrigued by the strangeness of the entire experience; the music, bells, candles, gold, and silver were so "calculated to take in mankind" that he wondered the Reformation had ever succeeded. The New Englander found remarkable both what he did and did not like: he felt pity for "the poor wretches fingering their beads, chanting Latin, not a word of which they understood," but the music and chanting went on "most sweetly and exquisitely," and he liked the "good, short moral essay" the priest gave on the duty of parents to see to

Revolution" of 1689, with the establishment of the Church of England in Maryland in 1692. The Quaker regimes in Pennsylvania and Delaware allowed Catholics unqualified and universal religious liberty, and many Catholics moved north from Maryland.

John Tracy Ellis, in his excellent survey *American Catholicism,* sums up the situation of the few thousand Catholics in colonial English America in these four points: (1) There was a universal anti-Catholic bias; (2) Catholics were few in number and clung stubbornly to their faith; (3) When they were twice their children's temporal and spiritual welfare. What is most interesting about this episode is how completely unfamiliar Adams was with Roman Catholic worship and how daring he imagined his visit to be.

Catholic leaders figured into the Revolution out of proportion to their actual numbers. Charles Carroll, a Catholic from Maryland, signed the Declaration of Independence. Catholics from France and Poland figured as heroes in the Revolution, including Lafayette, Pulaski, and Kosciusko. John Barry, the first commander of the American Navy, was a Catholic. In 1776, the Continental Congress asked Charles Carroll and his cousin John Carroll, a Jesuit priest, to accompany Benjamin Franklin and Samuel Chase to Canada to win Canadian support for the Revolution, which they were not able to do. About the same time, 1775, George Washington, commander of the Continental Army, forbade the popular tradition of burning the pope in effigy, condemning the "observance of that ridiculous and childish custom," because "insulting their religion is so monstrous as not to be suffered or excused."[8] Besides, the practice was not designed to endear Americans to the French or the French Canadians.

The American Revolution marked an advance in Catholic toleration in America. At the end of the war, several states willingly granted toleration for Catholics. According to Ellis, "The patriotic part played by the Catholics during the war, the influence of the French alliance, and the growing consciousness of the extreme complexity of the American Religious pattern—all helped to dilute the anti-Catholic-bias."[9] Indeed, Charles Carroll expressed the hope that "freedom and independence, acquired by united efforts and cemented with the mingled blood of Protestant and Catholic fellow citizens should be equally enjoyed by all."[10] While Carroll's cousin Daniel Carroll of Maryland and Thomas FitzSimons of Pennsylvania would both sign the Constitution of the United States, Charles's hope was not to be entirely realized. In 1789, George Washington became the new nation's first President and Father John Carroll was appointed the first Catholic bishop in the new country. Nevertheless, Catholics had equal citizenship with Protestants in only five of the original thirteen states. Religious liberty was spotty for Catholics in New England. Until 1833 they were barred from public office in Massachusetts, and in New Hampshire the religious test for holding public office was abolished only in 1877, twelve years after the end of the Civil War.[11]

In 1785 the United States had a population of almost 4,000,000 persons, only 25,000 of whom were Roman Catholics, located mostly in Maryland and Pennsylvania.[12] After 1820 the story of the country and the American Catholic Church was one of enormous and rapid population growth. Between 1820 and 1860, the general population grew from 8,000,000 to 27,000,000, and the Catholic population grew from 200,000 to 3,000,000. In 1789 roughly one half of 1 percent of the nation was Catholic; by the beginning of the Civil War the figure was 11 percent. (In 2002, 23 percent of Americans were Catholic.) By 1850, Catholics had become the largest religious denomination in the country. In that same year, Germans constituted one-half of all the foreign-born persons in the United States, but German Catholics settled in Midwestern villages and farms, thus attracting less attention. The Irish (numbering one million in mid-century) clustered in the cities of the Eastern seaboard and alarmed American Protestants as an "invasion" of persons who seemed alien in culture, ethos, worldview, and religious practice.[13]

Analyzing the situation of American Catholics in 1850, Ellis observes that they suffered from the traditional prejudice most Americans entertained for the Catholic Church, and the organized attacks of Protestants drove Catholics back among themselves in schools, in the press, and in social apartness. The Harvard historian Professor Arthur Schlesinger Sr. once remarked to Ellis, "I regard the prejudice against your Church as the deepest bias in the history of the American people."[14] In *Innocents Abroad,* the honest and direct Mark Twain admitted, "I have been educated to enmity toward everything that is Catholic, and sometimes, in consequence of this, I find it much easier to discover Catholic faults than Catholic merits."[15] Twain was probably speaking for many of his fellow citizens, though with considerably more self-awareness.

The lack of self-awareness in anti-Catholics in 1850 was important. Yet, the virulent antipathy toward Catholicism during the middle decades of the nineteenth century in this country must be understood in context. It cannot be excused but it can be better understood and explained. One Catholic historian has observed that because of the flood of newcomers and the rapid growth of the cities, "the feeling of a world awry easily slipped into a racist reaction against the new immigrants."[16] Another has remarked that the opposition to Catholics was more than bigotry and prejudice; it was "the turmoil of an entire society experiencing the stress of changing identity and self-definition."[17] Indeed, nativism, rapid economic change, population growth, and urbanization, coupled with religious bigotry, all factored into the conflicts between evangelical Protestants and Catholics throughout nineteenth-century America.

Beginning in the 1830s, nativism was a movement directed against foreigners in general and Catholics in particular. In the good times of expansion, before the financial panic of 1837, immigrants had been welcomed. In tougher economic times, hostile attitudes developed. For example, take Samuel F. B. Morse, of Morse code fame. As one Catholic writer has quipped, he electrified the country in more than one way. A passionate bigot, Morse founded and financed journals, such as *Foreign Conspiracy*, directed against Catholics.[18] Such publications had their effect, as did some of the preaching in Protestant pulpits. In 1834 in Charlestown, a suburb of Boston, the Presbyterian minister Lyman Beecher, father of Harriet Beecher Stowe, preached a sermon, "The Devil and the Pope of Rome." This and other sermons by Beecher are considered largely responsible for incitement of the mob that burned down the local Ursuline convent and school—the nuns and their students narrowly escaped with their lives.[19] For a year after the burning of the convent, Catholics in Boston and Charlestown had to post armed guards around their churches. In 1835, Bishop Fenwick was burned in effigy, and in 1837 another mob burned down most of the section of Boston where the Irish lived.

In 1844 conflicts between nativists and Irish, much of which focused on the use of Protestant Bibles in public schools, erupted into a three-day riot, during which two Catholic churches were burned down, many Catholic houses were plundered, thirteen people were killed, and fifty were injured.[20] During this same period, pitched battles between rival mobs were a feature of almost every big city election day. The fracas in Philadelphia emboldened anti-Catholic nativists in New York City, who had assumed, incorrectly, that the forceful Bishop John Hughes would be as mild and deferential as Philadelphia's Bishop Kenrick. Hughes stationed armed guards around the city's Catholic churches and threatened that the Catholics would turn New York into a "second Moscow" if Catholic churches were burned. The mayor and his council tried to put the blame for the dangerous situation on the bishop, pleading with him to restrain his flock. Hughes responded: "I have not the power; you must take care that they are not provoked."[21] The nativists decided not to provoke the Catholics, and the crisis passed.

Nativism, however, had not passed. In 1852 the nativists organized a national political party, pledged to "resist the insidious policy of the Church of Rome and all other foreign influence against our republican institutions in all lawful ways; to place in all offices of trust, honor or profit in the gift of the people or by appointment, none but native American Protestant citizens."[22] This resolve was often sealed with Masonic-style secret oaths and gestures, which gave the popular name "Know-Nothings" to the members. Between 1854 and 1856, the Know-Nothings were quite successful politically, electing governors in New York, Rhode Island, New Hampshire, Massachusetts, and Connecticut. In

1856 they ran former president Millard Fillmore as their candidate for president of the United States. A year earlier, the New York state legislature had passed the Putnam Act, forbidding Catholic bishops to hold property in their own names.[23] It was quietly repealed in 1863, when the government needed the Church's support for unpopular conscription procedures during the Civil War.

The heightened sectional tensions that were to erupt into the American Civil War overshadowed the nativist controversy and ultimately led to the downfall of the Know-Nothing party. Likewise, the violence and secrecy that Know-Nothingism engendered were decried by the majority of "native Americans." Further, many Americans did take seriously the American principle of freedom of conscience. Abraham Lincoln was one of these, and, as on most issues, was ahead of his time on the subject of religious bigotry. The political landscape was chaotic during the 1850s, populated by old-fashioned Whigs and Democrats and newly arrived Republicans and Know-Nothings. When challenged to declare his allegiance, Lincoln said:

> I am not a Know-Nothing. That is certain . . . How could I be? How can anyone who abhors the oppression of negroes, be in favor of degrading classes of white people? Our progress in degeneracy appears to me to be pretty rapid. As a nation we began by declaring that 'all men are created equal.' We now practically read it, 'all men are created equal, except negroes.' When the Know-Nothings get control, it will read, 'all men are created equal except negroes, and foreigners, and catholics.' When it comes to this I should prefer emigrating to some country where they make no pretence of loving liberty—to Russia, for instance, where despotism can be taken pure, and without the base alloy of hypocracy [sic].[24]

Years earlier, in 1844, at a meeting of the Whigs in Springfield, Illinois, Lincoln introduced the following resolution:

> Resolved, That the guarantee of the rights of conscience, as found in our Constitution, is most sacred and inviolable, and one that belongs no less to the Catholic, than to the Protestant; and that all attempts to abridge or interfere with these rights, either of Catholic or Protestant, directly or indirectly, have our decided disapprobation, and

shall ever have our most effective oppositions.[25]

Mr. Lincoln's was the direction the country chose, though not without detours aplenty. By the end of the Civil War, Americans had grown more comfortable with both immigration (western European at least) and the Catholic religion to which many of these immigrants adhered. Gradually Americans came to see that the melting pot may obscure, but it does not obliterate, our differences, including our religious differences—and the nation is the richer for it. The election of John F. Kennedy in 1960 marked a final triumph in the process of American acceptance of Catholicism. As one Catholic historian claimed, "The election . . . signified not only the decline of anti-Catholicism but also the fact that the country had actually redefined its identity in such a way as to render Catholicism compatible with America."[26] Thus, America's rocky progress toward religious tolerance had reached a major milestone.

Notes

1. Sydney E. Ahlstrom, *A Religious History of the American People* (New Haven, Conn.: Yale University Press, 1972), 527.

2. James H. Hutson, *Religion and the Founding of the American Republic* (Washington: Library of Congress, 1998), 2.

3. Quoted in Newman C. Eberhardt, *A Summary of Catholic History*, 2 vols. (St. Louis: Herder, 1962), 2:119.

4. Hutson, *Religion and the Founding*, 12–13.

5. John Tracy Ellis, *American Catholicism*, 2d ed. (Chicago: University of Chicago Press, 1969), 19.

6. Ahlstrom, *Religious History of the American People*, 339.

7. Quoted in David McCullough, *John Adams* (New York: Simon and Schuster, 2001), 88.

8. Quoted in Eberhardt, *Summary of Catholic History*, 2:418.

9. Ellis, *American Catholicism*, 37.

10. Hutson, *Religion and the Founding*, 65.

11. Eberhardt, *Summary of Catholic History*, 2:421–22.

12. Ellis, *American Catholicism*, 21.

13. Ellis, *American Catholicism*.

14. Ellis, *American Catholicism*, 151.

15. Mark Twain, *The Innocents Abroad*, in *The Writings of Mark Twain*, 37 vols. (New York: Harper and Brothers, 1929), 2:349, quoted in Ellis, *American Catholicism*, 85.

16. Charles R. Morris, *American Catholic: The Saints and Sinners Who Built America's Most Powerful Church* (New York: Times Books, 1997), 65.

17. Thomas Curry, *Farewell to Christendom: The Future of Church and State in America* (New York: Oxford University Press, 2001), 65.

18. Eberhardt, *Summary of Catholic History*, 2:511.

19. Eberhardt, *Summary of Catholic History*, 2:510.

20. Morris, *American Catholic*, 60. A full examination of

the "Philadelphia Bible Riot" can be found in Daniel Lee Crosby, "A Christian Nation: Evangelical Protestantism and Religious Conflict in Antebellum Philadelphia" (Ph.D. Diss., Washington University, St. Louis, 1997).

21. John R. G. Hassard, *Life of the Most Reverend John Hughes, First Archbishop of New York* (New York, 1866), 276, quoted in Ellis, *American Catholicism,* 68.

22. Eberhardt, *Summary of Catholic History,* 2:574.

23. Eberhardt, *Summary of Catholic History,* 2:575.

24. Abraham Lincoln, *The Collected Works of Abraham Lincoln,* ed. Roy P. Basler (New Brunswick: Rutgers University Press, 1953), 2:322–23, quoted in Ellis, *American Catholicism,* 86.

25. Lincoln, *Collected Works of Abraham Lincoln,* 1:338, quoted in Ellis, *American Catholicism,* 64–65.

26. Curry, *Farewell to Christendom,* 65.

EARLY JEWISH SINGERS OF THE AMERICAN DREAM
FROM PENINA MOISE TO EMMA LAZARUS

Rabbi Frederick L. Wenger

Rather than discuss how America treated the Jews, I've decided to address how Jewish speakers, Jewish singers, and Jewish poets treated America.[1]

In 1883, a campaign was under way to raise funds for the base of a giant statue to be placed in Bedloe's Island, at the mouth of New York Harbor. The statue, a gift from the Franco-American Friendship League, was the work of renowned sculptor Frederic Auguste Bartholdi. Its theme was "Liberty Enlightening the World" and was intended as a tribute to world friendship and liberty. At the suggestion of Ralph Waldo Emerson, an American Jewish poet named Emma Lazarus submitted a poem which raised $2,500. The statue was completed in 1886, installed, and dedicated by President Grover Cleveland. The poem was entitled "The New Colossus." In 1903, a plaque containing Emma Lazarus's poem was placed on the statue's base. As a preface to our theme let us review its immortal words:

> Not like the brazen giant of Greek fame,
> With conquering limbs astride from land to land;
> Here at our sea-washed, sunset gates shall stand
> A mighty woman with a torch, whose flame
> Is the imprisoned lightening, and her name

Mother of Exiles. From her beacon-hand
Glows world-wide welcome; her mild eyes
     command
The air-bridged harbor that twin cities frame.
"Keep, ancient lands, your storied pomp!"
     cries she
With silent lips. "Give me your tired, your poor,
Your huddled masses yearning to breathe free,
The wretched refuse of your teeming shore.
Send these, the homeless, tempest-tost to me.
I lift my lamp beside the golden door!"[2]

The title is a reference to the Colossus of Rhodes, one of the seven wonders of the ancient world. The "imprisoned lightening," which is the statue's flame, refers to the biblical general Barak, whose name means lightening and whom the prophetess Deborah urged to fight the Canaanite Sisera in Judges 4:4–7. The Hebrew description of Deborah—*Eishet Lapidot,* "wife of Lapidot"—also means "woman with a torch." In Judges 5, Deborah is referred to as a Mother in Israel. Emma Lazarus suggested subtly—but in terms that no educated nineteenth-century American could fail to understand—that the prophetess Deborah was a fit symbol for American Liberty. Emma's dream of America as a homeland for all the tired, huddled masses, yearning to breathe free, the homeless wretched refuse of all the ancient lands of the entire world, echoed an ancient Jewish dream. Ever since the days when the exiles of Israel sat down by the waters of Babylon and wondered, *How can we sing the Lord's song in a strange land?* they have expressed their yearning for God's kingdom here on earth in poetic expressions, poems, speeches, and songs.

THE JEWS IN EARLY AMERICA

The Jewish immigration to America from 1654 (or perhaps 1492) onward is no exception. I want to share with you some of the literary fruits of that encounter of the Jewish people with America. The theme of this exploration attempts to establish the obvious generalization that American Jewish literature in its early years identified the new world with God's promised kingdom in the days of the Messiah. Emma Lazarus closes this period, but in a sense, she also opens it, for she was born to Moses and Esther Nathan, a prominent fourth-generation Jewish family, one of the oldest in New York City. The Lazaruses proudly traced their genealogical roots back to the original immigration of Jews to the New World when, in 1654, twenty-three Jewish refugees landed in Dutch New Amsterdam. They were fleeing from Brazil, which had just been reconquered by the Portuguese, thereby reintroducing the dangers of religious oppression. Although these twenty-three Jews were Dutch subjects with civil rights in Holland, the New Netherlands governor, Pieter Stuyvesant, did not want to accept them. Those twenty-three struggled for the right to trade and practice Judaism. By 1657, they were able to carry on due to vigorous intercession on the part of Amsterdam Jewry, Dutch fear of English competition, and the imperatives of mercantilism. In a very few years, however, the new Jewish community began to fade because of larger opportunities, especially in the West Indies. By 1660, the community was moribund.

In 1664, the English eliminated the Dutch wedge between Long Island and Maryland. New Amsterdam became New York. Under the English, synagogue communities were established in six towns: Montreal, Newport, New York, Philadelphia, Charleston, and Savannah. By 1700 there were two to three hundred Jewish communities in the country. By 1776, there were twenty-five hundred. Until 1720, most were of Sephardic origin. After that year, central and eastern European Jews predominated. By 1700, under the English, Jews were permitted to sell at retail, to practice crafts, and to worship openly.

Some colonial Jews engaged in trades apart from the norm: a number were artisans, tailors, soap makers, distillers, tobacconists, saddlers, bakers, silversmiths, and farmers. Francis Salvador was a planter; some in Georgia ran cattle in the pine barrens. The economic aristocrats among the Jews were the army purveyors who provisioned the British armies on the North American continent. During the frequent wars of the eighteenth century, Jews also engaged in privateering. These economic activities were exceptional.

The typical Jew in the coastal colonies was a small shopkeeper selling hardware, dry goods, and liquors. If successful, he became a merchant or shipper. As an exporter, he might exchange American raw materials for English consumer wares. A merchant shipper (such as Aaron Lopez) was also an industrialist, contracting for anything from a work apron to a ship. A number of Jews were members of the United Company of Spermaceti Chandlers, the first American organization to attempt to control the production and price of candles. Some of the candle manufacturers sent out their own whalers. A few entrepreneurs were engaged in the slave trade. Most Canadian Jews were in the fur trade.

In the colonial period, the typical Jewish shopkeeper was an immigrant devoted to Judaism. He established a *Kehilla,* a congregation. Discipline, especially in matters of *kashrut* (dietary law), was constantly exercised but oftentimes ameliorated by the need not to offend, for there were too few Jews. Permanent cemeteries were established in 1678 in Newport and in 1682 in New York. No synagogue in North America had a rabbi until 1840, but each employed a *Hazan* (cantor), a *schochet* (slaughterer), and a *shamash* (servant). On occasion, the first two roles were combined in that of a *Mohel* (circumciser).

A sizable portion of the budget in these communities went for charitable works. Itinerants were constantly arriving from England, Europe, and Palestine. Impoverished members were granted loans, the sick and dying were provided for, and the community saw to burials. *Rebbes* (private teachers) were always available. By 1731, a school building had been erected in New York—Gershom Sexias, the first native-born American Hazan, received his education there. (His son, Joshua, taught Hebrew to a young man named Joseph Smith in Kirtland, Ohio.)

The typical American Jew of pre-Revolutionary America was of German origin, a shopkeeper, hard working, enterprising, religiously observant, uncouth, and untutored, but with sufficient learning to keep his books and write a simple business letter in English. By 1776, he had brought with him from Europe a sense of Jewish communalism, and he kept his congregation alive. He tended to be careless in matters of ritual. He seems not to have been in exile. America was home to him.

When the Revolution broke out in 1775, most Jews were Whigs. They had few ties to England and were determined to become first-class citizens. Many were fascinated by the Declaration of Independence. Quite a number were in the militia, and some served in the Continental Army as line soldiers and officers. Three officers attained relatively high rank. Jewish merchants ventured into privateering and blockade running. Most provided consumer goods during the British blockade. The most notable Jewish rebel was the Polish immigrant Hayim Solomon, who served as an underground agent for the American forces while working for the British. When discovered, he fled to Philadelphia, where he became a bill broker. As such, he made available to Robert Morris, superintendent of finance, the funds for the successful expedition against Cornwallis.

JEWS EMBRACE THE NEW REPUBLIC

Independence did not at once improve the political status of the American Jew. In 1787, the Northwest Ordinance guaranteed that the Jew should be on the same footing as his fellow citizens in all new states. The Constitution, adopted a year later, gave him equality on the federal level. But most of these rights were still resident in the states. As late as 1820, only seven of the original thirteen states had recognized the Jews politically. Ultimately, men of talent who were Jews were appointed or elected town councilors, judges, and members of state legislatures.

Eventually, the synagogues were enlarged, and the status of the Hazan was elevated to that of the Christian minister. The Revolutionary period saw special organizations arise to care for the poor, the sick, and the dead. Jews became planters, merchant shippers, and land speculators. The firm of Cohen and Isaacs of Richmond employed Daniel Boone to survey their holdings in Kentucky. Jews went from banking and money lending to the stock exchange. By 1820, they were in law, medicine, engineering, education, and journalism. Many Jews in the post-Revolutionary period, especially in South Carolina, were people of education and culture. Some were artists or playwrights; all were cultural nationalists. Patriotism was no guarantee against Judeophobia and anti-Semitism, which increased as the Jews rose in wealth, prominence, and visibility. Those who entered politics and joined the Jeffersonians were vilified in the Federalist press. Jews seeking public office, and even Christians of Jewish descent, were frequently and viciously attacked. In 1760, two English translations of Hebrew prayer books appeared. After the Revolution, there were printed sermons, eulogies, a Hebrew grammar, and by 1820 a rather good polemic entitled *Israel Vindicated*.

The typical American Jew of the post-Revolutionary period was native born and completely acculturated. Intermarriage was not uncommon. While he was nominally a follower of tradition, he was often indifferent to the practices of his religion. Basically he was loyal to his Jewish community, attached to American and world Jewry by a strong sense of kinship. By 1820, there were about four thousand Jews in the United States. Even distant St. Louis had some Jews. Many of these were recent German immigrants who had drifted in after the Napoleonic wars. By the turn of the eighteenth century, central Europeans had already started a little Ashkenazi synagogue in Philadelphia. Within a generation, Ashkenazi culture dominated the American Jewish scene.

Reviewing their past, the early American Jews came to see their immigration to this new world as part of God's divine plan for them. In 1784, David Franco Mendes wrote *A History of the Great Men of Israel,* which describes the early colonial period in biblical terms:

> And it came to pass in the year 5414 (1654) that the Portuguese came back to Brazil, and from the Hollanders took their land by force. And God had compassion on his people, granted them favor and grace. . . . And all our people went down to the sea in ships, and spread sail and God led them to their destination to this land, and they . . . reached the end of the inhabited earth called New Holland. (1784)

And everywhere this new community went, it sang the glories of the New World.

The Sheftalls were a prominent family in Savannah, Georgia, in the eighteenth century. Mordecai Sheftall's father, Benjamin, had emigrated from London in 1733 with the first group of Spanish Portuguese Jews. Benjamin Sheftall struggled to feed his family. Mordecai, however, became a well-to-do merchant. He used his substantial community influence and assets to secure land for the first Jewish cemetery in Georgia and later contributed heavily to the building of the first synagogue in the state. The Sheftalls organized the colonists' cause in their community. All the men of the family joined the Continental Army. At the fall of Savannah to the British in late December 1778, Sheftall and his sons were taken as prisoners of war. After their release, he sent one of his sons back to England to trade, but urged his return, upon the Continental victory, in the following letter:

My dear son: . . .

What my feelings are on the occassion is easier immagined than described. For it must be supposed that every real well wisher to his country must feel him self happy to have lived to see this longe and bloody contest bro[ugh]t to so happy an issue. More especially, as we have obetained our independence, instead of those threats of bringing us with submission to the foot of the throne whose greatest mercies to Americans has been nothing but one continued scene of cruelty, of which you as well as my self have experienced our shares.

But thanks to the Almighty, it is now at an end. Of which happy event I sincerely congratulate you and all my friends. As an entier new scene will open it self, and we have the world to begin againe, I would have you come home as soon after the [Passover] holidays as possibly you can.[3]

In 1790 the first president of the United States paid a visit to Newport, Rhode Island. On that occasion, the Jewish community there sent the following message to George Washington:

Sir,

Permit the Children of the Stock of Abraham to approach you with the most cordial affection and esteem for your person and merits—and to join with our fellow-citizens in welcoming you to New Port.

With pleasure we reflect on those days—those days of difficulty and danger, when the God of Israel, who delivered David from the peril of the sword—shielded our head in the day of battle:—And we rejoice to think that the same Spirit, who rested in the bosom of the greatly beloved Daniel, enabling him to preside over the Provinces of the Babylonish Empire, rests, and ever will rest upon you, enabling you to discharge the arduous duties of the Chief Magistrate in these States.

Deprived as we have hitherto been of the invaluable rights of free citizens, we now, (with a deep sense of gratitude to the Almighty Disposer of all events) behold a Government, [(] erected by the Majesty of the People) a Government which to bigotry gives no sanction, to persecution no assistance—but generously affording to All liberty of conscience, and immunities of citizenship—deeming every one, of whatever nation, tongue, or language equal parts of the great governmental machine. This so ample and extensive federal union whose basis in Philanthropy, mutual confidence and public virtue, we cannot but acknowledge to be the work of the Great God, who ruleth in the armies of Heaven and among the inhabitants of the earth, doing whatsoever seemeth him good.

For all the blessings of civil and religious liberty which we enjoy under an equal and benign administration we desire to send up our thanks to the Ancient of days, the great Preserver of Men—beseeching him that the Angel who conducted our forefathers through the wilderness into the promised land, may graciously conduct you through all the dangers and difficulties of this mortal life—and when like Joshua, full of days, and full of honor, you are gathered to your Fathers, may you be admitted into the heavenly Paradise to partake of the water of life and the tree of immortality.

Done and signed by order of the Hebrew Congregation in New Port, Rhode Island, August 17th, 1790.

To which Washington replied in echoing words and then added his own laconic blessing: "May the children of the Stock of Abraham, who dwell in this land, continue to merit and enjoy the good will of the other inhabitants, while every one shall sit in safety under his own vine and fig-tree, and there shall be none to make him afraid."[4]

And so the American Jewish community set about the task of building itself both materially and spiritually. In many of their earlier efforts, they viewed the new United States as part of God's redemptive plan for the world. So in 1784, Manuel Josephson petitioned the Philadelphia Congregation to build a *Mikve,* a ritual bathhouse.

It having pleased the Almighty God of Israel to appoint our lot in this country, the rulers where of he has inspired with wisdom and a benevolent disposition toward us as a nation, whereby we enjoy every desirable privilege and great preeminence far beyond many of our brethren dispersed in different countries and governments, and in order to manifest our gratitude for those peculiar favors and blessings, we ought in a very sincere manner, observe a strict and close adherence to those laws and commandments ordained by Him and

delivered to our master Moses, of blessed memory, which have been handed down to us in a regular succession to the present, wherein we are told that the almighty has made choice of our nation in preference of all others, on condition that we hearken unto his voice, and observe his covenants; . . . (so) we should endeavor with all our might to regulate our conduct in every respect conformable to His Holy Law, rectify every deviation there from and supply every omission so far as in our power, . . . In order thereto, we, the subscribers having taken these matters to heart, we find one matter which strikes us most forcibly and cannot but affect astonishment and horror every judicious and truly religious mind. This is the want of a proper Mikve or bathing place according to our Law and institution . . . so that the Almighty may look down in mercy upon us and send the redeemer to Zion in our days. Philadelphia 21 May 1784, Rosh Hodesh Sivan 5524.

Of course, the Mikve was built.

In Joseph's letters and thenceforth in American Jewish literature, the tension between Jewish and American life was identified from the start of our odyssey in this country. The twin dangers of assimilation and populist anti-Semitism were documented in a letter dated 1791 that Rebecca Samuel wrote to her parents back in Germany, the old country:

One can make a good living here, and all live at peace. Anyone can do what he wants. There is no rabbi in all of America to excommunicate anyone. This is a blessing here; Jew and Gentile are as one. There is no *galut* ["exile"— rejection of Jews] here. In New York and Philadelphia there is more *galut.*[5]

Soon the new Jewish community sought the right to fight in the militia and to hold public office despite state rules which mandated a Christian oath to secure these positions. In doing so, they appealed to the religious ideals which permeated the American value system. "If a man fulfills the duties of that religion which his education or his Conscience has pointed to him as the true one; no person, I hold, in this our land of liberty, has a right to arraign him at the bar of any inquisition," fulminated Jacob Henry in North Carolina in 1808. He prevailed, as the Bill of Rights became a part of the law of the land. This newfound liberty was glorified in sermons delivered in synagogues throughout the country. A typical example is the 1821 discourse of Dr. Jacob De La Motta, a friend of James Madison and Thomas Jefferson:

> *Here,* a liberal and tollerant [*sic*] spirit, pervades every individual. *Here,* unbiased protection, and friendly co-operation are alike extended, without consideration or reference to particular faith. *Here,* Justice presents her scale to public view, and guards its preponderance from the touch of illeberality [*sic*]. *Here,* a union of friendship and fellowship is promoted and encouraged. . . . It is *here,* that we are reasonably to expect the enjoyment of those rewards for our constancy and sufferings, as promised by the word of God, when he declared that he would not forsake us.[7]

PENINA MOISE

This history paved the way for the publication of the first book of poetry by an American Jewish author. In 1833, Penina Moise of South Carolina published *Fancy's Sketch Book.* Among her predecessors were Grace Sexias Nathan, Adah Isaacs Menken, Octavia Harby Moses, and Rebekah Hyneman. All of these were women who wrote salon pieces for reading in private parlors; many of their poems were later published in popular magazines. (Menken created another career as a flamboyant and controversial actress.) Penina was the child of French refugees who had fled from Haiti after the slave insurrection of the 1790s. She was born in Charleston, South Carolina, where she spent most of her life. She worked beginning at the age of twelve making lace and embroidery. Many of her eighty-three years were spent in genteel poverty. Hardship and deprivation were as common among antebellum Jews as they were later among the Eastern European émigrés. She was active in the Jewish life of her synagogue, serving as director of Beth Elohim's Sunday school. During the Civil War she went blind and contracted neuralgia. After the war, she ran a small private school for girls. She wrote hymns for synagogue use, including one which incorporated wording of the Declaration of Independence:

> O God! to Thy paternal grace
> That ne'er its bounty measures.
> All gifts Thy grateful children trace,
> That constitute Life's treasures.
>
> Light, being, liberty, and joy,
> All, all to Thee are owing;
> Nor can another hand destroy
> Blessings of Thy Bestowing. . . .
>
> Protector of the quick and dead
> Thy love THIS WORLD o'erfloweth:
> And when the "vital spark" hath fled,
> Eternal life bestoweth.[8]

In this hymn, Penina echoed the preamble of the Declaration that all men are created equal and endowed by their Creator with inalienable rights of life, liberty, and the pursuit of happiness.

This poem by Penina appeared in the wake of the 1819 riots in Germany:

> If thou art one of that oppressed race,
> Whose pilgrimage from Palestine we trace,
> Brace the Atlantic—Hope's broad anchor weigh,
> A Western Sun will gild your future day.[9]

ISAAC MAYER WISE

It was left to a single-minded organizational genius to take all of these pious and patriotic energies and mold them into a movement for a uniquely American Judaism. Though Isaac Mayer Wise is heralded as the founder of American Reform Judaism, he eschewed the word "reform," preferring to look upon himself as the crusader for American Judaism. Born in 1819 in Bohemia, he studied in European *Yeshivas* (schools) and then came to America in 1846. Forced out of his pulpit in Albany, New York, Wise moved out west to Cincinnati, where he founded a weekly English-language newspaper as well as an organization of rabbis and congregations and a school for the training of rabbis. He edited a prayer book and wrote voluminously. What was his passion? Hear his sermon written in honor of the Fourth of July 1858:

> Next to the Passover feast, the fourth of July is the greatest, because it is a memorial of the triumph of liberty. . . . The fourth of July tells us the glorious story of the second redemption of mankind from the hands of their oppressors, the second interposition of Providence in behalf

of liberty, the second era of the redemption of mankind, the second triumph of right over might, justice over arbitrary despotism, personal and legal liberty over the power of the strongest and the most warlike. . . .

"Moses forms one pole and the American revolution the other, of an axis around which revolves the political history of thirty three centuries." . . .

The spirit of God as revealed through Moses and the prophets as far as this earth is concerned, was incarnated in a modern and suitable form and destined to conquer the nations, to break the chains of servitude, dispel the clouds of despotism, conquer the night of prejudice and superstition, that every eye may behold the sacred sun of truth and be delighted with its glorious rays, that every mind perceive the great laws of God, the path of truth and salvation. Hallelujah! we exclaim, for the birth day of liberty, when man came to the conviction, "Have we not all one father, has not one God created us?" Hallelujah! for the day when God's law was verified, "One law and one judgment shall be for all of you." Hallelujah! for the day when man was restored to his rights, when conscience resumed its rightful throne and the dwarf of superstition was slain. Hallelujah, for the birth day of liberty to all nations![10]

ERNESTINE L. ROSE

No sooner did the Jewish people become established in the United States than they weighed in on all sides of the important issues of each age. Jewish literature boldly held a messianic vision of America up to scrutiny, weighed it in the balance, and found the reality wanting when compared with the American dream as they envisioned it based on their biblical heritage. Ernestine L. Rose, the most famous Jewish woman during the mid nineteenth century, provides an early example of the American Jewish prophetic spirit. After leaving Russian Poland, she wandered to England, where she became a disciple of Robert Owen, a Utopian Socialist. In 1838, she immigrated to America, where she became a temperance advocate, a suffragette, and an ardent abolitionist. When she gave this address in 1851, slavery was still in effect:

Even here, in this far-famed land of freedom and of knowledge, under a republic that has inscribed its banner the great truth that all men are created free and equal, and endowed with inalienable rights to life, liberty, and the pursuit of happiness,—a Declaration wafted like the voice of Hope on the breezes of heaven, to the remotest parts of the earth, to whisper freedom & equality to the oppressed and down trodden children of men, . . . yet in the very face of that eternal truth, woman, the mockingly so called "better half of man," has yet to plead for her rights, nay, for her life. For what is life without liberty? and what is liberty without equality of rights? . . . Permit me to say that the slaves of the South are not the only people that are in bondage. All women are excluded from the enjoyment of that liberty which your Declaration of Independence asserts to be the inalienable right of all. The same right to life, liberty and the pursuit of happiness, that pertains to man, pertains to woman also . . . emancipation from every kind of bondage is my principle. I go for the recognition of human rights, without distinction of sect, party, sex, or color.[11]

What a change in tone from the days of Peter Stuyvesant, when Jews modestly petitioned for the right to remain without pretending to be Christian. The only thing left was for an American Jewish poet to become a spokesperson for all of America.

EMMA LAZARUS

Born in 1849, Emma Lazarus was the daughter of a sugar merchant and the descendant of one of the original Sephardic families who established New Amsterdam. She was educated by private tutors. When she was seventeen, her father printed her first book privately. Soon after, she established a friendship with Ralph Waldo Emerson, who became her mentor. The publication of poetry, essays, short stories, and even a novel followed. Emma was a vital part of the artistic climate in New York, writing articles on music, art, and literature that were published in the *Century* and the *Critic.* She was a welcomed part of the cultural elite and traveled extensively throughout Europe. After the Russian pogroms of 1882, she visited Ward's Island, where hundreds of the victims of czarist persecution were waiting for admission to the United States. Immediately after this visit, Emma wrote a sharp response to an article in the *Century* that repeated traditional anti-Semitic canards. Her essay entitled "Russian Christianity versus Modern Judaism" launched her new path as one of the most outspoken Americans on Jewish issues. She used her celebrity to bring attention to the idea of the resettlement of Jews in Palestine. She created classes for Jewish immigrants and helped to find them housing in an overcrowded city. She started an organization called the Society for the Improvement and Colonization of East European Jews. She wrote articles on Jewish history and cultural life that were published in both Christian and Jewish publications.

"The Crowing of the Red Cock" was written in the wake of the Russian pogroms. It places the suffering of the Jews squarely on Christian shoulders, yet at the end calls for reconciliation and peaceful forgiveness here in America:

> Across the Eastern sky has glowed
> The flicker of a blood-red dawn,
> Once more the clarion cock has crowed,
> Once more the sword of Christ is drawn.
> A million burning rooftrees light
> The world-wide path of Israel's flight.
>
> Where is the Hebrew's fatherland?
> The folk of Christ is sore bestead;
> The Son of Man is bruised and banned,
> Nor finds whereon to lay his head.
> His cup is gall, his meat is tears,
> His passion lasts a thousand years.
>
> Each crime that wakes in man the beast,
> Is visited upon his kind.
> The lust of mobs, the greed of priest,
> The tyranny of kings, combined
> To root his seed from earth again.
> His record is one cry of pain.
>
> When the long roll of Christian guilt
> Against his sires and kin is known,
> The flood of tears, the life-blood spilt,
> The agony of ages shown,
> What oceans can the stain remove,
> From Christian law and Christian love?
>
> Nay, close the book; not now, not here,
> The hideous tale of sin narrate,
> Reechoing in the martyr's ear,
> Even he might nurse revengeful hate,
> Even he might turn in wrath sublime,
> With blood for blood and crime for crime.

> Coward? Not he, who faces death,
> Who singly against the world has fought,
> For what? A name he may not breathe,
> For liberty of prayer and thought.
> The angry sword he will not whet,
> His nobler tasks is—to forget.[12]

"In the Jewish Synagogue at Newport" is a response to Longfellow's poem of the same name, but, where Longfellow concludes his visit to the historic cemetery with the baleful cry "the dead nations never rise again," Emma's poem sees new life for the Jewish nationality here in America:

> Here, where the noises of the busy town,
> The ocean's plunge and roar can enter not,
> We stand and gaze around with tearful awe,
> And muse upon the consecrated spot.
>
> No signs of life are here: the very prayers
> Inscribed around are in a language dead;
> The light of the "perpetual lamp" is spent
> That undying radiance was to shed.
>
> What prayers were in this temple offered up,
> Wrung from sad hearts that knew no joy on earth,
> By these lone exiles of a thousand years,
> From the fair sunrise land that gave them birth!
>
> Now as we gaze, in this new world of light,
> Upon this relic of the days of old,
> The present vanishes, and tropic bloom
> And Eastern towns and temples we behold.
>
> Again we see the patriarch with his flocks,
> The purple seas, the hot blue sky o'erhead,
> The slaves of Egypt,—omens, mysteries,—
> Dark fleeing hosts by flaming angels led.
>
> A wondrous light upon a sky-kissed mount,
> A man who reads Jehovah's written law,
> 'Midst blinding glory and effulgence rare,
> Unto a people prone with reverent awe.
>
> The pride of luxury's barbaric pomp,
> In the rich court of royal Solomon—
> Alas! we wake: one scene alone remains,—
> The exiles by the streams of Babylon.
>
> Our softened voices send us back again
> But mournful echoes through the empty hall;
> Our footsteps have a strange, unnatural sound,
> And with unwonted gentleness they fall.
>
> The weary ones, the sad, the suffering,
> All found their comfort in the holy place,
> And children's gladness and men's gratitude
> Took voice and mingled in the chant of praise.

The funeral and the marriage, now, alas!
We know not which is sadder to recall;
For youth and happiness have followed age,
And green grass lieth gently over all.

And still the sacred shrine is holy yet,
With its lone floors where reverent feet once trod.
Take off our shoes as by the burning bush,
Before the mysteries of death and God.[13]

Her hope and expectation of renewed Jewish life here in America is stated again in "The New Ezekiel," which recalls the prophet's famous vision of the valley of the dry bones in Ezekiel 37:

What, can these dead bones live, whose sap is dried
By twenty scorching centuries of wrong?
Is this the House of Israel, whose pride
Is as a tale that's told, an ancient song?
Are these ignoble relics all that live
Of psalmist, priest, and prophet? Can the breath
Of very heaven bid these bones revive,
Open the graves and clothe the ribs of death?

Yea, Prophesy, the Lord hath said. Again
Say to the wind, Come forth and breathe afresh,
Even that they may live upon these slain,
And bone to bone shall leap, and flesh to flesh.
The spirit is not dead, proclaim the word,
Where lay dead bones, a host of armed men stand!
I ope your graves, my people, saith the Lord,
And I shall place you living in your land.[14]

Despite her proto-Zionist leanings, it is clear that for Emma Lazarus, that land is here in America. In her poem entitled "1492," Emma draws attention to the ironic fact that the same year that Columbus sailed to America, the Jews were expelled from Christian Spain and the inquisition was applied to those who remained. Meanwhile, a "virgin world," full of hopeful, freedom-filled redemption, awaited the Jewish people here in America:

Thou two-faced year, Mother of Change and Fate,
Didst weep when Spain cast forth with
    flaming sword,
The children of prophets of the Lord,
Prince, priest, and people, spurned by zealot hate.

(The two-faced god of Rome was Janus, who looked forward and backward in time. The flaming sword recalls the angelic guard who barred Adam and Eve from the Garden of Eden:)

Hounded from sea to sea, from state to state,
The West refused them, and the East abhorred.
No anchorage the known world could afford,
Close-locked was every port, barred every gate.
Then smiling, thou unveil'dst, O two faced year,
A virgin world where doors of sunset part,
Saying, "Ho, all who weary, enter here!
There falls each ancient barrier that the art
Of race or creed or rank devised, to rear
Grim bulwarked hatred between heart and
    heart!"[15]

This vision of America as the biblically promised land for the Jewish people was expanded by Emma in the famous "New Colossus." She picked up the spirit of Penina Moise, informed it with her own Zionist optimism, and inspired a vision of the American dream which still beckons in New York's harbor. Its roots are in the biblical vision of redemption when all shall sit under vine and fig tree with none to make them afraid. You see its relics in our exhibit. Now, in a time when every immigrant has become suspect as a potential enemy—in fact, ever since the 1920s America has ceased to be as hospitable to the huddled masses yearning to breathe free as she should be, or wishes she could be—Emma Lazarus and the expression of redemption embodied in her Jewish literary tradition going all the way back to the seventeenth century call us to make our own country what it should and must become. That tradition continues in our own time and gives us courage in the face of our national anxiety following the terrorist attack of September 11. Its most current, though not most recent, expression was given by a Russian Jewish immigrant in the spirit of Penina Moise and Emma Lazarus: the author is Israel Baline, born in Mogla, Russia, in 1888. He was the son of a poor cantor and came with his family to the United States in 1893. Baline's song begins:

While the storm clouds gather far across the sea,
Let us swear allegiance to a land that's free.
Let us all be grateful for a land so fair,
As we raise our voices in a solemn prayer.[16]

You might recognize these words as the beginning of "God Bless America" and know the author, Israel Baline, by his pen name, Irving Berlin. He stands in the same tradition as Penina Moise and also our beloved Emma Lazarus, singing the praises of a new world and wishing that all our ideals were realized.

Notes

1. This talk was given on February 26, 2002, at the opening of an exhibit at Brigham Young University. I spoke from notes and did not prepare a complete manuscript. The paper here is reconstructed from those notes and a transcript that the university provided at a later date. I want to thank the university and its library and museum staff for providing the transcript and for encouraging me to prepare it for publication.

I apologize for any errors or lack of adequate notation. The standard histories of American Judaism include Jacob R. Marcus, *Early American Jewry,* 3 vols. (Philadelphia: Jewish Publication Society, 1950); Salo Baron and Joseph Blau, eds., *The Jews of the United States,* 3 vols. (New York: Jewish Publication Society, 1963); Arthur Hertzberg, *The Jews in America* (New York: Simon and Schuster, 1989); Howard M. Sachar, *History of the Jews in America* (New York: Alfred A. Knopf, 1992).

2. Reprinted and annotated in Jules Chametzky and others, eds., *Jewish American Literature: A Norton Anthology* (New York: W. W. Norton, 2001), 106.

3. Marcus, *Early American Jewry,* 2:372–73.

4. Morris U. Schappes, *A Documentary History of the Jews in the United States, 1654–1875* (New York: Citadel Press, 1950), 79–80.

5. Chametzky, *Jewish American Literature,* 39, brackets in Chametzky's edition.

6. Chametzky, *Jewish American Literature,* 42.

7. Baron and Blau, *Jews of the United States,* 2:576–77; Schappes, *Documentary History,* 155.

8. "Hymn," reprinted in Chametzky, *Jewish American Literature,* 72–73.

9. Chametzky, *Jewish American Literature,* 70

10. Chametzky, *Jewish American Literature,* 85–86.

11. Ernestine L. Rose, *A Lecture on Woman's Rights* (Boston: Pamphlets in American History, 1886), 3–4.

12. *Emma Lazarus: Selections from Her Poetry and Prose,* ed. Morris U. Schappes (New York: Cooperative Book League, 1944), 30–31.

13. Chametzky, *Jewish American Literature,* 103–4.

14. Chametzky, *Jewish American Literature,* 105.

15. Chametzky, *Jewish American Literature,* 104–5.

16. Chametzky, *Jewish American Literature,* 970.

ROUTING THE REPUBLIC
RELIGION AND THE AMERICAN WEST

Laurie F. Maffly-Kipp

We all have images in our minds of the American West, be they the paintings of Frederick Remington, images of handcarts and covered wagons, or the natural geography of water-parched landscapes. In this lecture I want to highlight some important and lasting features of religious life in the early republic as settlers moved westward by using another kind of representation: maps and charts. I have been working on these graphics since I began doing work on religion in the West and began to understand the importance of maps to explorers and missionaries who were discovering the West for themselves in the nineteenth century.

Obviously there are many kinds of images that can give us important information about the past, but maps do this in a particular sort of way. They help us to project ourselves into the world. They are a forecast of hopes and dreams, and are a vision of the world as it ought to be or as we imagine it to be. They also allow us to pay attention to the early republic not simply as a glimpse of a people, but as groups of people who lived in relation to a specific location, to a specific space, and to landscapes filled with sacred meanings.[1]

I want to focus on the relationships between human beings and this continent to see how religious groups interpreted and interacted with the vast expanse of land that they increasingly claimed. The republic as it was established in the late eighteenth century had become a completely different landscape by 1850—it was a literally a different space, and it had been transformed by the presence of new human communities. There were new challenges and opportunities, and the land itself and people's projections of themselves onto the land played a role in shaping the future of the republic.

The early nineteenth century witnessed changes in more than landscape, of course. The major religious event of the new republic was the Second Great Awakening, an event that is often caricatured for its extremes of emotional revivalism—the enthusiastic praying, singing, dancing, falling down, and yelling that reportedly overtook participants in camp meetings and churches as they were felled by the power of the Holy Spirit.[2] Yet it was the slower and perhaps less sensational kinds of organizational changes in denominations that led ultimately to long-lasting change, particularly in the western parts

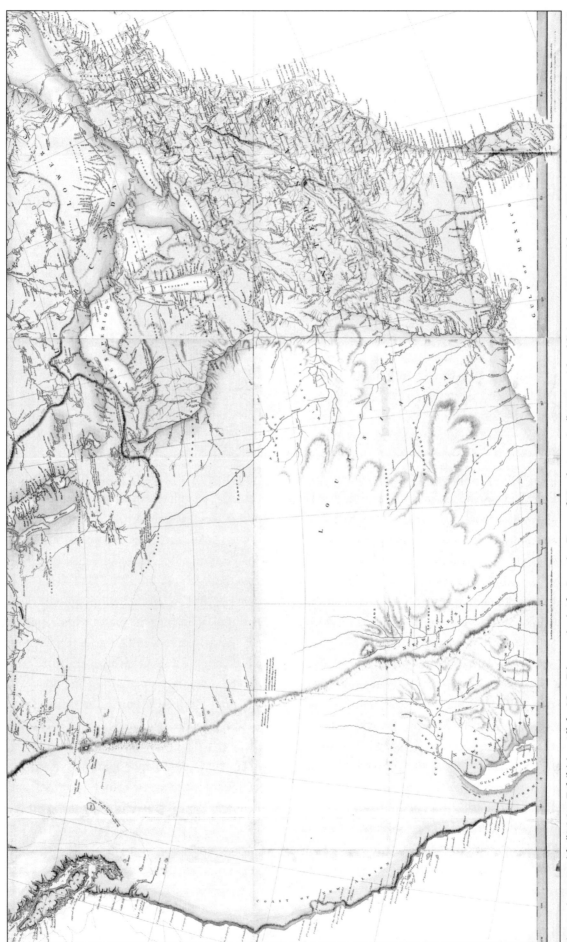

Aaron Arrowsmith, "A Map Exhibiting All the New Discoveries in the Interior Parts of North America." 1795, with additions to 1811. Held at the University of Virginia Library Special Collections. The Arrowsmith map was one of the most important maps of North America during the early republic.

of the nation. In other words, the revivals of the early republic resulted eventually in well-organized and motivated groups who saw newly opened western lands as a divinely ordained opportunity to build the kingdom right here on earth. In doing so, some of these groups that moved west were among the first to organize and settle western lands. They were far ahead of the federal government and even the more mainstream Protestant groups. Ironically, it was those people who were the outcasts religiously from the East who became the developers of the lands in the West and who ultimately paved the way for the infrastructure to develop later on in the West. These kingdom builders, as I call them, saw the land as both a means and an end. The land itself was sacred. The land itself had value. It was a consecrated holding that served as a physical manifestation of an ongoing relationship with God.

PERCEPTIONS OF THE WESTERN LANDSCAPE IN EARLY AMERICA

In order to understand the ways in which Americans on the eve of the Revolution were thinking about the landscape, we have to back up a little bit. Prior to the Revolution, the continent itself was more often seen by Euro-American Protestants as an obstacle, not as an opportunity. For the Puritans, the landscape itself was a dark, heathenish, even evil and forbidding land. In fact, in the earliest Puritan settlements, families were compelled to live within the towns. Even if the people worked lands elsewhere, they had to live alongside neighbors in an orderly and compact village. They shared the conviction that where the community is, God is. The Puritans weren't so sure that God was out there in the dark woods. Compact towns represented a way of preserving social order, obviously, but they also worked to buffer society from the evil influences that lay beyond the bounds of civilization as they knew it. Nathaniel Hawthorne's *Scarlet Letter* is a great example of this tendency to see the forest, the symbol for a natural world that was unimproved by Euro-American hands, as the primary location of evil and foreboding.

Bad things happened when people strayed off into the woods. The landscape itself was not a romantic image of something to be nurtured, but rather a chaos to be tamed or perhaps to be feared. This image held sway in both Europe and among Protestants in the New World for several centuries.[3]

Maps and the Development of the West

Not until the opening of more lands right around the time of the founding of the republic and the turn of the nineteenth century did exploration of those forbidding regions to the West begin in earnest. But even the exploration that began at this point, with Lewis and Clark's expedition being the most well-known example, was actually not intended to explore the land for its own sake. People were searching for something *beyond* the continent. Lewis and Clark were not seeking to discover the wonders of the wilderness in Nebraska or in South Dakota. They were looking for the Northwest Passage. They were looking for a way out the other side of the land. They were looking to get elsewhere. They were sponsored by merchants and other traders and financiers who for their own economic and political reasons wanted to establish ties with areas on the Pacific. The expedition was a way to find the other end of the continent, but not necessarily a way to explore the interior.[4]

One of the most popular maps of the western part of the United States available around the time that Lewis and Clark began making their journeys was created by Aaron Arrowsmith. Arrowsmith began his career as a surveyor in England. In 1790 he started his own map-publishing firm, and he soon had an international reputation for the maps and atlases that he created. The Hudson's Bay Company gave him access to the many journals and surveys of western Canada contained in its archives in London, and Arrowsmith printed his first map of North America shortly thereafter, in 1795. He made several revisions between 1795 and 1811. Many things are interesting about it, and many of the details are geographically incorrect.[5]

What might strike a contemporary observer, however, is how blank the map is. It reveals, in a single image, how little those Euro-Americans in the eastern part of the new United States knew about the western part of the continent. The Missouri River, for example, is completely off course. There is one single ridge of mountains in the West. The map situates the Great Lake River on the western side of the mountain range and then connects this to the Columbia River with a dotted line. The Arrowsmith map thus supported the incorrect assumption that explorers would encounter a relatively convenient route to the Pacific Ocean. This factual error may well reveal the extent to which our projections of what we would like to see shape our understanding of reality—in turn, these wishful thoughts then change history. Arrowsmith literally created the impression that there was an easy way to get to the Pacific Ocean, and in doing so he opened a door for exploration that eventually produced such a path.

Lewis and Clark, in fact, carried this Arrowsmith map along on their expedition, using it as their authoritative guide. (If you think Map Quest doesn't work, well, trust me, this was worse.) Arrowsmith's 1802 map was the most comprehensive map of the West available at this time, and it probably was the most important map that Lewis and Clark used in planning their expedition. Thomas Jefferson owned the 1802 map as well. All of this bespeaks the idea that people were looking to get around the West, to get past it to the other side. For most North Americans of the day, the West itself did not excite interest until sometime later.

Most early maps of the United States, in fact, point to a second reality. The West was not only considered uninteresting in and of itself, but it was also regarded as simply an appendage to the states along the eastern seaboard. Before the various colonies ceded land to the federal government beginning in the 1780s, all of the land to the west of Georgia all the way to the Mississippi River, for example, was considered to be the property of the State of Georgia. Most of the other states had similar boundaries. Colonial authorities simply extended lines due west to the edge of British territory, in order to divide up lands that were not seen to have intrinsic characteristics or value at the time. This demarcation demonstrates the way in which easterners were projecting their own possessions westward—they were seeing themselves projected west.

One of the most dramatic and ultimately the most consequential changes after 1787 that affected religious groups was the gathering and opening of all of these western lands up to the Mississippi as federal territory. The colonies all ceded their western lands to the newly established federal government, and those lands were held thereafter as common land. It was subject to federal jurisdiction, and, therefore, to the laws governing freedom of religion set by the federal government—laws that were decidedly more tolerant than those adhered to by many state governments. This new legal status created considerable ambiguity about what religious freedom was going to look like in those regions—would traditional churches simply move west, or would something new develop? As we'll see, this geographical and legal opportunity opened the door for religious dissenters to move into western lands.

If this notion of space and landscape was not terrifically important to the federal government in the early years after the founding of the republic, it should also be noted that the notion of America as an ideal of freedom was in many respects removed from the concrete realities of the landscape itself. The idea of freedom was not so much a freedom of place or freedom to be in a certain place. It was a freedom that was vested in the rights of individuals. Similarly, the notion of Manifest Destiny as it emerged in the first decades of the nineteenth century was a political ideal without reference to actual land. It did not contain any specific moral directives about how space should be used, and therefore, it left open the door for a wide variety of opportunities, for new kinds of expression. If America, therefore, had the divine mission to inhabit this continent, that right was an abstract one, formed with little reference to the landscape itself.[6]

As lands westward began to open for development in the decades after the Revolution, transformation occurred unevenly and in a way that reflected values that often lay beyond the American landscape. Even with the massive territorial expansion of the United States in its early years, the middle of the country was largely ignored. It was the edges that had very important political and economic potential. Again, the middle was just a way to get to other places. California became strategically important, for example, as a gateway to the Pacific world. The Oregon country became important in part for the agricultural value of its land, but also because of its strategic location near the Russians who were coming down from Alaska and the north. Texas, of course, provided an early political buffer from Mexico. But few Americans expressed any sense that the landscape of North America in and of itself was something to be valued. So we have this great donut-shaped approach to development of the country.[7]

The exploration and settlement of the United States from 1800 to 1820 illustrates this point. All of the early exploration took place with an eye towards getting out and getting across the ocean. The interior, particularly the western half of the country, remained largely undeveloped before about 1820. The routes taken by explorers all tended to be the river routes, which was obviously the easiest way to travel before the introduction of paved roads. The larger point to be made, however, is that the new nation developed unevenly and also strategically, in ways that allowed passage through interior spaces and abundant exit sites.[8]

Religion and the Landscape

For many reasons, then, the way was clear for outcasts from mainstream society to see value in a landscape where many other Euro-Americans did not. Not all religious believers, of course, saw western regions as sacred. Even for Protestant missionaries who did begin to move westward, the West in the earliest stages was an area to be circumvented on their way to fairer pastures, often the Pacific. Hawaii was the first place that Protestant missionaries looked for outreach. In 1819 and 1820 Protestants left New England and sailed all the way to Hawaii, because they understood it to be a strategic location close to Asia that would allow them some missionary activity. Shortly thereafter the west coast became important for Protestant missionaries. Methodists and Presbyterians both founded missions in the Oregon territory beginning in the mid-1830s and into the 1840s. These were all groups, however, that were pulled along by settlement. They were compelled by the many settlers moving west, so they were reacting to the slow movement of people onto the west coast rather than organizing pro-actively.[9]

The real evangelistic action, for Protestant missionaries at this time, took place in foreign lands, which were considered ripe for the harvest. One of the biggest foreign missionary associations, the American Board of Commissioners for Foreign Missions (ABCFM), expended much more money sending Protestant missionaries to other countries throughout the world in this time period than in trying to develop the landscape back home. Groups of missionaries traveled to India in 1813, to Sri Lanka in 1816, and to countries all around the Mediterranean in the 1820s and 1830s.[10] But again, they expressed much less interest, interestingly, in the North American continent itself. Some missions did reach out to western Native Americans, but relatively few missionaries or resources traveled in that direction.[11]

RELIGIOUS OUTSIDERS THAT EMBRACED THE WEST

Most people in the United States—Protestant missionaries, the federal government, merchants, and traders—were ignoring the middle of the country at this point. It is no surprise that the first major organizations to see land as an opportunity were religious outcasts, those dissenters who felt that the U.S. government was either actively hostile towards their interests or who simply sought to live out their religious convictions differently. In particular I want to focus on the Shakers, on African American communities, and finally on the Mormons, who represent the most familiar episode. But in fact, there are similarities among all of them not only in terms of their visions of what they wanted to build in the West, but also in terms of the outcome of what they were doing. They were, in large measure, groups who had been the most excluded from the promises of the Revolution and the founding of the republic. Ironically, it was the people left outside of the republican dream, religious dissidents such as Shakers, Mormons, and African Americans (among others) who saw the potential of the landscape itself to become redemptive. The land was sacred ground and would help them build spiritual dreams on the American landscape that would in turn shape the future of the continent and the nation as a whole.

Shakers

The Shakers were a small religious group founded in the 1780s. They came together under the leadership of a charismatic woman named Ann Lee, a British immigrant. Centered in upstate New York in the area that came to be known as the Burned-Over District, the community grew dramatically in the midst of the revivalist furor of the Second Great Awakening. Mother Lee, as she was called, was believed by her followers to be the second incarnation of Jesus Christ. Christ had returned to earth to the United States as a female to convince followers that the millennium had already arrived. Therefore, the job of members of the Shaker community was to build the kingdom and to live in it. All work, all cultivation was consecrated to this purpose of building the kingdom of God right here in the United States. For Shakers, new sets of rules and practices pertained in this kingdom and set Shakers apart from most other Americans of the time. They believed in complete celibacy and a strict division of the sexes. They also engaged in lively dancing and singing as part of their worship.[12]

The Shakers' neighbors in New York in the 1790s were not terribly thrilled with the group's unconventional approach to religion. Facing pressure, Lucy Wright, the successor to Mother Lee, authorized a missionary expedition into the Ohio Valley (which was considered the far west in 1805). This expedition was very successful at finding followers in southern Ohio and Kentucky, where the Shakers founded communities by the late 1820s.[13]

The Shakers employed a very systematic approach to constructing and establishing new settlements. They developed an extensive communications network to overcome the problems of distance that separated their eastern and their western groups so that they could coordinate better amongst themselves. In other words, the Shakers built an organizational grid that provided one of the first templates for the development of that first frontier. And in fact it was a template that outlasted their own communities. The numbers of Shakers dwindled rather quickly after the turn of the twentieth century. Nonetheless, this area boomed in the wake of some of these early settlements that set the pattern for settlement in its communities. The Shakers demonstrate westward movement instigated by religious dissidents.

African Americans

African Americans are obviously not in and of themselves one religious group. However, there are some similarities in their situation to what we see in the Shaker movement and what we also see among the Mormons. African Americans were also left out of the republican ideal. Although enslaved blacks were gradually freed in the northern states after the establishment of the republic, slavery still was practiced throughout the South.

African Americans, who had converted to Protestant religious traditions in large numbers during the Second Great Awakening, came to understand their plight as analogous to that of Israel. The South, then, became Egypt. African Americans developed a theology based on a reading of the Bible and projected a time when they would move out of Egypt, with the help of a Moses, to Canaan. African Americans sang about and discussed this future promise constantly during the antebellum era. On the one hand, the concept of communal suffering provided many African Americans with a sense of peoplehood. More important for our story, it led them to figure the land itself as sacred: somewhere there was a Canaan that God would preserve for them. Sweet Canaan's land was not only an idea of freedom for individuals; it was also an actual place.[14]

Throughout the antebellum period, African Americans talked about and wrote about where that Canaan might be and when they might go there. Some believed that it was Mexico, and several black leaders offered the suggestion that free blacks ought to migrate to Mexico en masse. For a brief period of time in the 1820s, many saw Haiti as the Promised Land. About six thousand African Americans migrated there in the 1820s, but most of them soon realized that it was not the land of freedom and they returned. Many believed Canaan to be Africa, and throughout the nineteenth century, a small number of African Americans lobbied for a collective return to that continent for religious reasons. The colony of Liberia was established in 1820 for African American migrants, and it was regarded by many settlers as a sacred site. Some thought Canaan was in Canada, and the growth of Canada West, an area in Ontario, was again a signal that African Americans were looking for that landscape.

Interestingly, though, many blacks found sacred space in western lands. Several African-American settlements were formed prior to the Civil War by settlers seeking Canaan. By the 1850s, a number of such towns were scattered around the eastern coast, and more developed in the Midwest. The height of the interest came, however, right after the Civil War. Between 1856 and 1915, over sixty predominantly black towns were founded in the Midwest, about a third of them in Oklahoma. This is a story of sacred movement that is not often told. Throughout the West, places like Blackdom, New Mexico; Hobson City, Alabama; Allensworth, California; Rentiesville, Oklahoma; and Mound Bayou, Mississippi, were settled by African Americans who based their migration on the premise that they were going into Canaan.[15]

Religious organizations moved right along with them. Sometimes, whole church communities picked up and resettled further west. As a result, the major black denominations of the time, the African Methodist Episcopal Church (AME) and the African Methodist Episcopal Zion Church (AMEZ) established churches throughout the western territories. The typical story we hear is that these denominations moved south in order to evangelize the newly freed slaves in the South. This story is true, but they simultaneously moved westward so that states such as Louisiana, Arkansas and Missouri became centers of African American religious life in this period.

Perhaps the most famous of all the Black towns established after the Civil War was a place called Nicodemus. The concept of Nicodemus came from two Black ministers, William Smith and Thomas Harris, both from Clarksville, Tennessee. They went west in the spring of 1877 to look for land. They were joined in that expedition by a man named W. R. Hill, a Kansas land speculator who went back with them to Tennessee after seeing this place out in Kansas. He spread the news among small rural Black churches in Tennessee of a beautiful land, a Canaan, on the south Solomon River in northwestern Kansas. They put up signs that talked about this as the Promised Land for Blacks. It is no wonder, then, that they named the town "Nicodemus," after the Pharisee to whom Jesus spoke of the importance of being "born again." Black settlers felt that they might literally be born again in this new place.

The first sixty recruits to Nicodemus arrived in June of 1877. In this new Canaan, African American migrants created a town layout similar in its conception to the early town plans of Puritan New England. Nicodemus was quick to establish its own infrastructure. The First Baptist Church of Nicodemus was organized approximately nine months after the first Black settlers arrived on the Kansas prairie land. In 1879 a sod structure, intended to serve as a church meetinghouse, was partly built over a dugout—revealing something about the conditions in Kansas at that day. By 1880 a small one-room stone sanctuary had been erected at the same site. This structure evolved from limestone to stucco and finally a brick sanctuary was built in 1975.[16]

Persecution and Expulsion of the Mormons from Nauvoo, Illinois, 1846, by G. W. Fasel, 1851, lithograph print, 22" x 28".

Other such communities formed around Nicodemus, and the pace of migration out of the South picked up speed. Probably the most famous participant in this settlement was a man named Benjamin Pap Singleton, who became known as the Moses of the movement. Singleton was a former slave, born in Nashville, Tennessee. Those who followed him came to be known as "Exodusters." In the late 1860s, Singleton and some of his associates had been urging Blacks to acquire farm land in Tennessee, but Whites wouldn't sell productive farm land to them, so they had to move further west. As an alternative, Singleton began scouting land in Kansas in the early 1870s. Soon several Black families had migrated from Nashville to Kansas. By 1874, Singleton and his associates has formed the Edgefield Real Estate and Homestead Association in Tennessee, which steered more than twenty thousand Black migrants to Kansas between 1877 and 1879.

The journey west was arduous, which only heightened the sense that it was in fact related to the original Israelite exodus. At the time of the exodus, yellow fever ravaged many river towns in Missouri, Mississippi, and Louisiana. Because many of the Black migrants who stopped over in these towns—they were coming by steamboat, by train or on horseback—were sick and were poverty stricken, city officials assumed that they must be potential disease carriers. This perceived threat caused alarm in cities such as St. Louis, which imposed all kinds of unnecessary quarantine measures to discourage future migrants from crossing that way. The trek, with its hardships, became an exodus of biblical proportions for the participants.

For many African Americans, including the Nicodemus settlers, the western lands represented Canaan. African Americans proceeded to establish self-sustaining communities that represented their vision of equality and spiritual freedom. They also were the first to settle these lands, and they developed the technology and strategies that would become common in this area.

Mormons

As several scholars have observed, Mormonism represents perhaps the archetypal example of the spacialization of religion. The sacred geography of the American West is a central and defining feature of Latter-day Saint identity. It has served to distinguish the Saints as a people almost from the very beginning. What is perhaps less often noticed are the contributions made by The Church of Jesus Christ of Latter-day Saints as an organizational body to the early development of the western United States.

The initial motivation for settlement was not unlike what we have seen in the Shaker movement and in the African American community. Early Saints agreed that America had a special role to play in sacred history. For the Shakers and for the Mormons, Jesus Christ had appeared here. For Mormons the gospel had been restored through Joseph Smith right here. Therefore, the Saints had a religious mandate to build the kingdom in this land, a new Zion. The Mormons were legally enabled, as were African Americans and Shakers, by the extension of federal jurisdiction over western lands. This federal statute allowed for freedom of religion in theory if not in practice. Of course, the Mormons met with fierce resistance from local officials and from popular crowds as they tried to establish themselves successively in New York, Ohio, Missouri, and Illinois. They were pushed westward gradually and eventually began to build Nauvoo, Illinois, in the late 1830s.[17]

The story of Nauvoo is a story often told. What is perhaps less noted is the extent to which the Mormon presence there helped to develop not just Nauvoo, but also the entire region. From 1840 to 1850, the only community that shrank in size in the Midwest was Nauvoo because of the exodus. Yet at the same time, and primarily because of the development of Nauvoo, this entire region grew dramatically and was affected by the Mormon migration to that area. Even after the bulk of the Mormon community had moved to Utah, the area experienced continued growth. (It would be interesting, in this regard, to study the extent to which Mormons who

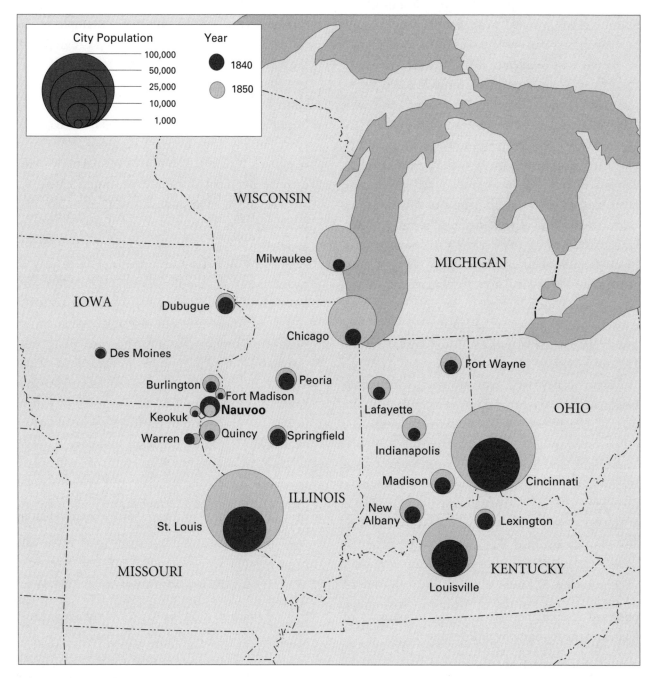

This map is based, with permission, on Edwin S. Gaustad and Philip L. Barlow, eds., *New Historical Atlas of Religion in America,* 3d ed. (New York: Oxford University Press, 2000), 297. Graphics by Kimberly Chen Pace.

stayed behind helped to develop those areas, but that's a subject for another day.)

By 1845, after the martyrdom of Joseph Smith, the Saints were once again on the move. This time they traveled under the leadership of Brigham Young, who like Moses would lead the new Israelites into the Zion of the Salt Lake basin. And this time they would find a lasting Zion, a place to build the kingdom of God. As was true for the Shakers, Mormons consecrated all their labor to the church and to God, seeing spiritual fulfillment in the material promise of the western landscape. Just as Kansas

Map depicting the similarities between Utah and Palestine, from William E. Smythe, *The Conquest of America*, rev. ed. (New York: Macmillan, 1905), facing 54.

was being promoted as a blessed destination for African Americans, so, too, did Mormon Saints gather in Utah to fulfill a religious destiny. Often the dream of land that flowed with milk and honey stood at stark odds with the sod houses or desert spaces. Nonetheless, their religious vision reinforced the connection between a sacred geography and their North American landscape. The Latter-day Saint view of Utah as Zion is reinforced by the often-observed resemblances between the topography of Utah and the topography of Palestine.[18]

In 1849 and 1850, The Church of Jesus Christ of Latter-day Saints proposed the creation of the State of Deseret, which was projected to occupy approximately half of the American West. Although Deseret never came to pass, Mormon settlement of the region nonetheless had marked effects well beyond the Salt Lake Basin. The colony aided in the development of much of the West in strategic and important ways. By the late nineteenth century, Mormons had established interconnected communities throughout the West. What began, then, as a religious protest against the American republic, and a forced march westward, developed into a culture area that continues to define the nation itself.[19]

CONCLUSION

What can we conclude from these examples? For one thing, all the movements we have discussed were migrations of American outcasts, people who had been shut out from the ideals of republican freedom. They all held significantly different understandings of what religious freedom could mean, and their very presence reinforces the fact that intolerance still existed in the United States even after the establishment of the nation. In important ways, each group was quite literally denied access to the space of America. Mormons and Shakers were pushed out of New York and later even further west. African Americans fled the South. In other words, space and landscape were never something that could be taken for granted. The land itself came to be seen by these groups as part of God's providential offering to the faithful. In western areas, all of these groups found a land that fit their religious visions, a Canaan, a Zion, or a millennial kingdom, and they marked the landscape with their sacred names. Even something as simple as the way we have named our towns and the significance and value that we attach to those names reveal the notion that religious dissidents have shaped the nation.[20]

In each of these cases, the religious visions of communities led Americans to the vast interior of the continent, setting it out not as a place of dark and hidden threats, or a place to be passed over and exited out the other side, but as a living temple. Americans were brought there by dint of these early visionaries, people who never intended to develop the nation, but were in fact fleeing many aspects of the republic. Thus, as one of the unintended consequences of history, religious dissidents shaped that republic in crucial ways.

Notes

1. For more on maps and the ways that they both reflect and construct reality for the viewer, see Jeremy Black, *Maps and History: Constructing Images of the Past* (New Haven: Yale University Press, 2000); and Mark S. Monmier, *How to Lie with Maps*, 2d ed. (Chicago: University of Chicago Press, 1996).

2. Definitive treatments of the Second Great Awakening include Robert H. Abzug, *Cosmos Crumbling: American Reform and the Religious Imagination* (New York: Oxford University Press, 1994); and Nathan Hatch, *The Democratization of American Christianity* (New Haven: Yale University Press, 1989).

3. On the Puritan ideology of the land, see William Cronon, *Changes in the Land: Indians, Colonists, and the Ecology of New England* (New York: Hill and Wang, 1984).

4. For more on the Lewis and Clark expeditions, see Stephen Ambrose, *Undaunted Courage: Meriwether Lewis, Thomas Jefferson, and the Opening of the American West* (New York: Simon and Shuster, 1996).

5. Arrowsmith was one of the founders of the Royal Geographical Society. See E. H. Brown, ed. *Geography Yesterday and Tomorrow* (New York: Oxford University Press, 1987).

6. Anders Stephanson, *Manifest Destiny: American Expansionism and the Empire of Right* (New York: Hill and Wang, 1996). For a classic, but much older, exploration of this theme, see Frederick Merk, *Manifest Destiny and Mission in American History: A Reinterpretation* (1963; reprint ed., Cambridge: Harvard University Press, 1995).

7. I am indebted to Jan Shipps for the metaphor of the donut, which she has used to describe the failure of many American historians to take seriously the history of the Mormon empire in Utah.

8. See Arch C. Gerlach, ed. *The National Atlas of the United States of America* (Washington, D.C.: U.S. Department of the Interior, Geological Survey, 1970), 136. This image may be viewd on-line at www.lib.utexas.edu/maps/united_states /explor ation_1800.jpg.

9. On early Protestant missionary efforts in the Pacific, see Arell Morgan Gibson and John S. Whitehead, *Yankees in Paradise: The Pacific Basin Frontier* (Albuquerque: University of New Mexico Press, 1993); and Tom Hiney, *On the Missionary Trail: A Journey through Polynesia, Asia and Africa with the London Missionary Society* (New York: Grove Press, 2001). On Methodists in Oregon, see Robert J. Loewenberg, *Equality on the Oregon Frontier: Jason Lee and the Methodist Mission, 1834–43* (Seattle: University of Washington Press, 1976).

10. See Bret E. Carroll, *The Routledge Historical Atlas of Religion in America* (New York: Routledge, 2001), 69.

11. For more information on the international scope of U.S. missions in this period, see William R. Hutchison, *Errand to the World: American Protestant Thought and Foreign Missions* (Chicago: University of Chicago Press, 1987).

12. Stephen J. Stein, *The Shaker Experience in America: A History of the United Society of Believers* (New Haven: Yale University Press, 1994).

13. See Carol, *Routledge Historical Atlas,* 79.

14. On the Exodus theme, see Eddie S. Glaude Jr., *Exodus! Religion, Race, and Nation in Early Nineteenth Century Black America* (Chicago: University of Chicago Press, 2000); and Albert J. Raboteau, "African-Americans, Exodus, and the American Israel," in *Fire in the Bones: Reflections on African-American Religious History* (Boston: Beacon Press, 1995): 17–36.

15. For more on the "exoduster" movement of African Americans, see Nell Irvin Painter, *Exodusters: Black Migration to Kansas after Reconstruction* (New York: Knopf, 1976).

16. For images related to Nicodemus, see the Library of Congress's on-line exhibition at www.loc.gov/exhibits/african/ afam010.html.

17. The story of Mormon movement westward is better documented than that of other religious groups. Still the most comprehensive study of the building of Zion in Utah is Leonard J. Arrington, *Great Basin Kingdom: An Economic History of the Latter-day Saints, 1830–1900* (Cambridge: Harvard University Press, 1958). For a more contemporary set of interpretations, see Thomas G. Alexander, ed., *Great Basin Kingdom Revisited: Contemporary Perspectives* (Logan: Utah State University Press, 1991).

18. For a scale comparision of Utah and Palestine, see Edwin S. Gaustad and Philip L. Barlow, eds., *New Historical Atlas of Religion in America*, 3d ed. (New York: Oxford University Press, 2000), 301.

19. For the extent to which Mormons currently reside in the western United States, see *New Historical Atlas,* 307; and Carroll, *Routledge Historical Atlas,* 82–83.

20. For a sampling of place names with religious significance in the United States, see *New Historical Atlas,* 336–39.

CONTRIBUTORS

Milton V. Backman Jr. is Professor Emeritus of Church History and Doctrine at Brigham Young University. He earned degrees in history from the University of Utah and the University of Pennsylvania. He is the author of numerous books, including *Christian Churches of America: Origins and Beliefs* (rev. ed., New York: Scribner, 1983); *American Religions and the Rise of Mormonism* (Salt Lake City: Deseret Book, 1965); and *The Heavens Resound: A History of the Latter-day Saints in Ohio, 1830–1838* (Salt Lake City: Deseret Book, 1983).

W. Cole Durham Jr. is Gates University Professor of Law at the J. Reuben Clark Law School, Brigham Young University, and the director of the BYU International Center for Law and Religion Studies. He earned his A.B. and J.D. at Harvard University. His work and service includes: law clerk, Judge Robert A. Ainsworth Jr., U.S. Court of Appeals, Fifth Circuit; Max Rheinstein Fellow, West Germany; secretary, American Association for the Comparative Study of Law Executive Committee; chair, Comparative Law Section, American Association of Law Schools; chair, Law and Religion Section; and member of several national advisory boards on church-state issues.

Matthew S. Holland is Assistant Professor of Political Science at Brigham Young University. He earned a B.A. at Brigham Young University and an M.A. and Ph.D. from Duke University. He was a Raoul Wallenberg Scholar at the Hebrew University of Jerusalem. He specializes in political philosophy and American political thought.

Richard C. Howe served on the Utah Supreme Court from 1980 to 2002. He was Associate Chief Justice from 1988 to 1993 and Chief Justice from 1998 to 2002. He currently serves on the Advisory Committee on the Rules of Appellate Procedure of the United States Judicial Conference. He received degrees in speech and law from the University of Utah and had a private law practice in Salt Lake City. Working twelve years in the Utah House of Representatives (1951–58 and 1969–72), he was Speaker of the House for the 1971–72 session. Elected to the Utah Senate in 1972, he served there until 1978. He was assistant minority leader in the 1973–74 session. During his eighteen years in the House and Senate, he served on every major committee. He introduced and sponsored legislation to establish a Judicial Council and Court Administrator in Utah.

James H. Hutson is Chief of the Manuscript Division at the Library of Congress. He has served on the faculty of the history departments at Yale University and the College of William and Mary. Dr. Hutson is the author of *John Adams and the Diplomacy of the American Revolution* (Lexington: University Press of Kentucky, 1980); *To Make All Laws: The Congress of the United States, 1789–1989* (Washington and Boston: Library of Congress, 1989–90; 4th edition, Washington, 1990); *The Sister Republics: Switzerland and the United States from 1776 to the Present* (Washington: Library of Congress, 1991; 4th edition, Washington, 1998); and *Religion and the Founding of the American Republic* (Washington: Library of Congress, 6th printing, 2003). He received his Ph.D. in history from Yale University.

Laurie F. Maffly-Kipp is Associate Professor of Religious Studies at the University of North Carolina–Chapel Hill. Her major publications include *Religion and Society in Frontier California* (Yale University Press, 1994), and *African-American Communal Narratives* (forthcoming). Her expertise is religious history of the American West, and African-American religious history. She serves on the editorial boards of *Church History* and *North Star*. She received a B.A. from Amherst College, an M.A. from Yale University, and a Ph.D. from Yale University.

The Most Reverend **George H. Niederauer, Ph.D.,** is Bishop of Salt Lake City. He was ordained a Roman Catholic Priest in Los Angeles in 1962. He is the author of *Precious as Silver* (forthcoming in 2004, Ave Maria Press). He serves as president of the Utah Coalition against Pornography; executive member of the National Board Religious Alliance against Pornography; chairman of the USCCB Sub-Committee for Catholic News Service; and a member of the USCCB Committee on Communications. He earned a bachelor of philosophy from St. John's Seminary, Camarillo, Calif.; a bachelor of sacred theology from Catholic University of America; a master's degree in English literature at Loyola University of Los Angeles; and a Ph.D. in English literature from the University of Southern California.

Elizabeth A. Sewell is Associate Director of the BYU International Center for Law and Religion Studies at the J. Reuben Clark Law School. She plays an active role in consulting with governments, nongovernmental organizations, and other academic institutions to promote religious liberty throughout the world. Prior to joining the Center and the faculty of the J. Reuben Clark Law School, Professor Sewell was an associate in the Washington, D.C., office of Mayer, Brown & Platt, where she was a member of the Appellate and Supreme Court Litigation Group. At Mayer, Brown & Platt, she briefed a variety of constitutional issues in federal and state courts of appeal and in the U.S. Supreme Court. She graduated from Brigham Young University and from the J. Reuben Clark Law School.

Andrew C. Skinner is Dean of Religious Education at Brigham Young University. He serves on the board of the Institute for the Study and Preservation of Ancient Religious Texts at BYU. He is a member of the Foundation for Ancient Research and Mormon Studies Research Committee and a senior editor of the Early Christianity Initiative, both at BYU. Dr. Skinner also acts as the director of the Religious Studies Center and is on several committees, including the Council on Religious Endeavors and the Joseph Fielding Smith Institute for Latter-day Saint History Executive Committee. He is on the board of directors for the Children of Israel Foundation. Dr. Skinner is the author of over 100 publications, including *Jerusalem, the Eternal City* (Salt Lake City: Deseret Book, 1996) and *Discoveries in the Judaean Desert XXXIII: Qumran Cave 4* (Oxford: Oxford University Press, 2001). He received his bachelor's degree in history from the University of Colorado. He earned a master of arts in Hebrew Bible–Judaic studies from Iliff School of Theology and a master of theology in Biblical Hebrew–Hebrew Bible from Harvard University. He received his doctorate degree in European and Near Eastern history from the University of Denver.

John S. Tanner is Professor of English at Brigham Young University, where he recently served as department chair and, prior to that, as associate academic vice president. His research interests lie in John Milton and, more broadly, in the intersection between literature and religion. His award-winning book *Anxiety in Eden* (Oxford University Press, 1992) examines Milton and Kierkegaard. He is currently working on a book about the concept of premortal existence in the Western tradition. Professor Tanner received a B.A. from BYU and a Ph.D. from the University of California–Berkeley. He has also taught at Florida State University and been a Fulbright Lecturer in Brazil.

Grant Underwood is Professor of History and Research Historian at the Joseph Fielding Smith Institute for Latter-day Saint History at Brigham Young University. He is the author of *The Millenarian World of Early Mormonism* (Urbana: University of Illinois Press, 1993). He earned a Ph.D. in history from the University of California–Los Angeles.

John W. Welch is Robert K. Thomas Professor of Law at the J. Reuben Clark Law School, Brigham Young University, and editor-in-chief of *BYU Studies*. He serves as director of publications for the Joseph Fielding Smith Institute for Latter-day Saint History at BYU and also on the board of the Institute for the Study and Preservation of Ancient Religious Texts, which oversees the Foundation for Ancient Research and Mormon Studies. He has authored numerous books and articles and serves on the executive committee of the Biblical Law Section of the Society of Biblical Literature. He received a B.A. in history and an M.A. in classical languages from Brigham Young University, studied Greek philosophy and history at Oxford University as a Woodrow Wilson Fellow, and earned a J.D. from the School of Law at Duke University.

Rabbi **Frederick L. Wenger**, of Rock Island, Illinois, served as Rabbi at Congregation Kol Ami in Salt Lake City from 1987 to 2003 and now serves as its Rabbi Emeritus. Rabbi Wenger began his rabbinate as a U.S. Army chaplain serving in South Carolina and Vietnam. Upon completing his chaplaincy, he returned to serve as assistant Rabbi at Congregation Emanu-El B'Ne Jeshrun, Milwaukee, Wisconsin. After a year spent in further studies in Jerusalem, Rabbi Wenger served as first Rabbi at B'nai Sholom Congregation, a merged synagogue congregation in Overland Park, Kansas, and at Temple Beth Israel, Skokie, Illinois. Before coming to Salt Lake City, Rabbi Wenger served as vice chairman of the Huntington Human Relations Commission and taught religious studies at Marshall University. He has also served as the secretary of the Northwest Suburban Synagogue Council in the Chicago area, and the Black-Jewish Relations Task Force of the Chicago Board of Rabbis. In Utah, Rabbi Wenger has served on the Martin Luther King Human Rights Commission, the Religious Freedoms Committee of the Utah State Legislature, and many other civic organizations. He also sits on the boards of all major Jewish organizations in Utah. He volunteered at Hadassah Neurim Youth Village in Israel. He also serves as adjunct faculty at Westminster College and Brigham Young University.

INDEX